Jamie McGuinness left Auckland University in 1985 for a spell of travel that lasted seven years. Numerous and varied occupations included prospecting for gold in Australia, training huskies in the Swedish Arctic, leading tours around North Africa and Central Asia and selling Trans-Siberian train tickets for the Hong Kong agency, Monkey Business.

Addicted to the Himalaya, he finds every excuse to return. He wrote the first edition of this book in 1992 and has since started a trekking agency that specialises in treks off the beaten track. He is currently working on a guide to adventure trekking in Nepal.

Trekking in the Everest Region
First edition 1993
This second edition 1996

Publisher Trailblazer Publications
The Old Manse, Tower Rd, Hindhead, Surrey, GU26 6SU, UK
Fax (+44) 0428-607571

British Library Cataloguing in Publication Data
McGuinness, Jamie
 Trekking in the Everest Region. -
 (Nepal Trekking Guide Series)
 I. Title II. Series
 915.49604

ISBN 1-873756-08-9

Maps by Jane Thomas from sketches supplied by the author
Edited by Patricia Major
Typesetting by Bryn Thomas and Anna Jacomb-Hood

Set in Times and Helvetica by Trailblazer Publications, UK
Printed and bound by Technographic Design & Print, Colchester, UK

★ TRAILBLAZER

TREKKING
IN THE
EVEREST
REGION

J A M I E   M^cG U I N N E S S

NEPAL TREKKING GUIDES

Acknowledgements

I am particularly grateful to the people of Nepal, who did much more than simply help with the research for this guidebook; living in their country has provided me with a diverse insight into life itself. The Sherpas and the mountains, especially of the Khumbu, hold a special place in my heart.

In Kathmandu, I should like to thank Dr Tom Deets and Dr David Shlim for pointing the medical section in the first edition the right way. For this edition, Dr Bir Bahan Rana of the Everest International Clinic edited the medical and health sections, kindly providing the most up-to-date advice. My frequent sojourns in Kathmandu have been immeasurably more entertaining with the assistance of the delightful Mr Puru of Hotel Karma and many of the hotel's guests. The staff at the Ministry of Tourism and the Department of Immigration also deserve special mention for so graciously allowing me to stay so long in Nepal.

Several of my treks have been enlivened by the guides and porters of Langtang Ri Trekking, in particular Ang Dawa Sherpa, Kajee Sherpa and Gyaljen Sherpa (whose sometimes riotous exploits can't be repeated here).

In the Khumbu, Lhakpa Sonam Sherpa provided much historical information, numerous naming corrections and several slides from his extensive photo library and Nga Gyalgen Sherpa of Chourikharka provided accurate detail for that region. Mr Pandy, the Sagarmatha National Park warden, discussed many excellent tourism ideas, none of which his budget will allow.

Each year the volunteer doctors staffing the Himalayan Rescue Association posts share their accumulated knowledge on altitude sickness and the region with infectious enthusiasm and deserve a thousand thank-yous not just from me but from all trekkers who have visited the posts.

I am also particularly grateful to Kerry Moran, James F Fisher, Margaret Jefferies and Stanley Stevens whose eloquent and appreciative works on Nepal immeasurably broadened my insight.

Thanks also to Jane Thomas for drawing and updating the maps, Patricia Major for editing the text, and Bryn Thomas for updating the Kathmandu section. Along the trails in the Khumbu there are so many Nepalis that I'd like to thank by name but the vast majority are more easily recalled by their smiles and helpfulness, as too are the many foreign trekkers I met.

And many thanks to my long-suffering mother.

A request

The author and publisher have tried to ensure that this guide is as accurate and up-to-date as possible. However things change quickly in this part of the world. Prices rise, new lodges are built and trails are rerouted. If you notice any changes or omissions that should be included in the next edition of this book, please write to Jamie McGuinness c/o of the publisher (address on page 2). A free copy of the new edition will be sent to persons making a significant contribution.

Front cover: Mt Everest (photo: Jamie McGuinness).

CONTENTS

PART 3: KATHMANDU

The city

Trek preparation

PART 4: THE EVEREST REGION

Mountaineering history

The Sherpas

National parks

Facilities for the trekker

Minimum impact trekking

PART 5: TRAIL GUIDE AND MAPS

Using this guide

Jiri to Namche

INTRODUCTION

The Solu-Khumbu region of Nepal has been a magnet for mountaineers, adventurers and travellers ever since its opening to foreigners in the 1950s, and with good reason. They may primarily be drawn by a desire to see the world's highest mountain but Everest is only one of a myriad of beautiful peaks in the area and there are many other attractions here.

Passing through populated areas, a trek in Nepal is very different from a wilderness hike in the USA or New Zealand, or a radonaire route in the European Alps. The hills in Nepal are the life and soul of diverse ethnic groups, the most famous of which are the hospitable Sherpa people. What further sets trekking in Nepal apart is the low cost and the ease with which a trek can be arranged. There can be few countries where you can set off for a month-long walk carrying no food or shelter yet be 100% sure that every day you will be able to find these essentials, and on a budget of just a few pounds or dollars a day. Alternatively, if you want an organised trek with an entourage of guides, cooks and porters to transport you back to the time of pukka sahibs and memsahibs, this can be quickly arranged with competent staff for a very reasonable cost.

Three areas in Nepal have become popular with trekkers, for their scenic attractions and their established network of local lodges for accommodation and food. As well as the Everest region, there's the Annapurna region, north of Pokhara, which may have a greater range of terrain and cultures but receives three times as many trekkers as the Everest region. The third area is Langtang, north of Kathmandu, which is quieter but there are no mountains over 8000m here. What sets the Everest region apart from these two other areas is the fact that, once above Namche and Lukla you are right among the mountains, continuously above 3000m/10,000ft with many chances to ascend above 5000m/16,400ft. This area also holds greater scope for exploration.

One of the world's classic long trekking routes, the first part of the trek to Everest crosses ridge after ridge of painstakingly-terraced hills populated by subsistence farmers. Mediaeval villages cling to the hillsides with mysterious gompas (Buddhist temples) above them. Rural life, unchanged for centuries, surrounds the trekker, thought-provoking and very different from the Western way of life. You soon settle into the trekking life-style leaving the world of portable telephones and fax machines far behind and rediscovering simple pleasures like the enduring glow of a sunset, the magic of flickering flames and the bliss of sleep to soothe naturally exercised muscles.

Namche, the capital of the Khumbu and a focal point for trekkers, is juxtaposed between the old and the new with traders well versed not only in the various types of Tibetan *tsampa* but also in the different brands of titanium ice screw. From the alpine valleys above Namche, the scenery is awesome: Ama Dablam, Machermo, Cholatse and numerous other peaks while the 8000 metre giants, Makalu, Cho Oyu, Lhotse and Everest command respect for their sheer height.

The highest mountain on earth has several different names. To the Western world it became Mt Everest in 1865 but to the Tibetans and the Khumbu Sherpas it has always been Chomolungma. The Chinese have wisely used the local name (transliterated as Qomolangma). Much more recently the government of Nepal has given it the name Sagarmatha. In this guide, it's referred to as Everest only because this is the name most readily recognised by readers. I personally prefer the original name, Chomolungma.

PART 1: PLANNING YOUR TRIP

With a group or on your own?

Nepal, long suspicious of foreign influence and colonial powers, began opening its borders only in 1948. The first tourists (as opposed to mountaineers and researchers) arrived in 1955 but it was not until 1965, when Colonel Jimmy Roberts set up Mountain Travel, that the first commercial treks began. The concept was similar to the expedition approach used by mountaineers, with guides, porters and tents. These holidays proved to be a great success and essentially the same format is still used today by most trekking companies.

Alongside this self-sufficient approach to trekking is a second locally-based tourism industry catering to the needs of a different type of visitor. Along the main trade routes the hill peoples of Nepal traditionally had a code of hospitality towards travellers. It was only a matter of time before small groups of adventurers started using this, staying in the basic teahouses and lodges. In 1964, 14 foreigners visited the Khumbu but by the 1970s the numbers were rapidly increasing. Now more than 6000 people trek this way each year, staying in the much improved lodges and teahouses along the routes.

The trekking infrastructure in the Solu-Khumbu has now developed to a stage where many options are possible: from a full-scale expedition with tents and porters to an independent trek using the local lodges and carrying only a sleeping-bag and jacket. It is simply a case of choosing the option most appropriate for you.

TEAHOUSE TREKKING

Dotted along the main trails the privately-owned teahouses and lodges cater specifically for independent trekkers. They can provide anything from a cup of tea to a full meal and a bed so, for the entire trek, there's no need to carry food or shelter. Teahouse trekking, as it's usually called, is easy to organise: just a day or two planning and bureaucracy-bashing in Kathmandu, and away you go. It's also cheap: luxuries aside, US$10/£6.50 a day easily covers food and accommodation.

The level of comfort and facilities in the lodges has improved greatly. Many once infamously smoky and rather too authenticallymediaeval inns are now modest hotels which generally offer better facilities than the expedition approach.

As well as being economical, teahouse trekking gives you the freedom to alter your schedule and stop where you wish. This is particularly handy if you are sick for a day or two or you feel like a rest; commercial group treks have to push on. The freedom to explore is, however, limited by the location of lodges and the restricting geography of the region. In practice most trekkers follow a few standard routes and similar itineraries, as do the trekking companies. This means that during the peak season the lodges in popular stopping places are crowded, although a meal and bed can always be found.

The main difference between the approaches is the style of interaction with the local people. Staying in a lodge provides the rewarding opportunity to mix with your Nepali hosts, many of whom speak reasonable English. How much you interact depends on you; some trekkers seem happy to spend all their time only in the company of other trekkers. On an expedition-style trek, although being self-sufficient removes the enjoyable need to interact with the villagers, this is redeemed by the crew, an often substantial team who look after, entertain and add local colour to a guided trek.

Trekking alone

Many people trek by themselves. Unless trekking during the monsoon or off the standard routes you constantly meet other trekkers in the lodges or on the trail. While you can remain by yourself most people end up walking in small groups and staying at the same lodges. This process often begins on the bus out to Jiri, or on the flight to Lukla, and more friendships evolve during the rest of the walk, one of the special joys of Nepal trekking.

There are few risks in hiking alone. Villagers often ask how many people you are trekking with and if you want to be cautious you can always say your friend is just behind; violent crimes against foreigners are still rare. As a woman you are slightly more vulnerable and locals do caution against hiking alone. Many lodges, however, are managed solely by the woman of the household while her husband is away, and women sometimes herd cattle and collect leaves alone or walk just with their children. Dressing sensibly and behaving modestly is essential. When stopping for the night, check that there is another woman staying there or pick busier lodges; if heading off the main routes you should definitely team up with someone else.

If you would prefer to begin your trek with a partner advertise on, or scan, the noticeboards around Thamel, especially at the Himalayan Rescue Association (HRA) office. You'll also meet lots of other trekkers at the Department of Immigration as you get your permit. Other alternatives are to hire a porter-guide through a trekking company or try to join an existing group.

Is a guide or porter necessary?

Assuming you will be taking this book with you, there's no need for a **guide** of the human kind on the established trekking routes. The lodges are impossible to miss, route finding presents few problems and basic English is widely understood. However, trekking with some local people can be an enlightening, entertaining and rewarding cultural exchange.

Hiring a **porter-guide** is an option that gives you the advantages of both the independent approach and the group trek. You retain control with the opportunity for the greater insight and interaction that a guide can provide, and you have your load pleasantly lightened. A porter-guide should speak reasonable English, know the region and carry 10-15kgs plus their equipment. Usually they are younger and aspiring to become a full guide or sirdar. They are happy to work for one person or a small group or if you have several loads to be carried you could hire an additional porter to accompany the group. See p86.

A cheaper option is to hire a normal **porter**, who will probably speak little English but know the route well. Once at a lodge they tend to look after themselves but on the trail they can be helpful, especially in route-finding and deciding on a lunch stop. You shouldn't feel the least bit guilty, however, if you do hire a porter-guide or a porter. For US$5-15/£3.30-10 a day, it directly benefits the local economy and it can be an enjoyable cultural exchange (see p86 for details).

Trekking the wild way

For climbers and experienced trekkers the region has an incredible amount to offer. At any major village on the main trekking routes you can pick up enough food (provided you're not a fussy eater) to disappear into the wilderness for a week . Climbing gear can be rented at a few strategic spots so the scope for exploring off the beaten track is immense. The main decisions boil down to selecting exactly what to take and deciding if you have enough experience for some of the wilder route options.

Commercial teahouse trekking

Recognising the improvements in lodges, some trekking companies now also offer teahouse style treks. Peregrine, an Australian outfit, has even bought a series of strategically placed lodges. While a dining room is a vast improvement on an often frigid dining tent and the bedrooms have more headroom than a tent, you pay dearly for the privilege compared to doing the same thing independently. The advantages are that everything is already arranged in Kathmandu and the length of the trek is fixed. The quality of the trek then rests on the leadership: a good Western leader backed up by a local sirdar or guide is a powerful combination. Many companies, however, particularly if the group is small, provide only a local guide and you are equally as likely to land a good one hiring through a Kathmandu trekking agency as through the foreign trekking companies. Often, the best local leaders form their own trekking companies or work as expedition sirdars.

COMMERCIAL GUIDED TREKS

The traditional idea of trekking evokes images of armies of heavily-laden porters catering to the every needs of a few pampered sahibs and memsahibs. Sherpas pitched the tents and kitchen staff served magnificent dinners on tables complete with table linen. This is still, in fact, the basic format of the ordinary commercial or package trek, but the scope of trips on offer is increasingly varied.

A day in the life of a group member

You're normally awoken with 'bed tea' followed by hot washing water. Sufficiently encouraged, you are expected to rise and pack your kit bag before a hearty breakfast. As you consume this the tents are struck and the porters set off, halting at around 10am for their traditional twice-daily meal of dal bhat (rice and lentils).

On the trail after breakfast, you carry just a day pack containing little more than your camera and jacket. Sherpas are on hand to assist and accompany you and the sirdar or leader sets a measured pace with occasional tea stops and breathers. While you leapfrog with the porters the kitchen crew races ahead to prepare the lunch. This is an ample and leisurely affair usually with time to explore around a village, play a hand of cards or read.

Camp is established following the afternoon's walk, sherpas erect the tents and the cook crew is busy once again, preparing a three-course dinner. Some camp sites now have a kitchen shack and sometimes a rough dining room that the crew will also sleep in. Most trekkers turn in early. The two-person tents are comfortable enough and slightly warmer than the dormitories of the high-altitude lodges, but space is at a premium. After a good day's walking sleep comes quickly.

What you're paying for

The expedition style is a pleasant routine suited to those who enjoy being looked after and, with everything planned in advance, is perfect for people with limited time. Normally the package includes airport pick-up, a guided tour plus a day or two in Kathmandu, hotel accommodation, and everything while trekking.

What sets one company above another is the quality of the trek leaders. The better companies will always provide a Western leader (who is also always backed up by a local sirdar), or an exceptional local leader. Treks operated by more ordinary companies will be led by a guide or sirdar who may have excellent organisational abilities but be less able to act as a cultural interface between trekkers and Nepalis.

A selling point for companies is the independence that trekking with tents allows. In reality, on the standard trails porters prefer to stay in the villages so the group is just as reliant on these as is the teahouse trekker. Off the main trails, however, and in the true wilderness areas, the expedition approach is the best and only alternative for a group.

Adventure treks

A few professional trekking companies offer itineraries that would be difficult or expensive for an individual to organise. These are expeditions that would need a supreme amount of confidence to tackle alone; their experienced leaders make climbing the easier trekking peaks and crossing the tougher mountain passes relatively safe for newcomers to the Himalaya.

Trekking peaks and expedition peaks

In 1981 the government of Nepal streamlined group climbing permit applications for 18 mountains which it calls 'trekking peaks'. The name is not well-chosen for some of these peaks are challenging technical climbs but a handful are 6000m or 20,000ft peaks within the ability of the experienced hill-walker/hiker (with a guide). This form of recreational mountaineering took off at the end of the 1980s and expeditions can now be organised at a similar cost and within a time frame similar to a less adventurous trek.

The best professional operators offer full expedition-style treks with experienced mountain guides and staff with medical training to ensure a safe trek. **Expedition peaks** are now also on a few company programmes, Ama Dablam (6856m) is popular and several even offer guided attempts on Cho Oyu and Everest.

Arranging a guided trek in Nepal

Armed with the addresses of trekking companies in Nepal a number of people have tried arranging a trek by mail or fax from their home country. Some have had success, others experience frustration. In fact it's better simply to arrive in Nepal and start making arrangements there. You won't be met at the airport but that's about all that will be missing. Allow a couple of days comparing companies, then a few more for the trekking company to get a crew and supplies together, and you'll be ready to go. Complications do arise if you wish to fly in to begin your trek as the crew must walk in, taking longer (chartering a helicopter is an option) but if time is so important consider a package trek booked in your home country.

This approach is cheaper than a packaged tour. You are not paying for office services in your home country, which may amount to more than the actual trek cost, or a set standard of luxury that you may not entirely desire. Other advantages are greater flexibility on the choice of itinerary and changes en route. Try to talk to other trekkers who have used a company's services: some pretend to specialise in everything (trekking, rafting, climbing) rather than sticking to what they do best.

Climbing trekking peaks (see above) can be arranged on arrival in Kathmandu but unless you are an experienced climber who would prefer to lead and be responsible for safety you are better booking with a competent adventure trekking company. The reason for this is that there are many cowboys in this industry; skilled guides are likely to have been booked in advance and hard to find at short notice.

If your intention is to join a group trek arranged on arrival, you must be prepared to wait. The majority of pre-arranged treks are organised by foreign tour operators and are considered exclusive: bookings via the overseas agent only. There are a few companies that advertise set trekking dates but these usually depart even if only two people book. Sometimes, although not always, this is just a different way of advertising trek-organising expertise.

TREKKING AGENCIES OUTSIDE NEPAL

Some companies offer a general range of treks while others specialise in climbing and adventure treks. Brochures usually stress the level of experience required for treks and climbs advertised. Don't, however, lose sight of the fact that although trekking is made easier by the need to carry only a day pack, it is your legs that do all the walking. Don't be afraid to quiz the company on who is leading the trek, their group numbers policy, and on the detailed itinerary. All profess to following comfortable acclimatisation rates but the hard reality is that many don't. They may have a good safety record, saving people before it's too late, but many itineraries cause undue and unnecessary discomfort.

Costs

US companies quote land-only costs. For the shortest treks that fly to Lukla and explore as far as Tengboche, they charge US$1500-2000. The longer standard treks start at US$1900 but most are around US$2500 and climbing treks cost US$2600-3000. US companies that offer UK or Australian operated treks are usually a little cheaper.

In the UK, trek costs are generally quoted including return airfares. Treks start from £1400 with most around £1700 and the longer climbing treks ranging between £1800 and £2300. US companies (bar one) don't operate in Europe because they are not competitively priced; the Australian and UK markets, however, seem to mix well.

Australian companies quote air and land costs separately. A return flight to Nepal is around A$1700. Short treks are A$1300 and upwards, and the standard treks are from around A$2000 to A$3000. Trekking peak expeditions cost A$2500-3500.

Trekking agencies in the UK

• **Classic Nepal** (☎ 01773-873497, fax 01773-590243) 33 Metro Ave, Newton, Derbyshire, DE55 5UF, feature a good mix of standard routes and adventure treks.

• **Encounter Overland** (☎ 0171-370 6845, fax 0171-244 9737) 267 Old Brompton Rd, London SW5 9JA, offers guided treks in the region.

• **Exodus Expeditions** (☎ 0181-675 5550, fax 0181-673 0779) 9 Weir Rd, London SW12 OLT, have a wide range of guided treks with accommodation in tents or tea-houses.

• **ExplorAsia/Abercrombie & Kent Travel** (☎ 0171-973 0482, fax 0171-730 9376) Sloane Square House, Holbein Place, Sloane Square, London SW1W 8NS offer a large selection of standard and adventure routes.

• **Explore Worldwide** (☎ 01252-319448, fax 01252-343170) 1 Frederick St, Aldershot, Hants GU11 1LQ, offers a number of treks.

• **Guerba Expeditions** (☎ 01373-858956, fax 01373-858351) Wessex House, 40 Station Road, Westbury, Wilts BA13 3JN, leads small group treks in the region.

• **Himalayan Kingdoms** (☎ 01179-237163, fax 01179-74493) 20 The Mall, Clifton, Bristol BS8 4DR, have several treks in the region. Their expeditions section (☎ 01142-763322) organises more ambitious adventure trekking and mountaineering holidays.

• **Himalayan Quest** (☎ 01926-450835) 12 Euston Place, Leamington Spa, Warks CV32 4LY.

• **KE Adventure Travel** (☎ 017687-73966, fax 017687-74693) 32 Lake Rd, Keswick, Cumbria CA12 5DQ) offers treks and trekking peaks including Mera.

• **Naturetrek** (☎ 01962-733051, fax 01962-733368) Chautara, Bighton, Nr Alresford, Hampshire SO24 9RB offer bird-watching tours in several regions of Nepal including the Everest area.

- **OTT Expeditions** (☎ 01142-588508, fax 01142-551603) 62 Nettleham Rd, Sheffield S8 8SX, specialises in trekking peaks and mountaineering expeditions, including Everest at US$25,000.
- **Roama Travel** (☎ 01258-860298, fax 01258-861382) Shroton, Blandford Forum, Dorset DT11 8QW specialise in individual treks.
- **Sherpa Expeditions** (☎ 0181-577 2717, fax 0181-572 9788) 131a Heston Rd, Hounslow, Middx TW5 0RD, have over 20 years experience in Nepal and a wide range of guided treks.
- **World Expeditions** (☎ 01628-74174, fax 01628-74312) 7 North Rd, Maidenhead SL6 1PL feature a range of standard treks.
- **Other operators** offering tours in the Annapurna region include **Bales Tours** (☎ 01306-885923, fax 01306-885991) Bales House, Junction Rd, Dorking, Surrey RH4 3HB; **Ramblers Holidays** (☎ 01707-331133, fax 01707-333276) Box 43, Welwyn Garden City, Herts AL8 6PQ.

Trekking agencies in Continental Europe

- **Austria Okistra** (☎ 0222-347526) Turkenstrasse 4, A-1090 Wien. **Supertramp Reisen** (☎ 01222-5335136) Helferstorfer St 4, A-1010 Wien.
- **Belgium Connections** (☎ 02-512 50 60) Kolenmarkt 13, rue Marche au Charbon, Brussel 1000 Bruxelles, with branches in Antwerpen (☎ 03-225 31 61), Gent (☎ 091-23 90 20) and Liege (☎ 041-22 04 44). **Joker Tourisme** (☎ 02-648 78 78) Boondaalsesteenweg 6, Chaussee de Boondaal 6, Brussel 1050 Bruxelles. **Divantoura** (☎ 03-233 19 16) St Jacobsmarkt 5, 2000 Antwerpen. **Roadrunner** (☎ 03-281 16 50) Belgielei 209, 2018 Antwerpen. **Divantoura** (☎ 091-23 00 69) Bagattenstraat 176, B-9000 Gent.
- **Denmark Green Tours** (☎ 33-13 27 27) Kultorvet 7, DK-1175 Kobenhavn K. **Inter-Travel** (☎ 33-15 00 77) Frederiksholms Kanal 2, DK-1220 Kobenhavn K. **Marco Polo Tours** (☎ 33-13 03 07) Borgergade 16, 1300 Kobenhavn K. **Topas Globetrotters** (☎ 86-89 36 22) Skaersbrovej 11, 8680 Ry.
- **Germany Explorer** (☎ 0211-379 064) Huttenstrasse 17, 4000 Dusseldorf 1. **SHR Reisen** (☎ 0761-210 078) Kaiser Joseph Strasse 263, D-7800 Freiburg.
- **Iceland Icelandic Student Travel** (☎ 01-615656) V/Hringbraut, IS-101 Reykjavik.
- **Ireland Maxwells Travel** (☎ 01-779 479) D'Olier Chambers, 1 Hawkins St, Dublin 2. **Funtrek** (☎ 01-733 633) 32 Batchelors Walk, O'Connell Bridge, Dublin 1.
- **Italy CTS** (☎ 06-46791) V. Genova 15, 00184 Roma.

• **Netherlands NBBS** (☎ 071-22 1414) Schipholweg 101, PO Box 360, 2300 AJ Leiden. Branches in Groningen (☎ 050-126 333), Amsterdam (☎ 020-20 5071), Utrecht (☎ 030-314 520) and Rotterdam (☎ 010-414 9822). **De Wandelwaaier** (☎ 020-622 6990) Herngracht 329, 1016AW Amsterdam. **Terra Travel** (☎ 020-275129) Singel 190H, 1016AA Amsterdam. **Royal Hansa Tours** (☎ 050-127799) Stoeldraalerstraat 11, 9712 BT Groningen.
• **Norway Terra Nova Travel** (☎ 47-2 42 14 10) Dronningens Gate 26, N-0154, Oslo 1. **Eventyrreiser A/S Adventure Travel** (☎ 22-11 31 81) Hegdehaugsvn 10, 0167 Oslo.
• **Spain Expo Mundo** (☎ 03-412 59 56) Diputacion, 238 Stco, 08007 Barcelona.
• **Sweden Aeventyrsresor** (☎ 08-654 1155) Hantverkargaten 38, PO Box 12168, S-102 24 Stockholm. **Himalayaresor** (08-605 5760) Box 17, S-123, 21 Farsta.
• **Switzerland S.S.R.** (☎ 01-242 30 00) Backerstr. 52, CH 8026, Zurich. **Suntrek Tours** (☎ 01-462 61 61) Birmensdorferstr. 187, CH-8003 Zurich. **Case Depart Voyages** (☎ 021-311 13 61) Avenue de Bethusy 4, Case Postale 107, CH-1000, Lausanne 4.

Trekking agencies in the USA

• **Above the Clouds Trekking** (☎ 508-799 4499, fax 797 4779) PO Box 398, Worcester, MA 01602.
• **Adventure Center** (☎ 415-654 1879, ☎ 800-227 8747, fax 654 4200) 1311 63rd St, Suite 200, Emeryville, CA 94608 – agents for Explore (UK).
• **Geeta Tours & Travels** (☎ 312-262 4959) 1245 West Jarvis Ave, Chicago IL 60626.
• **Himalayan Travel** (☎ 800-225 2380, fax 203-359 3669) 2nd Floor, 112 Prospect St, Stamford CT 06901 – agents for Sherpa Expeditions (UK).
• **InnerAsia** (☎ 415-922 0448, ☎ 800-777 8183) 2627 Lombard St, San Francisco, CA 94123.
• **Journeys** (☎ 313-665 4407, ☎ 800-255 8735, fax 665 2945) 4011 Jackson Rd, Ann Arbor, MI 48103. Also includes some treks specially for families.
• **Mountain Travel & Sobek Expeditions** (☎ 510-527 8100, ☎ 800-227 2384) 6420 Fairmount Ave, El Cerrito, CA 94530. Wide range of upmarket treks.
• **Narayan's Gateway to Nepal** (☎ 303-440 0331, fax 440 6958) 948 Pearl St, Boulder CO 80302 is run by a Nepalese family based in Colorado and Kathmandu. Study programmes are offered.

• **Overseas Adventure Travel** (☎ 800-221 0814) 349 Broadway, Cambridge MA 02139 offer a number of treks in this area.
• **Safaricentre** (☎ 310-546 4411, ☎ 800-223 6046, fax 546 3188) 3201 N Sepulveda Blvd, Manhattan Beach, CA 90266 – agents for Exodus (UK).
• **Wilderness Travel** (☎ 510-548 0420, ☎ 800-368 2794) 801 Allston Way, Berkeley, CA 94710.

Trekking agencies in Canada
•**Adventure Centre** (☎ 416-922 7584) 17 Hayden St, Toronto, Ontario M4Y 2P2.
• **Mountain Travel & Sobek Expeditions** (☎ 604-876 5511) 101 511 West 14th Ave, Vancouver BC V5Z 1P5, offers upmarket treks.
• **Market Square Tours** (☎ 800 661 3838) 54 Donald St, Winnipeg, Manitoba, R3C 1LC – agents for Exodus (UK).
• **Travel Cuts**, also agents for Exodus (UK), have offices in **Edmonton** (☎ 403-488 8487) 12304 Jasper Ave, Edmonton, Alberta, T5N 3K5, **Toronto** (☎ 416-979 8608) 187 College St, Toronto, Ontario M5T 1P7 and **Vancouver** (☎ 604-689 2887) 501 602 West Hastings St, Vancouver BC, V6B 1P2.
• **Trek Holidays**, agents for Explore (UK), have offices in **Calgary** (☎ 403-283 6115, 336 14th St NW, Calgary, Alberta T2N 1Z7), **Edmonton** (☎ 403-439 9118, 8412 109th St, Edmonton, Alberta T6G 1E2), **Toronto** (☎ 416-922 7584) 25 Bellair St, Toronto, Ontario M4Y 2P2 and **Vancouver** (☎ 604-734 1066, 1965 West 4th Ave, Vancouver BC V6J 1M8.
• **Worldwide Adventures Inc** (☎ 416-963 9163, from USA ☎ 1-800-387 1483) 920 Yonge St, Suite 747, Toronto, Ontario M4W 3C7 – agents for World Expeditions (Australia).

Trekking agencies in Australia
• **Adventure World** has branches in **Adelaide** (☎ 231 6844, 7th floor, 45 King William St, Adelaide SA 5000), **Brisbane** (☎ 229 0599, 3rd floor, 333 Adelaide St, Brisbane Qld 4000), **Melbourne** (☎ 03-670 0125, 3rd floor, 343 Little Collins St, Melbourne Vic 3000), **Perth** (☎ 221 2300, 2nd floor, 8 Victoria Ave, Perth WA 6000) and **Sydney** (☎ 956 7766, toll free 008-221 931, 73 Walker St, North Sydney, NSW 2059).
• **Ausventure** (☎ 02-960 1677, fax 969 1463) Suite 1, 860 Military Rd, (PO Box 54) Mosman, NSW 2088. This long-established adventure travel company offers a comprehensive range of treks.
• **Back Track Adventures** (☎ 07-368 4987) 226 Given Terrace, Paddington, QLD 4064.

• **Exodus Expeditions** (☎ 02-552 6317) 81A Glebe Point Rd, Glebe, NSW 2037 – agents for Exodus (UK).
• **Outdoor Travel** (☎ 03-670 7252, fax 670 3310) 55 Hardware St, Melbourne, Vic 3000 – agents for Sherpa Expeditions (UK).
• **Peregrine Adventures** is a Nepal specialist with branches in **Melbourne** (☎ 03-663 8611, fax 663 8618, 2nd floor, 258 Lonsdale St, Melbourne, Vic 3000) and **Sydney** (☎ 02-241 1128, 5th floor, 58 Pitt St, Sydney, NSW 2000) and offers a good range of treks.
• **Peregrine Travel** (08-223 5905) 192 Rundle St, Adelaide, SA 5000.
• **Summit Travel** (☎ 09-321 1259) 1st floor, 862 Hay St, Perth WA 6000.
• **World Expeditions** (☎ 02-264 3366, fax 261 1974) 3rd floor, 441 Kent St, Sydney NSW 2000. The main competition for Peregrine. As well as range of standard treks, some climbing expeditions are offered.

Trekking agencies in New Zealand
• **Adventure World** (☎ 09-524 5118, 0800-652 954, fax 520 6629) 101 Great South Rd, Remuera, PO Box 74008, Auckland – agents for Exodus and Explore (UK).
• **Suntravel** (☎ 09-525 3074, fax 525 3065) PO Box 12-424, Penrose, Auckland – agents for Peregrine Adventures (Australia.)
• **Venture Treks** (☎ 09-379 9855, fax 770 320) PO Box 37610, 164 Parnell Rd, Auckland – agents for Sherpa Expeditions (UK).
• **Himalaya Trekking** (☎ 06-868 8595, 025-466 465), 54a Darwin Road, Gisborne.

Old clothes needed by Kathmandu charities
If you have a little space in your luggage there are a couple of worthy local charities that would be very grateful for some old clothes.

Kumbeshwar Technical School in Patan was set up to cater specifically for the very low caste groups. It incorporates a small orphanage, a primary school and a technical school where carpet weaving and carpentry are taught. High quality sweaters are on sale in the showroom here. The principal is Karuna Khadgi (☎ 536483).

Child Workers in Nepal (CWIN) is a charity working for the rights of children and the abolition of child bonded labour (16% of children in the country are bonded labourers). They also run a 'Common Room' to support the 1000 children who live on the streets of Kathmandu. Clothes are always needed; children's clothes are best but they can alter adults' clothes. They can also make use of any medicines you may have left after your trek. CWIN is near the Soaltee Holiday Inn in Kalamati. It's run by Gauri Pradan (☎ 271658).

Route options

Since ancient times caravans have followed trade routes across many parts of Asia. The advent of motorised transport brought great changes but these developments passed Nepal by until the 1950s. The first road link, the Rajpath, between Kathmandu and India was opened only in 1956 but road construction is now a government priority (rail is impractical). With much of the countryside being not far off vertical, only the low-lying Terai and the Himalayan foothills have been penetrated but the roads are still very rough.

The rest of the country still relies on the footpaths and mountain trails that form an age-old surface transportation network across the country. So extensive is this network that it's easy to plan some weird and wonderful routes in wild and isolated areas. However, only a few major routes are suited to trekkers wanting to stay in lodges, but what routes some of them are!

Planning

Most people start planning with the intention of seeing Everest. Basically this entails going to the Khumbu region and up a hill to view the mountain. So the majority of trekkers walk in from Jiri or fly to Lukla, trek to the top of Kala Pattar, then fly out of Lukla or Syangboche. This standard route is popular with reason but options are broadening. All routes to Everest pass through **Namche** (except a few tough options mentioned later) so first it's a question of getting there. If you plan to fly one way then flying out is best since the walk in gives helpful acclimatisation (the process of getting used to altitude, see p240). If flying in and out, flying in to Phaplu rather than Lukla is more sensible; you shouldn't fly direct to Syangboche. For sample itineraries see p227.

GETTING TO NAMCHE

The main options plus approximate time to walk to Namche are:
> Bus to Jiri (1 day) then walking (6-9 days)
> Flying to Lukla (2 days + 1 or 2 extra acclimatisation days)
> Flying to Phaplu (4-5 days)
> Flying to Syangboche (not recommended)
> Bus to Hille (1 day) then walking (9-12 days)
> Flying to Tumlingtar then walking (7-10 days)

Main Routes to Namche

Walking from Jiri to Namche

Jiri, a day's journey by bus or taxi from Kathmandu, is still the most popular starting point for trekkers who prefer to walk in. This route (see p125) features numerous lodges and teahouses catering for trekkers and is well trodden for good reason: it's a pleasant and rewarding walk that prepares you for the higher altitudes ahead.

Flying to Lukla (2850m/9350ft)

This is the most popular place to fly into because it's only one and a half day's walk from Namche. However, the risk of altitude sickness is double that of alternative routes unless at least one extra acclimatisation day is scheduled. In the past there were nightmarish flight-booking queues but the problem has now largely been alleviated.

Flying to Phaplu (2350m/7710ft)

If you wish to fly, flying to Phaplu is an under-used route and yet the most sensible choice. It saves what some consider an arduous day on a bus (ie to Jiri) and a few days walking. Compared with flying to Lukla, it allows a safer and more gentle introduction to altitude and reveals a richer cultural variety with the added bonus of being able to visit Junbesi. The government has recognised the potential and introduced tourist priority flights but trekking companies have yet to adapt. Flying to Lukla saves that extra day or two, all-important in today's package trek market, so the safer approach (flying to Phaplu) has been overridden. See p187.

Flying to Syangboche (3700m/12,139ft)

The advent of helicopter services has meant that this short airstrip just above Namche now takes commercial flights. However, arriving directly at Namche, at 3450m or 11,319ft, is a dangerous altitude to fly to directly. You should spend at least 2-3 nights between 2000 and 3000m before ascending higher, ie to Namche.

The eastern route from Hille/Basantpur or Tumlingtar

On this route, compared with the Jiri to Namche walk, the number and height of the hills are similar but the overall distance is slightly greater. Route-finding is more challenging and many lodges are a half or full day's walk apart so it's better attempted by trekkers with some experience. It was, until 1992, a little-trekked route because of misleading information about lodges and trails and it is still very much in the process of developing to trekkers' needs. See p211 for more details.

Walking from Hille or Basantpur first involves a rough 24-hour bus ride from Kathmandu, then a short but hot two-day walk to Tumlingtar airport. If the on-again, off-again huge Arun III hydro scheme up-river is ever begun the road will be extended along the ridge above Tumlingtar, saving a day and a half's walking. Flying directly to Tumlingtar is cheap and reliable and generally the better option.

THE ROUTES ABOVE NAMCHE

Altitude sickness

The key to planning an itinerary above Namche is awareness of altitude sickness: going up too fast causes a medical condition serious enough to kill you. The higher the altitude, the less oxygen there is in the air. On the summit of Kala Pattar (5554m/18,222ft), for example, there is 50% less oxygen than at sea level. Your body needs several days to adapt to this phenomenon so for a safe trek it is absolutely essential that you allow sufficient time for acclimatisation. See p240 for more information.

The choices

There are four main valleys (see **map p24**), each spectacular and worthwhile exploring. The upper Bhote valley is closed at present but a day or overnight trip from Namche to Thame, in the lower section, gives useful acclimatisation and is a good introduction to the Khumbu. The Gokyo Valley is particularly beautiful and offers incredible potential for exploration. The popular standard route to Lobuche and Kala Pattar is also spectacular and the Chukhung valley offers good exploring and climbing. There are also several high passes that can be crossed in between the major valley systems for a greater challenge.

The amount of time spent above Namche varies with your ambitions. To spot Everest from the top of Kala Pattar, or Gokyo Ri in the Gokyo Valley, a minimum of nine days must be allowed (Namche to Namche). This includes several consecutive nights spent at the same point while ascending, essential for adequate acclimatisation. Lovers of grand mountain scenery and explorers, however, could spend weeks wandering up the high valleys above Namche, only returning to hunt down a hot shower and Namche cuisine. In addition to incredible scenery wherever you trek, staying in quieter lodges and spending time with Sherpas and other local people is all part of a rewarding experience. It is this that separates trekking in Nepal from trekking in wilderness areas in Western countries.

Lobuche vs Gokyo

Years ago, heavy marketing for treks to Everest Base Camp excluded other less goal-orientated options. This is still reflected in the brochures of many trekking companies which barely mention a trek up Gokyo valley. It is, however, well worth considering but it makes choosing an itinerary limited by time difficult.

The pros and cons The views from Kala Pattar (near Lobuche and Everest Base Camp) are fantastic. Although only the upper part of Everest can be seen, spectacular sheer mountains and glaciers entirely surround you. For the fit, climbing another of Pumori's spurs offers more extensive views of Everest in similarly-inspiring terrain. Most people don't end up visiting Everest Base Camp since the trail there is rough and the only view is of the fearsome icefall.

From Gokyo Ri the mountains are just as spectacular but not so close with views extending into the distance. Close to Gokyo there's a more extensive view of Everest than from Kala Pattar or Gokyo Ri and it doesn't even require climbing a hill, but from there the other mountains are not as impressive so the overall effect is not as satisfying.

Trekking to Gokyo or Lobuche takes the same amount of time. If you plan to spend only a single day at one or the other, Lobuche is possibly the better option because the views are great from nearby Kala Pattar and the walk is perhaps more spectacular. If you have three or four extra days the options broaden. Having been to one of either Gokyo, Lobuche or Chukhung you should now be acclimatised sufficiently so that you no longer have to plan with this in mind. The distances in the Khumbu are not in fact very great with each valley only being a day or two apart. Deciding between visiting Chukhung en route to Lobuche or going to Lobuche first and then Gokyo, is such a difficult choice you might as well add a couple more days and visit all of them. Examples of itineraries are given on p227 and can be joined together to create even more interesting combinations.

Chugima La/Cho La The Cho La (p190) is a tempting option when contemplating visiting both Gokyo and Lobuche valleys but the conditions must be good. The walk around via Phortse is less alpine but probably as rewarding while taking a day longer.

LEAVING THE REGION

Flying out

The majority of trekkers fly out of Lukla. Although the walk from Namche to Lobuche or Gokyo takes a week going up, the return trip takes most trekkers only two days, then one more to Lukla. Asian Airlines began helicopter services out of Syangboche in 1994 and this service has the potential to become the main exit route as more trekkers become aware of it.

Walking in and out

The most obvious route is to walk from Jiri to the Khumbu, then exit via Tumlingtar or Hille/Basantpur. It is slightly better attempted in this direction because the Jiri route is a more gentle introduction to trekking. However, retracing your steps to Jiri is not a boring alternative; returning, the views are different and the seasons change the colours of the countryside. You'll get a warm welcome from lodges you return to, and being wiser to the ways of the land you'll probably find this part of the walk more rewarding than before.

Instant Everest

If you merely wish to spy the very summit of Everest this can be seen from the National Park headquarters above Namche, the path between Namche and Khumjung, or from Tengboche. The same cautions on acclimatisation apply, however, and many group members have suffered through ignoring these. A minimum of seven days from Lukla to Tengboche to Syangboche (or eight, back to Lukla) is needed, and still the rapid altitude gain is likely to be troublesome. This short itinerary is often part of an 'all Nepal' tour encompassing Chitwan, the Annapurnas and Everest. These tours try to let you see and do everything but in the rush miss the real essence of Nepal. Concentrating on one or other of the regions brings deeper and more satisfying rewards.

With the advent of **helicopter charter services**, however, you no longer have to trek the hills to reach the National Park headquarters or Tengboche Gompa. From either Kathmandu or Lukla a helicopter can whisk you up for a picnic backdropped by the summit of Mt Everest. Since you stay above 3000m for only a few hours, you might feel breathless but there is little risk of life-threatening altitude sickness.

The chances are, if as you flew in to Kathmandu the majestic Himalaya greeted you in regal glory, one of the peaks was the big one. For a closer look you could take one of the morning **mountain flights** from Kathmandu (see p88). These flights are absolutely breath-taking and are definitely worth it, especially after a trek.

OTHER OPTIONS

Other non-technical routes into the Khumbu
The standard routes (Jiri and the Arun) are the most logical and direct, reinforced by chains of lodges. However, walking from Barabise to Jiri is feasible, as is flying into Lamidanda, Okhaldhunga, Bhojpur or Taplejung, or trekking up from the road to the south. These alternatives are not on difficult or dangerous trails but they traverse hot low country and lack lodges, so they are better attempted after acquiring some Nepalese trekking experience.

Technical passes into the Khumbu
There are four challenging 5700m+/18,700ft+ passes that drop into the Khumbu and require mountaineering competence. The tough and dangerous **Trashi Labtsa** is at the head of the Rolwaling Valley and can

be reached from Barabise or Dolakha. If you're trekking with a group, a climb of the trekking peak Ramdung-Go is usually included as acclimatisation and to ensure that you are capable of the crossing. The **Mingbo La** and **Amphu Labtsa** are technically difficult and isolated, and are generally only crossed in conjunction with climbing the trekking peak Mera (6476m/21,246ft) or crossing a couple of 6100m/20,013ft passes from Makalu Base Camp. Generally it's better to visit the Khumbu first and acclimatise properly, then exit via one of the high passes. Read the detailed route descriptions on pages 198, 195 and 193 for 'scare' factors.

The **Nangpa La** (5716m/18,753ft) is the highest and one of the more arduous trading passes in the world. It links Tibet with the Khumbu but is closed to foreigners, except to those on Cho Oyu expeditions.

The high passes of the Khumbu and the trekking peaks should be attempted only during the October to end of December season. Later the numbing cold and increasing snowfall make these already tough propositions highly dangerous or impossible.

Trekking peaks
These are dotted around the Khumbu, Rolwaling and Hinku areas, and present satisfying objectives. Their level of difficulty varies considerably but they are not all the exclusive domain of tough mountaineers. A couple are little more than a high altitude walk requiring an ice-axe and crampons plus rope for the snow fields. See the individual descriptions beginning on p230. For competent alpinists and serious mountaineers there is endless potential limited only by the government regulations.

Alternative treks
The psychological omnipotence of Everest is so great that few people contemplate trekking in this region without the aim of seeing it from close quarters. However, apart from the star attraction there are other areas that offer fantastic trekking amid stunning mountains. These all require a degree of self-sufficiency and camping out. Many would be particularly suited to the classic style of Nepal trekking – a crew to carry the excess, and a few Sherpa companions to round the experience. Going without local support is for the tough and experienced and even so a porter for some sections would be invaluable. The best suggestions are:

• **Exploring above Junbesi**, to Dudh Kund (Milk Lake) below the holy mountain of Numbur and in the Lumding Kharka area, below Kongde and Nupla. This could be combined with the trek to Namche.

• **South of the Rolwaling valley** hides untold exciting possibilities – high kharkas and ridges littered with mountains a touch under 6000m/19,685ft. Several circuits are possible over unused passes.

• **The Hinku and Hongu valleys** offer challenging and remote treks amongst mind-blowing mountains. A circuit including Mera would be attractive.

The Barun and Makalu region

This is an isolated area with only a fraction of it used for grazing and expedition access to Makalu. Otherwise it's impenetrable forest topped by savage mountains. A trek to **Makalu Base Camp** is the only feasible option and the route is outlined on p222 with enough details to whet your appetite but not detract from the adventure of visiting a little explored area.

Budgeting

Nepal is undoubtedly one of the cheapest countries to travel around. It's possible to survive on US$5/£3.50 a day but for under US$15/£10 a day you can live really quite comfortably. There's also a tempting array of services and souvenirs to mop up any excess funds.

COSTS IN KATHMANDU

Your choice of hotel will largely determine the amount spent on basics. A spartan double room with communal bathroom facilities goes for US$2-5/£1.30-3.50 a night, and with attached bathroom US$5-10/£3.50-7. A pleasant 1 or 2 star room is about US$20/£13. The 4-5 star hotels are not quite to international standards but at around US$110/£70 a night neither are their prices.

Food is of a more uniform price. If you avoid the ten most expensive restaurants, meals are US$1-5/£0.60-3.50, so US$5-8/£3.50-5.30 a day is plenty. What you spend on drinks depends on your poison: large bottles of beer and double nips of cheap spirits are around US$1.50-2/£1-1.30 while soft drinks cost less than US$0.50/£0.30.

For a budget traveller, around US$100/£65 a week is adequate for cheap hotels, good food, sightseeing, visa extensions/trekking permits, and other necessities such as chocolate, bicycle hire, newspapers and a quick call home. It is the avoidable one-off expenses, such as flights, rafting trips and quality souvenirs that will have a large impact on your budget plans. With much less than US$100/£65 per week careful budgeting is required.

THE TREKKING BUDGET

Independent trekkers

Once it was difficult to spend even US$5 a day but there are now double rooms and extensive menus in lodges, tempting trekkers to spend more. Around US$10/£6 a day per person gives you good food and accommodation, plus a few treats. Lodges charge under US$1/£0.70 for dormitory accommodation while doubles go for US$1-2/£0.70-1.30, and main courses are around US$1/£0.70. Chocolate, beer and Coke are not so cheap but even with an excess of these luxuries spending more than US$15/£10 daily would be a challenge. At the tight end it is still possible to trek in relative comfort on US$6/£4 a day on the trail.

There are, however, other things than day-to-day survival to allow money for: extra films, souvenirs and emergency situations (a porter to carry your backpack if you twist an ankle) so it's best to take perhaps US$100-200/£70-130 more than your budget. If you intend to take advantage of leftover mountaineering gear sold in Namche (see p43) you'll need dollars not rupees.

If you're planning to organise a guided trek on arrival in Nepal or to hire a porter see p84-6 for the costs.

Commercial treks

With all the money paid up front it's simply a case of following company guidelines and allowing for the few extras. While trekking there are no expenses bar the odd bottle of beer and tips for the crew so just allow for souvenirs, extra film and bars of chocolate.

Currency

US, Canadian, Australian, Hong Kong and Singapore dollars are accepted, plus all the main European currencies, cash and travellers cheques (any major brand although only American Express has an office in Kathmandu). Major credit cards are accepted by star-class hotels, in some shops and for cash advances at a few banks. Eurocheques and Post Giros are not accepted. As in the rest of Asia some US$ cash is handy. Nepal's once thriving black market is slowly being eroded by more realistic exchange rates and currency regulations, and by banks opening exchange counters where tourists need them. There are, however, still plenty of touts who will take you into a shop and exchange dollars (even travellers cheques), for rupees at marginally more favourable rates. You should, however, be aware that exchanging money on the black market does nothing to help the country's balance of payments.

When to go

Trekking the standard routes in the Khumbu is possible and can be pleasant at almost any time of the year; just tailor your route and your expectations to the prevailing seasonal conditions. However, for climbing and crossing high passes the classic trekking time (October – December) is best, followed by March to May a distant second. During the depths of winter and the monsoon some areas are all but inaccessible and finding willing crew is difficult because of the greater risk involved.

The post-monsoon season (October and November edging into December) offers the clearest weather and stunning views but since it's also the busiest time many lodges are full. The winter perils are of an elemental kind – cold and the occasional snow fall at altitude but for the well-prepared, trekking is still rewarding. Winter thaws to the spring reawakening: the flowers bloom, leaves sprout and the rhododendrons blossom for the March to May trekking season. During this increasingly warm period the afternoons are hazy unless there's been a shower of rain to clear it away. By the end of May and into June it's hot and the approaching monsoon occasionally rattles its sabre. When this does arrive, at the end of June or the beginning of July, everything flourishes under the life-giving rain. Except at high altitudes, leeches abound and coupled with the humidity are enough to put off all but the most determined trekkers.

SEASONAL CONDITIONS

One constant is the lack of wind. Although Everest expeditions are frequently hampered by high wind, in the trekking regions anything more than a stiff breeze is rare. As the morning sun strengthens, thermal currents waft up but the evenings are often so still that outside a candle will stay lit. On high passes and trekking peaks the wind sometimes whistles, but is often more noisy than blustery.

Early Autumn (mid-September to mid-October)

The monsoon has dwindled but a few tail-end clouds and showers (or short-lived snow at altitude) must be expected. Locals and trekkers simply take cover in the nearest teahouse and wait the afternoon shower out. Every few years, though, the remnants of a Bay of Bengal hurricane unload in a downpour lasting a day or two. There's also a chance that the monsoon may not quite have ended, staging a dramatic return for a few weeks. The Jiri to Namche section is hot and sweaty under the fierce sun, while higher up it's pleasant with cool but mostly frost-free nights. If you skip the lower country, this is a particularly pleasant and under-trekked season.

The approach of winter (mid-October to Christmas)
This is classic trekking time, famed for clear skies and fantastic fine weather. Early October through to late November is also the busiest period with most lodges and camp sites brimming with trekkers.

The long fine periods are occasionally broken for day or two by a front sweeping overhead causing high cloud or cloud banks that roll up the valleys, then usually clear at altitude with the sunset. The odd stronger front brings a spot of wet weather as well but it is impossible to tell (even the locals can't) whether a front contains rain. Barring unusual conditions during this trekking season perhaps two or three periods of showers and drizzle, or short-lived snow at altitude, can be expected.

Tengboche begins receiving frosts in October and by November at altitude evenings are chilly. During a cold clear snap in the up-valley lodges (Lobuche, Gokyo and Chukhung) a water bottle will partially freeze overnight and the lakes above 5000m/16,404ft begin to freeze. Shorts can still be worn above Namche on windless days by the determined; but light pants feel more comfortable. December is probably one of the most pleasant months for trekking because statistically it is the driest month of the year and the vast majority of trekkers have already headed down. The shorter winter days are cooler but on the walk in you'll still sweat on the hills. Above Namche it is cold but a thick down jacket, good sleeping bag and lots of hot drinks can ward the cold off effectively.

Winter (January through March)
New Year usually brings a week or so of disturbed weather and frequently this is the snowfall that puts a stop to the easy pass-hopping and climbing or at least brings more challenging conditions. This almost regular fall is followed by more winter storms breaking the fine periods. Two closely spaced storms can lead to snow drifts above Namche. A bad year will see the high lodges snowed in for a few days and a sudden rush on plastic boot rentals in Namche. The shaded snow has no chance of melting while the rest of the snow patchily clears over a week or two. In other years there'll be only light falls that burn off quickly in the sunny spots. Air temperatures stay around 0°C/32°F during the warmer days, and nights are all below 0°C/32°F and can even

hit -30°C/-22°F at 5000m/16,404ft. All the high altitude lakes sport ice thick enough to skate on and many (for example Gokyo lake) will not thaw until May. March has a reputation among the Sherpas as being colder than December, and with snow lying around, trekking is more challenging. Below Namche, down to an altitude of about 2600m/8530ft, periodic snow falls and ice can occasionally be expected. Flights to Lukla are sometimes disrupted by snow during January and February but only for a day or so. Since helicopters can land on snow, flights begin as soon as the weather clears.

Early summer (April to early June)
The second trekking season commences at the end of March and continues into May with the atmosphere becoming increasingly hazy. The fine periods will be broken by lots of cloud rolling up the valleys during the afternoon, often bringing drizzle that clears during the evening. On the trekking peaks and above this is a pattern of daily light powder snow that shortens the useable part of the day. Also, a torrential pre-monsoon downpour is possible though rare. The temperatures warm up considerably and by the end of April are sweltering at low altitudes and sometimes on the warm side higher up. The rain, sun and warmth spark a flourish of growth with rhododendrons painting the hillsides, beginning in late February at lower altitudes and blooming ever higher during March and April.

By May the sun is intense and it's hot everywhere, only pleasant high up. In the middle hills everyone is waiting for the cooling relief of the monsoon rains.

The monsoon – (late June to mid-September)
Below 3000m/9843ft it's oppressive, muddy and leeches abound but the helicopters still operate flights (on an irregular schedule) so it's possible to avoid the worst areas. There are frequent showers, mainly in the afternoon and at night, and occasional heavy deluges, especially in July. Everybody dives under the nearest shelter to drink tea and wait it out. Infrequently these cloudbursts create dangerous flash-floods and mud slides which can put paid to the day's walking.

Above Namche the days are hot and the nights are frost-free although short-lived snow can fall on Kala Pattar and even down as far as Chukhung. Rainfall is uneven with the southernmost mountains bearing the brunt; this is the reason the glaciers on Numbur and in the Hongu/Hinku are so big. Above Namche is a partial rain-shadow area and consequently in the higher reaches of the main valleys the rain is

---

(**Opposite**) A smiling welcome is assured from most lodge-owners.

reduced to occasional showers and drizzle. The rain pattern is not regular; it might be misty and rain every afternoon for a week, then clear for days. Slippery trails can be a problem, particularly for porters.

Overall, the almost perpetual cloud cover is more of an annoyance than the drizzle. The views are stunning when they clear but you often wait days for this to happen; although Kala Pattar does clear more frequently. The rewards of this season are lush green valleys carpeted by flowers. For a person who likes wandering, rather than trekking to a schedule, it's a wonderful time to observe the other way of life of the Sherpas, the monsoon cycle of agriculture.

By September the monsoon is in retreat. Usually the rains stop around mid-September but they sometimes cease as early as the beginning of the month or as late as early October.

Climatic statistics for Tengboche (3867m/12,687ft)

In October an average night minimum of -4°C/24°F and an average day maximum of 10°C/50°F can be expected. For January the average night minimum is -9°C/16°F and the average day maximum is 4°C/ 39°F . Average monthly rainfall for Tengboche is as follows:

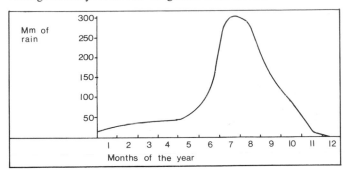

THE KATHMANDU CLIMATE

At the moderate altitude of 1400m/4600ft, the capital's climate is quite mild. The monsoon showers keep the temperature down to the high 20s°C/80s°F during summer, although it's quite humid and uncomfortable if it does not rain. By the end of September the tropical temperatures cool and by late October the evenings are a little cold for just a

---

(Opposite) Top: Pangboche village in September; the buckwheat harvest is underway. **Bottom left:** Junbesi: the monsoon brings a profusion of flowering plants. **Bottom right:** Harvesting buckwheat in Khumjung.

shirt. The early winter days are sunny and agreeable, the evenings require a thick jacket and there's the occasional frost. From Christmas onwards a morning fog often settles on the valley making rising early a challenge. This also disrupts some flights but by 10 or 11am schedules are back to normal. Visiting Kathmandu is pleasant during any of the seasons although spring and autumn are the most popular, and crowded, times.

What to take

The bare necessities

What to take is simply a question of what is essential. I met some Tibetans travelling without yaks over the 5716m/18,735ft Nangpa La. We looked at each others' lunches (my biscuits and their *tsampa*) and then compared rucksacks: my fancy expedition-sized pack versus their grubby day-packs. One Tibetan unpacked the rest of his bag to show me what the essentials were: gloves, an extra pair of socks and shoes (Chinese shoes are not known for durability), a jersey and grass (for starting yak dung fires). After lunch into the bag went a 2kg sack of tsampa, a stomach of butter, a brick of tea, spoon, cup and the ancient teapot, and on top went the all-too-thin bedding roll. A hat was already on his head and his jacket pockets held a knife and lighter. They laughed as I shouldered my 20kg backpack and followed them.

FACTORS AFFECTING EQUIPMENT SELECTION

If you plan to stay only in lodges then camping equipment (tent, foam pad, stove, food, cutlery, plate and mug) is not needed. For the trek in (if you are not flying), regardless of the season, you'll want mainly cool loose clothes for the warm days. Above Namche the days are cooler and a set of interchangeable warm/windproof layers is best. These layers will also do for sitting around in the high lodges from late April to October but at other times a thick down jacket for cold mountain tops and fridge-like lodges is essential. An important key to staying healthy is sleeping well and warmly so that your body doesn't waste energy trying to keep you warm. Don't skimp on your sleeping bag.

During the main trekking season, October to December, it is nearly always dry so you need one set of clothes, ie only what you can wear at once (plus an extra shirt and a change of underwear). During late winter into April clothing may get wet so an extra thermal or light fleece might be appreciated.

All this can add up to a lot of equipment and since you (or a porter) must carry it all consider carefully how to keep it to a minimum. RNAC domestic flights enforce a 15kg limit; on helicopters they allow 25kg for foreigners and 15kg for locals.

Dress standards

These vary considerably around the country. Kathmandu is the most liberal and culturally diverse place though Western women will find dressing modestly attracts far less attention. The well-off (locals and foreigners) are expected to dress conservatively, casual but clean.

Along the regular trekking routes the Nepalese are used to (though have never understood) the comparatively odd and occasionally inde- cent ways in which Westerners dress, but in less frequented areas locals may still be quite shocked. Even with the Khumbu Sherpas' familiari- ty with foreigners, you will rarely see more than their head and fore- arms. Being dressed in a culturally acceptable way gains you much greater respect among the local people, a fact that many trekkers have commented upon.

For men, shorts are more or less acceptable although often you will be looked upon in a strange way because the only Nepalese that wear shorts are the porters (for the caste conscious, a low caste). T-shirts are OK, but singlets, running shorts or cycle pants, despite the fact that some porter-guides wear them, are going too far; bare chests are rude.

For women double standards exist. Long baggy shorts are worn although a skirt that falls at least to the knee, or light baggy trousers, are definitely more appropriate. A T-shirt is the minimum for modesty but Lycra pants invite unwarranted attention.

The layering principle

If you wear a number of thinner layers of clothing you can simply shed a layer if you get hot or add a layer if the temperature drops. In spite of the fact that this keeps your clothing dry (more comfortable and much warmer than if wet) you still see many people wearing a fleece jacket and dripping with sweat during the day. Of course the layer next to your skin will probably get wet with sweat so you should carry an extra T-shirt. When you stop, change the wet top for a dry one and then put an extra layer or two on to keep warm. This is a good principle for walking during the day but cold Himalayan nights require another. Forget the layers and simply put on dry thermals and the thickest down jacket you can find. Down is comfortable over a large range of tem- peratures, so even during a mild evening, thick jackets are still func- tional.

What to sleep in when it's cold

Surprisingly, if you put on all your clothes to go to bed you feel constricted and not a lot warmer. Using a sleeping sheet and thermal underwear is better and if that's not enough put your down jacket over your sleeping-bag. Alternatively, wear the down jacket but with only a T-shirt or thermal top on underneath. What keeps you warm is trapped air not the materials themselves. Pull the draw-cords tight and ensure your head is well insulated.

The Khumbu cold

The colder air gets, the less moisture it can hold, and the drier the air, the less it conducts (or feels) cold. Its impact is further reduced because the air density is much less than at sea level (a vacuum is, of course, the best insulator). This means that, although it is certainly cold in winter, warm clothes (especially good quality down) are very effective.

There are, however, several factors that work against this. As you breathe in through your nose, the nasal passages moisten the air and warm it to near blood temperature. In cold climes this means that as you breathe out you lose a lot of heat and water. Breathing through your mouth dries your throat out leaving you more susceptible to the Khumbu cough (p000). At sea level, at -40°C/-40°F, the heat you breathe out is roughly equivalent to the maximum heat your body is capable of producing at rest; hence the need for efficient insulating clothes (and the Eskimos' fat-rich diet, the richest source of calories). This heat loss is compounded by your needing to breathe more in the thinner air and, with less oxygen in the blood, your work rate and ability to generate heat are lowered. When tanked oxygen was first used for scaling Everest climbers immediately noticed that they felt warmer.

In short, don't let yourself get cold. Staying warm in the cold is much easier to manage than having to warm yourself up.

Foot care

Your feet will be doing far more work than they're probably used to so take great care of them. The rest of your body has the luxury of changes of clothes but your feet are confined to a single pair of boots that must cope with the extremes of heat and cold. So air them, and your socks and boots, frequently – lunch in the sun is an ideal time. Consider changing your socks more than once during the day and wash your feet and socks, if nothing else, at least every few days. If you feel a hot spot or a blister developing, you should stop immediately and cover it with a plaster/bandaid before it's too late to prevent damage.

EQUIPMENT LIST

• **Sleeping-bag** – essential. A down bag is lighter and more compact than a synthetic one of the same warmth. From April to the end of

October a three season bag is adequate. For the cold months, November to March, take particular care to choose a warm (four season) bag. When buying a down bag look for good and even thickness; the down should be fluffy and light. A muff around the top of the bag makes a big difference to overall warmth.

In Kathmandu you can easily rent ordinary sleeping-bags and there are also a few good down bags. Trekking companies often provide bags but if you already have a good one it's worth taking it instead.

• **Sleeping-bag liner** (cotton or silk). Saves washing your sleeping-bag, adds warmth and can double as a towel. In Kathmandu, these can be easily and cheaply made up from light cotton. Light-weight silk is harder to find and the more easily available imitation silk is not as good.

• **Rucksack/backpack** It's important to have a comfortable one. The feature that will help most in this respect is a good waist band – it should fit snugly without riding up your stomach (which interferes with breathing). At the same time it must not sit too low and touch your walking muscles. Small backpacks are neat and look trendy but are not really big enough. A larger pack is preferable since gear does not have to be tightly compressed and this makes packing easier. Group trekkers will need only a day pack but once you put a down jacket, wind pants, camera and water bottle in, plus more odds and ends, you need a big one, 30 litres or slightly more and a proper waist band will make it far more comfortable. It's possible to rent these in Kathmandu. Renting full sized rucksacks is not so easy, although there are plenty for sale.

• **Boots** One of the most important things for ensuring a happy trek is having comfortable feet. Carrying a backpack places a greater load on your feet than normal so rigid supportive boots will feel more comfortable in the long run. It's possible to trek in running shoes but the new generation light-weight trekking boots are far superior. Trekkers seem to get away with these boots even in winter but this can be dangerous during a snowfall. Sturdy but fairly light all-leather boots are better for cold weather (although they must be treated with water-proofing agents between January and the end of the monsoon).

When choosing boots look for good ankle support, plenty of toe room (essential for the long descents), a stiff sole (helps prevent tired feet by lessening twisting), and the boots should not be too heavy. Check the inner lining – leather is good and Cambrelle (which can destroy some of the bacteria that cause foot odour) is even better. Light-weight trekking boots generally have good shock-absorbing qualities but some foams can actually be crushed if too heavily loaded.

Leather boots, even with Sorbothane inserts, transmit shock via the outer edges so some extra shock-absorbing insoles are a good idea and will leave your feet feeling less tired at the end of the day. The Spenco range is best but sometimes hard to find. Boots must be worn in before trekking and this should include some steep hills.

For independent trekkers weight and space are of prime importance so a single pair of comfortable boots is generally enough. If trekking with a group, another pair of shoes for relaxing around camp can be useful. In cold weather down bootees are an option worth considering.

• **Socks** Most of the time your feet will be warm or even hot while walking so quality cotton mix sports socks are fine. Three to four pairs are enough. It's during some evenings and a few cold days that you will need good warm socks. Light-weight trekking boots generally fit snugly so wearing two pairs of socks at the same time (originally used in stiff boots to prevent blisters) is not practical. Instead a single pair of thick high quality socks is quite adequate, with an extra pair in reserve.

• **Down jacket** This is essential during the cold months and for sitting around in during the evenings. Find one of bum-warming and hand-warming length, big and thick with a hood. If trekking during the warmer months you will not need it until above Namche and even then a hat and a jersey or fleece combined with a rain jacket may well be adequate.

• **Down pants/trousers** – a luxury that may be appreciated above Namche from December to March.

• **Wind/rain jacket** – essential. High up, if the sun is shining, it can be wonderfully warm. When a breeze picks up the true air temperature becomes apparent and wind protection is a necessity. Since it rarely rains all day – or even at all in peak season – having an expensive, totally waterproof jacket is not necessary. When it starts raining everybody simply takes cover in the nearest shelter. Plastic ponchos are only of use during the monsoon.

• **Jersey/Fleece top/Polarplus top** Opinions vary – when it's cold people with down jackets consider down essential, but those with only fleece say it's adequate. Fleece is no substitute for a down jacket in real winter, however. From May to October, the wet times, fleece is a better choice. Kathmandu is a great place for buying luxuriously thick wool jerseys but they are very heavy to take trekking.

• **Shirt/blouse** T-shirts are popular but thin long-sleeved cotton shirts/blouses are more versatile: the collar protects the back of your neck and the sleeves can be rolled up or down. Take two so that you have a dry one to change into after trekking.

• **Underwear** Along the trail into Namche washing every day or two is never a problem. Higher up, when it is cold, the inclination to change your underwear and wash may occur less frequently. Four to five pairs is plenty. If you frequently wear a sports bra bring two, otherwise what you normally wear is fine.

• **Thermal underwear** Longjohns and a top are essential unless substituted by fleece for the warmer times, and in winter thermals should be used with fleece. Modern materials are extremely comfortable and functional.

• **Pants/trousers** Light material, loose and dark-coloured is best. These are easily bought in Kathmandu. Cotton/polyester travel pants or rock-climbing baggies in nylon or cotton/nylon mixes are best. Jeans are not practical; they are restricting and cold when damp.

• **Fleece pants/trousers** These are not needed during the warm seasons since longjohns with walking pants/trousers over the top will do. In winter they are almost a necessity, though.

• **Windproof/waterproof pants/trousers** If your trekking pants are partly windproof an additional pair isn't needed. They may, however, be useful during winter.

• **Warm hat** If your jacket does not have a hood then a warm hat is essential.

• **Sun hat** You need something to protect your head in hot sunny weather, particularly from April to the end of October. A light hat with a wide brim is good, as is a cotton scarf with a visor.

• **Mittens/Gloves** – essential except during the monsoon. The hand-knitted gloves available in Kathmandu are fine. If you already have ski gloves these will do. In particularly cold conditions a pair of thin liner gloves is invaluable.

• **Gaiters** Leggings that protect from the ankle to the knee are useful in Nepal only when it has snowed heavily. On the main trails, after a large fall of snow a path is cleared quickly so if you can wait you can survive without gaiters. Off the main trails or when climbing, they are essential.

• **Towel** Doesn't need to be big. Quick-drying sarongs are the best. A T-shirt makes a reasonable substitute (and gives it a little wash into the bargain).

• **Bathing suit** – only useful while walking along the Arun, where the water is less than glacial in temperature.

• **Insulating pad** – not needed unless you plan to spend a night or two outside.

• **Water bottle** A one-litre water bottle is essential and should be leakproof, tough and able to withstand boiling water.

• **Sun screen** – essential. The ultra-violet (UV) concentration increases around 4% for every 300m gain in altitude and snow reflects 75% of UV. Apply frequently and extensively at higher altitudes.

• **Sunglasses** These are essential and must be able to protect against UV. For prolonged high altitude sojourns side pieces are useful but ski goggles are not. If you wear prescription glasses it's best to get a pair of prescription sunglasses made. Alternatively detachable dark lens have proved adequate.

Contact lens wearers report problems with grit and pollution in Kathmandu but few problems in the hills except cleaning them in cold conditions. To prevent the cleaning solution from freezing it's best kept in your sleeping-bag on very cold nights. Also bring your glasses.

• **Torch/flashlight** – essential. A quality torch is invariably better, as are Western-quality batteries. Head torches are particularly handy for group trekkers in tents. Independent trekkers may get by with a cheap Kathmandu torch.

• **Ski pole** Useful for stiff descents on rough terrain. One for each hand is unnecessary. The telescoping variety is best.

• **Umbrella** Most useful during late spring and the monsoon through to the end of September, an umbrella is great protection against the sun and, coupled with a good rain jacket, is essential for surviving the monsoon. Available in Kathmandu.

• **Pack cover** – useful from January to the end of September. A large, carefully cut plastic bag can be a reasonable substitute. Both are available in Kathmandu; you can also buy plastic bags in main villages on the trail.

• **Toiletries** This is where you can really save some weight. There is no need for a half litre bottle of shampoo; chances are you will only wash your hair a few times. Finding hot water for a shave is not always easy and there are no plugs for electric razors. The smallest size of toothpaste sold is perfect for a month. Don't forget your deodorant ('the trekkers' shower'). Natural anti-bacterial mineral crystals are available, but hard to find, in the markets.

• **Toilet paper** Available on main routes so start with only one roll.

• **Lighter** – essential for burning used toilet paper and handy for lighting candles in lodges.

• **Moisturiser** A small tube for sensitive or well cared for skins is useful as the air is dry and the sun harsh.

• **Lip balm/Lypsyl with sunscreen** Essential to prevent chapped and blistered lips, this should be used frequently especially above Namche, and even on cloudy days.

• **Tampons/sanitary napkins** The supermarkets in Kathmandu always have limited stock, Namche generally has some but they're unavailable elsewhere.

• **Pre-moistened towelettes ('Wet-ones')** Handy for group trekkers but bulky for individuals.

CHECKLIST		
sleeping-bag	shirts/blouses	moisturiser
sleeping-bag liner	pants/trousers	lip care
rucksack/backpack	warm hat	tampons
boots	sun hat	camera & film
socks	mittens/gloves	first aid kit
down jacket	gaiters	water purification
down pants	towel	book
wind/rain jacket	bathing suit	money pouch/belt
jersey/fleece (Polartec)	water bottle	
top	sun screen	**Monsoon additions**
fleece pants	sunglasses	umbrella
underwear	torch/flashlight	pack cover
thermal underwear	toiletries	extra socks and optional
(top & bottom)	toilet paper & lighter	second pair of boots

• **Camera** If you bring one always keep it with you. Thieves are well aware of the value of cameras so check your insurance policy to ensure your camera is fully covered.

The modern compact, especially with zoom lens, is light and convenient but lacks the versatility of the SLR (interchangeable lens camera). A zoom lens provides brilliant flexibility. For portraits and stunning landscape details take a telephoto zoom (70-210mm) as well as a wider lens. Experienced photographers will appreciate a very wide angle lens. Today's auto-everything camera places high demands on batteries which sometimes give out in the cold so take several spare sets. One trick is to keep a set warm in a pocket ready to substitute. Don't dispose of batteries in the hills and bring some cleaning equipment as lenses can get very dusty.

A polarising filter is very useful and learning its tricks can be fun. It can significantly cut down reflection, giving skins, landscapes (tree leaves in particular) and the sky a deeper, richer colour. It does this best when used in bright sunlight at 90 degrees to the sun. It should not be used for every shot and it's possible to overdo the effect.

New to the market are cheap disposable cameras with panoramic lenses. While of inferior quality to a good camera they can produce reasonable results in the Himalaya.

• **Film** Kathmandu stocks a wide variety of the standard films (Kodak, Fuji, Konica, Agfa) at competitive prices. Slide film is available everywhere but supplies of Kodachrome are erratic. Black and white film is scarce.

• **First aid kit** See the medical section, p247.

• **Water purification kit** – essential, see p240.

• **Reading matter** Owing to the lack of night light and the social nature of trekking, there's not much time for reading. One paperback is usually enough and this can be exchanged in Namche or with another trekker.

• **Diary** Many people like to write a diary while they trek.

• **Money pouch/belt** Most people find wearing one while trekking a hassle and keep it buried in their pack until they stop for the evening.

If you plan to stay exclusively in lodges or are trekking with a group then a tent, foam pad, stove, cutlery, plate and mug are not needed.

Modern equipment aside, in Kathmandu it's possible to buy a thick jersey, cotton thermal underwear, socks, and hit the trail having spent little money. Whatever else you don't already have can be rented.

RENTING OR BUYING EQUIPMENT IN NEPAL

In Kathmandu

There's a great variety of rental equipment here which saves buying expensive specialised gear. Easy-to-rent items include down jackets, down pants, sleeping-bags, insulating pads, ice-axes, crampons, ski poles and day-packs. Also available (although stocks often run low) are water bottles, stoves, fuel bottles and large backpacks.

Many items can also be bought here, for less than in the West. You can rely on finding lightweight trekking boots (mainly HiTec brand, and only a few models), thick down jackets, locally-made rucksacks, inferior down sleeping bags, good quality head torches and their batteries, Maglite torches, fleece jackets (little variety, though), woollen mittens, gloves, socks and hats, jerseys, low quality longjohns, large 'porter' or duffel bags, telescoping ski poles and sunglasses. To check if sunglasses are UV protective, look on the inside of the lenses for a purple film, the coating necessary on plastic lenses to protect your eyes.

The items that are better brought from home include high quality socks, boots, thermal underwear, liner gloves, fleece and good quality rain gear.

Increasingly, equipment is being made in Nepal. While much of it is serviceable, the quality is much inferior to outdoor equipment from home. Disturbingly, local manufacturers have chosen to copy Western labels but these fakes are generally easy to pick out from the originals. The stitching is uneven, the webbing and fabrics feel inferior and are less well colour-coordinated, logos are on plastic labels and the designs are less innovative. All locally made Gore-Tex jackets and pants are definitely not made from Gore-Tex; and you can be sure that all brown 'The North Face Made in USA' labelled backpacks and sleeping bags are fakes – real North Face gear has the name on zip rings and pops, machine-embroidered logos and labels difficult to duplicate. Similarly, real Lowe and Wild Country rucksacks were once common but now are mostly fakes. If using a locally-made rucksack take a sewing kit. Dental floss (with several large needles) is the strongest and easiest to use thread.

Locally-made sleeping bags use either Russian or Korean down, offering reasonable quality, although since it is untreated it often smells after a while. Local 'down' is not worth buying.

In Namche

If you are flying in and out of the Khumbu then it's better to rent most of the equipment you require in Kathmandu. Comparing daily rates, renting gear in Namche tends to be marginally more expensive than in Kathmandu; but you don't have to carry it up or pay for the time it's not in use. You can rent good sleeping-bags, down jackets, down pants and down boots. Gloves and hats can also sometimes be rented or more usually bought. Quality socks and thermal underwear are usually unobtainable.

Left-over expedition equipment is also available for sale or rent, sometimes enough virtually to equip a serious expedition with high quality gear – ice-axes, crampons, plastic boots, climbing hardware, tents, down suits, the latest Gore-Tex clothing and more. The only problem is you never know exactly what will be there, and in what sizes. Some of this amazing equipment is dumped by expeditions to save the cost of having it carried out and some comes from the high altitude porters who must by law be given full equipment. This is often worth many times their minimal wages so it's a valuable part of their income. The prices are not dirt cheap but are generally cheaper, often quite significantly, than in the West.

ADVENTURE TREKKING EQUIPMENT

Group trekkers are provided with extensive lists. Climbers and experienced adventure trekkers planning to camp out frequently really need to plan very carefully: too much is horribly heavy unless you recruit a porter, and too little is limiting.

If trekking alone, or in a small group without a full trekking crew, it's really worth employing a porter who has trekked the route before. Not only will all your packs be lighter (often making the difference between an enjoyable trek and an endurance test) but experienced porters know the bivvy caves, the local herders, the track details and the latest on where you can find supplies in unusual places.

In Namche it's possible to rent everything necessary to climb a trekking peak: harnesses, snow stakes, ropes, crampons, tent etc. There's also left over expedition equipment for sale (see above).

High altitude – October

Day temperatures rarely drop below zero, except above 6000m, so good fleece and thermals are enough though lighter down jackets are still handy. Although the weather is mostly fine you should be prepared for a fall of snow. Leather boots are quite adequate for 6000m peaks and the high passes in fine weather; however, most people attempting trekking peaks do wear plastics.

High altitude – November and December

Day temperatures range from 10°C/50°F to -10°C/14°F and at night expect -10°C/14°F to -25°C/-13°F .

• **Day wear for climbing** should include thin/mid-weight longjohns plus semi-windproof trousers, T-shirt or mid-weight top with expedition weight top (or fleece) and a Gore-Tex shell. Liner gloves (thin and not windproof), backed up by something more substantial. The higher you go the better your mittens must be. Semi-windproof pants are generally enough without carrying extra Gore-Tex pants, even to 6500m.

• **Boots** This is the most difficult choice. You have to be planning a lot of pass-hopping and peak-bagging in rough country to wear plastics the whole time above Namche. Walking from Jiri in plastics is absolutely out of the question. Tough well-insulated leather boots backed by full gaiters (eg Yeti) are more manageable, even for a single trekking peak or high pass in reasonable conditions. Insulating shock-absorbing inner soles can make the world of difference to the comfort of big boots. The often hard to find Spenco range is the best. Foot care is incredibly important and should never be neglected. If there is only one part of you that you wash in weeks at high altitude, it should be your feet.

• **In the evening** you'll need a substantial down jacket, thin balaclava, and perhaps thick longjohns or fleece pants. Down pants are a luxury.

• **At night**, for several people a tent might be comfortable but a bivvy bag will do. However, if your sleeping-bag is exceptionally warm even a bivvy bag is superfluous (provided you have an emergency space/survival blanket for an unexpected snowfall). If using a Thermarest self-inflating mattress, an ultra-lite with a very thin back-up pad is a comfortable combination, otherwise a thick foam pad will suffice.

High altitude – January to April
Light down jackets or, better, thermals with fleece, and expedition-weight longjohns are comfortable to walk in. Plastic boots above 4000m/13,123ft are good for trekking, with some trekking crews and most lodge owners wearing them; and they are essential for climbing. If trekking in leather boots use full gaiter protection and take care to keep them dry. Down pants are almost a necessity and a tent is essential. You must be prepared for savage cold and snow-storms. Above 5000m/16,404ft a cold clear night can put thermometers off the scale.

Frostbite is something to be aware of. For hands, tough liner gloves are invaluable. Take great care of your feet: lacing boots tightly compresses the lining and the socks that are meant to keep your feet warm and restricts vital circulation. Inner boots may need lacing only around the ankle. The soles suck heat out and insulating inner soles are invaluable. A single extra layer of material around the whole boot (like a stuff sack) can make a big difference on the coldest mornings when wearing crampons.

High altitude – April and May
The warmer conditions are tough with soft, wet and often deep snow. Bring an alarm clock for early starts and a few novels for long snowy

afternoons. Tents and clothing should be waterproof and plastic boots are still best for climbing. Gore-Tex pants/salopettes and fleece are in their element; carry plenty of spare dry clothing and perhaps some camp shoes.

General gear
• **Stoves** Kathmandu and Namche have 'Blue Gaz' and most other canisters, with matching stoves for rent. Dirty, low quality kerosene is available in small quantities at virtually every lodge, and there is a reasonable chance of finding petrol at two or three lodges above Namche. Petrol is easier to light and significantly cleaner than kerosene. All fuel should be filtered.
• **Water bottles/bags** A total capacity of $1^{1}/_{2}$ 3 litres per person is useful for camping.

Climbing gear
See the trekking peak descriptions for recommendations. For a first trip in the Himalaya, many climbers strongly advise beginning with a trek and a light climb or exploration rather than focusing on the vertical. With this approach you need technical gear basically just for walking on glaciers. There's lots of second-hand climbing gear for sale in Namche and Kathmandu. Always available are cheap titanium ice-screws, snow stakes, jumars, karabiners, slings, ice-axes, crampons (step-in and strap-on) and used ropes (fixed and climbing).

Excess gear can be stored at Namche, or flown back to Kathmandu from Syangboche (US$2/kg) or Lukla (US$0.50/kg) in a few days.

Don't neglect your crew's equipment
While you may have the latest and best equipment your crew certainly will not. Sirdars usually have reasonable gear although it is worth checking their climbing gear and sleeping bag. The sherpas and kitchen hands are less well-equipped and generally appreciate cast-offs, perhaps a Kathmandu fleece or a good piece of clothing as part of the tips. Porters have nothing and appreciate clean serviceable clothes of any sort and especially old running shoes or boots. See p84-6 for notes on employing and looking after crew.

RECOMMENDED READING

Kathmandu has the world's best selection of books on Nepal and the surrounding mountain areas. Prices can be below normal cover prices so it's also an attractive place to buy them. The Thamel area boasts many second-hand bookshops so finding cheap paperback novels and guidebooks is easy.

Guidebooks

For exploring the Kathmandu Valley and the rest of the country there's a wide range available. Apa's *Nepal Insight Guide* has beautiful coffee-table photos and an informative text but is, however, of limited use as a practical guide. Apa also have a *Kathmandu Insight Guide* covering the Valley and a *Kathmandu* city guide suitable for a flying visit.

Lonely Planet's *Nepal – a travel survival kit* is an exhaustive guide to the Kathmandu Valley with good practical information and ideas on what to do after your trek. Moon Publications' *Nepal Handbook* is a literate in-depth guide to the country and the *Rough Guide to Nepal* has interesting background information and a chatty style.

If you take one other book to the Khumbu it should be *The Story of Mt Everest (Sagarmatha) National Park* by Margaret Jefferies. This is an interesting and educational introduction to the park, with profits going to conservation.

Trekking/mountaineering books

Hundreds of expedition accounts have been published but many are of interest only to avid climbers. The books that I particularly enjoyed are listed below.

Bill Tilman and Eric Shipton are names closely linked with much of the early exploration of the Himalaya and Karakoram. It's incredible, even judged by modern standards, the ground they covered and the peaks that they conquered. Their second legacy is a series of books written in elegant prose with vivid and interesting descriptions that twinkle with penetrating insights, often curiously and hilariously funny. Their individual books have been reprinted in several volumes. Eric Shipton's *The Six Mountain-Travel Books* (The Mountaineers, Seattle, 1985) includes two books about Everest: *Upon That Mountain* and *The Mount Everest Reconnaissance Expedition 1951*. HW Tilman's *The Seven Mountain-Travel Books* (The Mountaineers, Seattle, 1983) includes *Everest 1938* and *Nepal Himalaya*.

Everest by Walt Unsworth (Oxford Illustrated Press, 1989) is a climbing history capturing the hopes and fears of the attempts on Everest.

Everest: the best writing and pictures from 70 years of human endeavour, edited by Peter Gillman (Little, Brown & Co, London 1993) features interesting historical snapshots of the climbing of Everest.

Cho Oyu by Favour of the Gods by Herbert Tichy covers the first ascent of Cho Oyu. With only three members this was not the usual grand expedition, and neither is the book written in the traditional heroic style.

Nothing Venture Nothing Win by Sir Edmund Hillary is an interesting autobiographical account of his adventures including the scaling of Everest. His *Schoolhouse in the Clouds* offers an insight into the development of the Khumbu and other Sherpa areas.

Sherpas: Reflections on Change in Himalayan Nepal by James F Fisher is an interesting and readable investigation into the changes in the Khumbu that tourism and schooling have brought, with perceptive feedback from local people.

MAP RECOMMENDATIONS

This guide specifically includes many maps, enough to cover a normal trek to the Khumbu from Jiri or Lukla. However for identifying the many surrounding peaks and features, detailed topographic maps are invaluable and virtually essential for exploration off the beaten track.

The Schneider 1:50,000 series published by Freytag-Berndt und Artaria, Vienna covers the entire area in beautiful four-colour topographic maps. The *Khumbu Himal* is the most useful for all trekking, exploring and climbing from Namche to the north. *Tamba Kosi* covers Jiri to Junbesi (and the approaches to the mountains south of the Rolwaling but not the range itself), including from Dolakha. *Shorong/Hinku* includes the trekking routes from Junbesi and Lukla to Namche as well as north of Junbesi, the Hongu (the area surrounding Mera peak) and the eastern Arun trekking route from Lukla/Kharikhola to the Surkie La. *Dudh Kosi* covers Phaplu to Junbesi, and also from the Rumjatar and Lamidanda airports up the Dudh Kosi. *Rolwaling Himal* includes the area from the Trashi Labsta to Simigoan and the Tamba Kosi, and is useful for exploring the Rolwaling range. *Lapchi Kang* covers from the Tamba Kosi to Barabise. These maps are available in Kathmandu (Rs600-850) but occasionally stocks run low so they are safer purchased at home from specialist bookshops.

The National Geographic Magazine (USA) published a beautiful map of the area surrounding Everest but, unfortunately, it does not cover the Gokyo valley, or even below Pangboche. Inserted in the 1988 centennial issue, it was the most accurate and detailed 1:50,000 map ever made. Use it for the Amphu Labtsa, Mingbo La, Sherpani Col and climbing around Chukhung. It's stocked by most bookshops in Kathmandu.

Also readily available in Kathmandu are several cheap general maps covering either Jiri to Kala Pattar or Lukla to Kala Pattar. There is little to choose between them, and even up-dated '96-97 editions are loaded with minor inconsistencies but they are adequate for trekking.

Health precautions and inoculations

The physical aspects of trekking

Trekking means walking almost every day for four to seven hours, often for three weeks or more. Many people begin only moderately fit but generally cope well and end the trek feeling amazingly healthy. A few find the reality of continuous walking difficult. If you lead a sedentary life then plan an exercise programme well before you go. Brisk walks are a good start, building up to include walking up and down hills with the boots you plan to wear trekking, to introduce your body to the rigours of hill walking. Jogging and aerobics are reasonable substitutes. Muscles strengthen fairly quickly, although painfully if you overdo exercise. Stretching should be included in your training programme: once you've warmed up stretch gently, without bouncing, holding each pose for 20-30 seconds.

It is important to realise that while trekking you can be a long way from help. Sometimes you will have to be your own doctor, there is no other choice. However, the Khumbu region is better endowed with medical facilities than anywhere else in rural Nepal. There's a hospital at Kunde (an hour above Namche) staffed by two Western doctors. The Himalayan Rescue Association post at Pheriche is staffed by two more Western doctors and open during the two busy trekking seasons. On the walk in, there's a large health post at Junbesi and a hospital half a day below at Phaplu. There are also health posts but these are not staffed by doctors.

MEDICAL CONDITIONS

Anyone with heart, lung and blood pressure abnormalities or a continuing medical condition should have a check-up and get a medical opinion before setting off.

• **Older people** Many recently-retired people have made it to the top of Kala Pattar (5554m/18,222ft) so age need not be a barrier. The older you are, the more important prior fitness preparation is.

• **Children** Caution should be exercised when taking children trekking. Younger people can be slower to adapt to altitude, and very young children have difficulty in communicating exactly how they feel. The limit generally considered the safe maximum for pre-teenage children is 3000m/9843ft. Within the limitations, trekking with children can be very rewarding and bring you even closer to the locals. You share a common bond for there are few people without children in Nepal. Little legs are easily carried by a porter when tired, and Sherpanis are good babysitters. Teenagers have significantly more chance of succumbing to the effects of altitude than adults so school groups should allow an extra day or two over the most conservative itineraries and be particularly watchful.

• **Asthma** is no reason to avoid trekking. Except in polluted Kathmandu there are fewer irritants in the air so most asthmatics actually feel better while trekking. Look after your medication – wear your inhaler on a chain around your neck or keep it in a pocket. There is still the normal risk of a serious attack so brief your companions on what to do.

• **Diabetes** – again no reason to avoid trekking but you cannot afford to lose the medication so keep it with you at all times and warn you friends on the procedures in case there's an emergency. It's very important to monitor your glucose levels frequently and carefully and to keep blood sugar levels well controlled.

• **High blood pressure** Blood pressure will fluctuate more and be higher than usual while on a trek. You should seek the advice of a doctor who is aware of the history of your condition.

• **Previous heart attacks** Studies have yet to be conducted but it is likely that the level of exertion required on a trek is more significant than the altitude factor. Get the advice of your doctor.

• **Pregnancy** You are unlikely to be near medical care if complications should arise so it's probably not a good idea to go trekking while pregnant. The effects of reduced oxygen at high altitude on the foetus have not yet been studied.

INOCULATIONS

The majority of Nepal's population has no access to doctors or modern medicines so the health situation is extremely poor. Disease and malnourishment are rife and even sickness easily cured by medicine often leads to death without it. Visitors arriving with immunisations, healthy bodies and access to clean water are much less at risk. A bout of diarrhoea, however, is almost inevitable, no matter how careful you are. There are no official immunisation requirements to enter Nepal but the following should be considered. The best people to consult about the vaccinations currently recommended are clinics specialising in travel medicine. They will have access to more up-to-date information than a normal general practitioner.

• **Hepatitis A** Usually passed on in contaminated water; immunisation is considered a must by most doctors unless you have had hepatitis A before. The new vaccine is Havrix and a full course will give up to ten years protection. A cheaper alternative is a gamma globulin injection which should be given just before departure and be repeated every 4-6 months while travelling. Although this is a blood-based product there is no chance of contracting AIDS from this immunisation.

• **Hepatitis B** This disease is avoidable since, like AIDS, it's passed by unsafe sex or contaminated blood products. A vaccine is available.

• **Meningitis** Occasional cases of meningococcal meningitis occur in Nepal. It is an often fatal disease but the vaccine is safe and effective and should be obtained.

• **Cholera** The World Health Organisation no longer recommend this vaccination. It is only partially effective and often causes a reaction. The risk of travellers acquiring cholera in Nepal is extremely low.

• **Typhoid** is prevalent in Nepal. There are now a variety of vaccines and one should be obtained.

• **Tetanus-Diptheria** This vaccine is recommended if you have not had a booster in the last 10 years. Many doctors advise a tetanus booster every time you intend to travel for any length of time.

• **Polio** If you escaped immunisation as a child a series of vaccinations is recommended. If you have not had a booster as an adult, one may be required. Check with your doctor.

• **Measles, mumps and rubella** If you did not have these diseases (or the vaccinations) as a child you may need a vaccination.

• **Japanese Encephalitis B** This disease is transmitted by mosquitoes and there have been sporadic outbreaks in the Terai (lowland Nepal) and India. Western doctors based in Kathmandu suggest the vaccination only for people visiting the Terai for extended periods.

• **Rabies** This deadly virus is transmitted by the bite of an infected animal, usually a monkey or dog. The risk of being bitten is minimal, probably greatest in Kathmandu since some of the street dogs are certainly rabid. A vaccination is available but even if you've had it you'll then need a follow-up course of two further injections. If you've not been vaccinated and are unlucky enough to be bitten, a series of injections is available only from the CIWEC clinic in Kathmandu and should be started within a week.

• **Malaria** Carried only by the lowland *Anopheles* mosquito, malaria exists in the Terai in Nepal (ie below 1000m/3281ft), and across much of the rest of rural Asia. There's no risk in Kathmandu or while trekking (except possibly at low altitudes during the monsoon). If visiting Chitwan or going rafting then consider taking tablets to protect against malaria. The drug of choice for different areas changes as resistance builds up in the parasite. If you have just visited a malarial area, for example India or Thailand, then it's vital to continue taking your medication for the recommended length of time.

The first line of protection, however, is to avoid being bitten. The *Anopheles* mosquito is active only between early evening and dawn so you should cover up well between these times and use mosquito repellent on any exposed skin.

If you are behind on any of the immunisations listed above, they can be safely obtained at clinics in Kathmandu.

MEDICAL INSURANCE

A combined travel/medical insurance policy is a sensible choice for any traveller and a requirement for most tours booked in your home country. Since trekking may require helicopter rescue which is not always covered by general travel schemes, trekking companies have specially-tailored policies. Independent trekkers should register with their embassy which will be contacted if helicopter rescue is required. Forms are available at the Himalayan Rescue Association in Kathmandu. Note that a rescue mission does not take place unless there is a guarantee of payment by a trekking company or your embassy (see p248).

For health precautions in Kathmandu see p79, and see p240 for a detailed discussion of staying healthy on the trek.

PART 2: NEPAL

Facts about the country

GEOGRAPHICAL BACKGROUND

Perilously placed between the Asian superpowers of India and China, Nepal is a land-locked rectangle roughly 800km by 200km (500 by 120 miles). It straddles the hills and mountains between the enormous Ganges plain and the high Tibetan plateau. In the south is a narrow strip of flat land known as the Terai. Rising abruptly from this are the small Siwalik hills and the Mahabharat range. Between are broad valleys, the Inner Terai, which were once infested with malaria. Thanks to DDT spraying in the 1950s that threat has been eradicated and this rapidly developing area is now the fertile bread basket of Nepal. The wide band of steep middle hills sheltered the older centres of population – Kathmandu, Pokhara and smaller towns like Jiri. To the north are the majestic Himalaya, including Kanchenjunga, Makalu, Lhotse, Everest, Cho Oyu, Manaslu, Annapurna and Dhaulagiri – eight of the ten highest peaks on the planet.

The Himalaya

As well as being the world's highest mountains, the Himalaya are also the youngest. What fascinated early explorers was the fact that they did not form the continental divide. This is, in fact, to be found further north on the Tibetan Plateau.

The Himalaya were formed by the collision of two continental plates, with the Indian plate being forced under the edge of the Asian plate, pushing up part of the Tibetan Plateau into jagged mountains. However, as fast as the Himalaya rose, the rivers to the north cut their southern paths faster, which accounts for the great depth of many of the valleys in the region.

The patterns of formation can be seen on many of the rock faces, especially the Lhotse-Nuptse wall (where distorted sedimentation lines are quite obvious) and from Kala Pattar (where continuation of the yellow band near the top of Everest can be seen in Changtse/Bei Peak, the mountain to the north in Tibet).

CLIMATE

Nepal is at the same latitude as Florida and Cairo so the climate in the lowland areas is hot with temperate winters. The trekking areas are, however, well above sea level and consequently temperatures vary considerably. The climate comprises distinct seasons but with an important additional feature: the monsoon. This moisture-laden wind amasses in the Bay of Bengal and sweeps up across India to spend its forces on the Himalayan mountain chain between late June and mid-September. It does not rain continuously or even every day. Rather there may be a couple of heavy downpours during the day that usually last less than an hour, keeping the summer heat down to bearable levels. Sometimes it rains only at night. After the monsoon retreats, the climate is dry and sunny for the remainder of the year. Autumn is renowned for clear skies and pleasant temperatures. By winter the high hills take on dry brown shades and the mountains are occasionally dusted with fresh snow. The colourful spring, March to May, is punctuated by the odd shower of life-giving rain but the heat builds until the monsoon relief arrives. The trekking seasons are detailed on p30.

HISTORICAL OUTLINE

Facts and fables

Nepal's early history is clouded in folklore and legend. One story relates how the Kathmandu Valley, then a huge sacred lake, was emptied through a channel cut by the stroke of a god's sword. The Chobar Gorge, which drains the valley, indeed fits the description and geologists maintain that the soil in the valley gained its renowned fertility as a lake bed.

At the time of the Buddha, in the second half of the 6th century BC, the Kirati ruled the Kathmandu valley. They were a Mongol race whose descendants include the Rai and Limbu now settled in the east of Nepal. Buddhism spread slowly and the arts and architecture developed under the 28 successive kings. Around 300 AD the Indian Licchavi dynasty invaded Nepal, introducing the caste system and Hinduism, which intermingled with Buddhism, a process continuing to this day. Around 900AD power struggles enveloped the valley and it was not until 1200AD that the Malla dynasty became established. The caste system was rigidly defined and (although there was occasional infighting that laid the towns of the valley to waste) trade, cottage industries and the enduring Newar culture blossomed. The 1400s left the wealth of architecture, carving and sculpture that surrounds the Durbar Squares in Kathmandu, Patan and Bhaktapur. Known then as

Kantipur, Lalitpur and Bhadgoan, respectively, these three cities divided into separate flourishing but quarrelsome kingdoms in 1482 on the death of Yaksha Malla.

Unity, treachery and extravagance

In 1768 Prithvi Narayan Shah of Gorkha (a princely kingdom between Kathmandu and Pokhara) conquered the Kathmandu valley and began the Shah dynasty that continues by direct blood line to this day. He started by consolidating the many individual kingdoms that now form the basis of Nepal. His successors, although 'honourably defeated' in the 1814 war with British India were able to resist colonial domination, a fact that the Nepalese are proud of to this day.

Overall control by the Shah dynasty was undermined by the rich nobles whose constant struggle for power often led to violence. However in 1846 unequivocal control was seized by Jung Bahadur Rana who killed all the ministers and high officials in what became known as the 'Kot Massacre'. He declared himself Maharajah, and the founder of a second line of Nepalese kings. To ensure continuity of the line his family married into the Shah dynasty and other high caste families. Jung Bahadur Rana alone fathered over 100 children. He and his heirs effectively ruled the country, although the King, kept in seclusion, was the highest authority. The Rana family amassed incredible wealth, visible in the numerous European-style palaces (inspired by Jung Bahadur's visit to Europe) which now house various government departments in Kathmandu. This feudal dynasty held Nepal in its grip for over a century until 1950, when the puppet king Tribhuvan escaped to India.

The post-war period

Following the end of the Second World War much of Asia was in turmoil. Newly independent India, and China, both seemed to have their hungry eyes on the tiny neighbour that divided them. Political discontent and fear were growing in Nepal.

Now known as the father of democracy in Nepal, BP Koilara managed to undermine the Ranas' control and India assisted in engineering the return to power of King Tribhuvan in 1951. Keen to establish its independence as a country in its own right and not an Indian vassal, Nepal quickly invited foreign countries to open consulates in Kathmandu. Thus ended more than a century of isolation.

The panchayat system

In 1955 King Tribhuvan died and was succeeded by his son, Mahendra. The constitution was reformed and in 1957 the people of Nepal voted in the Nepal Congress Party with a decisive majority.

However, bribery and corruption played a large part in the country's first elections and continued in the new government. This gave King Mahendra the excuse to step into power and at the end of 1959 he arrested the entire cabinet. He took direct control himself, later instituting the *panchayat* system. Under this system the locally-elected leaders of village councils nominated the candidates for higher posts, all ultimately under the King. In theory, this was quite a reasonable system and was endorsed by the new Eton-educated King Birendra (still the reigning monarch) when his father died in 1972.

Democracy established

Corruption and self-interest prevailed and popular discontent spread again, erupting in 1979 with rare violence in Kathmandu. The panchayat system was put to the test by public referendum and survived but only just. Its days were numbered and the government's inability to solve a serious trade dispute with India in 1990 and its continued persecution of the opposition caused public protest. Meetings dispersed with bullets became riots and the palace was surrounded by machine-gun toting soldiers.

The soldiers were supposedly there to protect the King but soon let it be known on which side their sympathies lay, as did the foreign aid donors. Cornered, the King lifted the ban on political parties in April 1990. He agreed to become a constitutional monarch and a temporary government was formed.

In 1991 the promised elections were held. The Nepal Congress Party (symbol: the tree) won, putting the Communist Party (the sun) in the role of opposition party.

Congress versus communists

After the elections the new government announced considerable changes. The price of subsidised foods (eg rice) was freed to stimulate production. Tourism was targeted for development and the Nepalese rupee gently floated on the open market, dealing a death-blow to the flourishing black market.

Expecting the promised improvements and a rise in living standards to come quickly once the democratic machine was in place, Nepalis soon lost confidence in their new government. The opposition parties were quick to take advantage of this, stirring up riots in which several people were killed. The government itself was torn by internal dissent and Nepal's second general election was called 18 months early, in November 1994. The communists took power, ruling in a coalition government under the leader of the United Marxist-Leninist Party, Man Mohan Adhikari.

Nepal's experiment with communism lasted till September 1995 when Adhikari's party lost a vote of no-confidence in parliament. A tripartite coalition government composed of the Nepal Congress Party, the right-wing Rastriya Prajatantra Party and the pro-India Nepal Sadbhavana Party, was sworn in under prime minister Sher Bahadur Deuba.

ECONOMY

Nepal's rural backwardness may be attractive to tourists but the mediaeval way of life is not easy for most Nepalese. In the past tenant farmers, the majority of the population, paid crippling taxes to landlords in a vicious semi-feudal system. The 1964 reforms sought to redress this by land redistribution and reducing rental to a (still unbearable) 50% of the crop. They were only partly successful. Even now 90% of the population lives off the land with the majority existing at subsistence level. It's a simple, hard life virtually without money, the reason that the average annual per capita income is so low – around US$150.

This legacy means the prospects for the farmers' children are indescribably bleak. Nepal's astronomic birth rate and a lack of new arable land are the main problems. The ever-expanding population has been partly absorbed by the Inner Terai but the amount of arable land available per person continues to drop. Crop yields have increased but cannot keep pace with demand so Nepal has become a net food importer. There are dire predictions about the decline of land fertility and the destruction of the forests; already there are food and firewood shortages. Without development miracles this situation can only get worse.

Nepal is barely industrialised. Demand for jobs far outstrips supply resulting in exploitative wages and appalling working conditions. With no manufacturing base all machinery and construction materials must be imported which means paying hard currency or Indian rupees, and earning these is difficult. Of the few exports, the majority go to India since reliable and cheap shipping is problematic for greater distances. The hard currency earners are carpets, tourism (250,000 people a year), and Nepalese working overseas, particularly the Gurkha soldiers. Foreign aid programmes are, however, big business in Nepal and a third of government funding comes from this source.

DEVELOPMENT

There is no doubt that considerable development is needed in Nepal, if only to avert tragedy. The root of the problem is the spiralling population growth. Nature's harsh natural balance was upset by the introduction of a few simple life-saving measures such as oral rehydration salts and basic hygiene principles. The 5 million people that lived in Nepal in 1950 have multiplied to 21.5 million, and this population is expected to double in the next 30 years, with catastrophic results.

It's difficult to get the message of birth control across to Nepal's peasant farmers when to them more hands are an asset and extra children an insurance against others that may die. Obviously education and health care are a good start. If you are secure in the knowledge that your children will live (their health protected by vaccines and clean water) and believe that their quality of life may be better (with education) you will be more interested in trying to limit the size of your family. Electricity and roads provide opportunities for diversification from agriculture and a move to a more cash-orientated society, where the benefits of birth control become more obvious.

Such massive changes don't happen overnight, certainly not in Nepal, despite vast quantities of foreign aid. As with aid programmes the world over, not all the money or aid gets through to where it's most needed. Charlie Pye-Smith's *Travels in Nepal* is an interesting assessment of the successes or otherwise of some of the aid programmes in the country and includes the Khumbu region.

The people of eastern Nepal

A cultural bridge between Tibet and India, Nepal is a colourful patchwork of ethnic groups, castes and clans. Although officially the only Hindu kingdom in the world, tides of history have also deposited Buddhists and even a few Muslims and Christians. Unlike in India the caste system is not institutionalised and is generally only observed by the beneficiaries, the higher castes.

Newars, with their rich urban-based culture and separate language, are the traditional inhabitants of the Kathmandu valley, responsible for much of the famous architecture and art. Outside Kathmandu they are mainly merchants, particularly shop owners. **Brahmins** are the high Hindu priestly caste rather than an ethnic group. Traditionally they earn money from performing religious rituals and must avoid being polluted by people of a lower caste. Many now work in the government and in business. In the hills they are often little better off than the lower castes and intermarriage has taken place.

Sherpas (see p104), Kirat (Rai and Limbu) and Tamangs are the ethnic groups most commonly encountered on the Everest trek. **Rais** are found south of Solu and Pharak, particularly in the area between the Khumbu and the Arun. The villages of Bung and Gudel are exclusively Rai and you'll also meet them at the Namche Saturday market. Usually stocky and short, the Rai have Mongoloid features, a round face and a tanned but fairly light skin and they wear light-coloured clothing. The diet staples are rice, maize, wheat and millet, mixed with a variety of vegetables. The Rais are well represented in Gurkha battalions of the Indian and British armies. **Tamangs** are people of the middle hills and very often act as porters. The women are distinctive with nose jewellery that hangs over their lips while the men wear a rough sleeveless woollen tunic when it is cold. They are Buddhists and like the Sherpas have their roots in Tibet.

Practical information for the visitor

VISA AND TREKKING REGULATIONS

Visas

All visitors require a visa for Nepal, easily obtained at the airport or border on arrival (one passport-sized photo required) or at Nepalese embassies abroad, sometimes the more expensive option.

At the airport a single entry visa valid for 15 days costs US$15 and a 30 day visa costs US$25, payable only in US$ cash. A double entry visa costs US$40 for an initial 30 days for the first visit and provides another 30 days on re-entry. Similarly, a multiple entry visa for US$60 is valid initially for 60 days. All visas can be extended in Kathmandu.

Trekking permits

To go trekking you need a trekking permit, obtainable from the Department of Immigration in Kathmandu. For the first month of a permit you're charged the equivalent in Nepalese rupees of US$5 per week, and for the following months, the equivalent of US$10 per week. In addition you need a permit (Rs650) to enter the national park.

If trekking through a trekking agency they will organise the permit, national park entrance fee and visa extensions as required. For trekking peak permit costs, see p230.

Visa extensions and trekking permit applications

Visa and trekking permit applications are accepted at the Department of Immigration, conveniently located in Thamel. It's open Sunday to Friday, 10.30am to 12.30pm, closed Saturdays and the main public holidays. If you apply in the morning you can usually collect your permit/extension in the afternoon of the same day.

Visa extensions cost US$1 per day (paid in equivalent Nepalese rupees), for up to a maximum of five calendar months in one year. Visas for children under 10 years old are free.

Leaving the country

Immigration officials will fine you if your visa has expired by more than one day. When leaving by air, you're entitled to cash back into hard currency only 15% of the rupees for which you have money changing receipts. For those heading to India excess Nepalese rupees are easily converted into Indian rupees.

GETTING TO NEPAL

By air

The quality airlines that fly into Kathmandu are Lufthansa and Singapore Airlines. Other carriers include Thai, Pakistan International Airlines, Indian Airlines, Royal Nepal, Bangladesh Biman, Aeroflot and Dragonair. Apart from Royal Nepal and Indian Airlines, which operate daily flights into Kathmandu, most airlines have only two flights a week.

• **From the West** For the cheapest flights check the travel advertising section of the major papers. From the UK the cheapest return ticket is on Bangladesh Biman at around £400. The fastest flight from London is on Royal Nepal which touches down only in Frankfurt and the Gulf. Lufthansa also flies between Kathmandu and Frankfurt, with connections to London.

• **From India** On Indian Airlines there are daily flights between Kathmandu and Delhi (US$142/£95) or Varanasi (US$71/£47). On Tuesday, Thursday and Sunday there are flights between Kathmandu and Calcutta (US$96/£64). Royal Nepal also operates flights between Patna and Kathmandu.

• **From Thailand** Since the border with Burma is closed the only way is to fly. There are direct flights or the cheapest combination is to fly from Bangkok to Calcutta, then take surface transport.

• **From Tibet** The surface route is the more interesting but you can fly between Kathmandu and Lhasa for US$190/£125. See p91.

See p69 for information on arrival at Kathmandu airport.

Overland from India

From Delhi or Varanasi the most convenient border crossing is Sunauli/Belahiya, reached via Gorakhpur. There are no through buses; whatever the agents in Kathmandu or Delhi may say you have to change at the border. It's not difficult to arrange your own tickets along the way and doing it yourself gives you the option to stop where you want to. Doing the trip from Delhi to Kathmandu all by bus is for masochists only and can take up to 60 hours. It's better to travel between Delhi and Gorakhpur by train (approximately US$4/£2.50 in 2nd class) then take a local bus for the three-hour journey to the border at Sunauli.

Immigration is staffed from dawn to dusk although the border does not physically close at night. If you arrive late simply walk across and stay at the better hotels on the Nepalese side, then visit immigration the next morning. Without a visa and entry stamps you'll encounter many problems in Kathmandu. Buses to Kathmandu (US$2/£1.30, 12 to 14 hours) leave from 5am to 9am for the day service and from 4pm to about 8pm for the night buses. For much of the way the route follows the Trisuli River and the scenery is an impressive introduction to the hills of Nepal. The road is being rebuilt over large sections and conse-quently is rough.

From Calcutta the usual route is via Patna to the border at Raxaul/Birganj. From there the direct Hetauda-Naubise road is narrow so buses take the longer route via Mugling to Kathmandu. The border crossing at Kakarbhitta, near Darjeeling, is open but the road is partic-ularly rough and often washed out during the monsoon.

LOCAL TRANSPORT

• **Air** Nepal has an extensive domestic network to make up for the lack of roads. With four competing airlines, services, although basic, are efficient. Since radar is not used bad weather can postpone flights, sometimes for several days. Tickets can be bought direct from the air-line offices, travel agents, however, can normally get them for the same price, saving you a taxi trip. Fares must be paid in hard currency, cash or travellers cheques, not rupees. For more details see p88.

In 1992 Asian Airlines pioneered the use of the large MI-17 Russian helicopters in Nepal. Designed for the military, they can carry around 26 people or 3500kgs of cargo and are big enough to drive a jeep into. Delivered new, these helicopters were flown all the way from Russia to Nepal loaded with spares and crew. Everest Air and Nepal Airways soon followed suit with used versions of these workhorse helicopters. At present all the pilots and flight engineers are Russian,

---

Helicopter etiquette

Never approach a helicopter while the rotor is moving; the flight attendant will show you when to board. Sometimes this is before the engine is warmed up, some-times as it is noisily started. Luggage is loaded via the back doors and simply piled up in the middle while passengers sit along the two bench seats. Sweets and cot-ton wool (to plug your ears) are given out. Lift-off is rapid, the rotors clatter, the whole machine throbs and the ground is left far below. The flights have a wild feel to them: no personal in-flight video here: not even a padded seat!

Although safety is paramount the helicopters sometimes run in cloudier weather than the planes could previously. They are able to dodge clouds and can hunt up or down the valleys for a way through. Occasionally, they may land at an airport along the way and wait for a clearing in the cloud cover. So, if you wake up to thick cloud in Lukla, the choppers may well get through but it could be a wild ride back.

and exceptionally experienced, while the co-pilots and flight attendants are Nepalese. Behind the scenes are two or three Russian ground crew per helicopter, responsible for maintenance. There are plans to replace the Russians with Nepalese but since years of experience are required this will not be for some years.

• **Long distance buses** Services are run using sturdy Indian buses that cope well with the rough roads. Night coaches are for masochists and better avoided since sleep is impossible. The day buses are often filled to bursting point and feature a variety of seating, mostly unsuitable for long legs. The spectacular scenery can, however, make up for the lack of comfort. It's important to realise that you pay to get from A to B, whether you have a seat or not.

A few tourist coaches have been organised. These cost a little more and are much less crowded. See a travel agent for tickets.

• **Taxis** are plentiful and cheap to use. Following the taxi strike and rate hike in 1995, all are now required to have meters and to use them. Don't accept any stories about meters being broken or needing recalibrating.

• **Hiring a vehicle** is best organised directly with a taxi driver for a taxi, or through a travel agent for mini-buses.

• **Local buses**, usually large Mercedes vans that have seen better days, these are cheap and unbelievably crowded.

• **Tempos** are small three-wheeled vehicles. There are two types: auto-rickshaws which are black and yellow, and fixed-route tempos with enough space in the back for eight Nepalis, or a single foreigner with a backpack!

• **Cycle-rickshaws** are found in all major towns and bargaining is required before you depart.

• **Bicycles** are a convenient and cheap way to get around Kathmandu. Standard bikes and mountain bikes are easily hired in the Thamel and Freak Street areas. The place would make a perfect bicycle city if it weren't for the pollution and the lack of road rules.

LANGUAGE

Nepali, a Sanskrit-based language similar to India's Hindi, is the country's official language. For approximately half the population Nepali is not the mother-tongue, ethnic languages such as Sherpa and Newari being widely used in local areas. Nepali is the medium for schools but English is also taught and you'll meet a surprising number of children who know at least a few English words. In the tourism industry English is the main language, although it is by no means fluently spoken. In the main trekking areas it's quite possible to get by speaking only English.

It is handy to learn a few phrases if trekking without a guide (see Appendix D). Learning more is very rewarding and will provide many amusing reactions. Simple spoken Nepali is not difficult and most Kathmandu bookshops sell small phrase-books.

ELECTRICITY

The electricity grid covers only the major towns and cities, and power cuts are frequent. The supply is 220V and 50Hz using old-type round-pin sockets (two-pin and three-pin). Rural Nepal has no electricity, apart from a few very small-scale private or foreign aid hydro schemes. On a trek it is impossible to recharge batteries for video recorders, other than with a solar panel because even if a village has electricity, the power is rationed to a few bulbs per house and turned on only for the evening. An efficient new system is now operational in Namche, facilitating the recharging of batteries here.

TIME

Nepal is 5 hours and 45 minutes ahead of Greenwich Mean Time (GMT), and 15 minutes ahead of India (as a show of independence). There is no special summer time.

MONEY

The Nepalese rupee (Rs) comes in banknote denominations of 1, 2, 5, 10, 20, 50, 100, 500 and 1000 rupees. It's divided into 100 paisa but as a tourist you will seldom have to deal with anything less than a rupee. There's a nickel coin worth a rupee and some aluminium coins for lesser denominations.

Rates of exchange vary depending on whether the exchange is an official government transaction or a transaction being made by a tourist in a commercial bank, and there's also a third, black market, rate. Current tourist rates are US$1 = Rs54.5, UK£1 = Rs85, A$1 = Rs41, DM1 = Rs38.5, Indian Rs1 = Rs1.60.

Changing money

This is supposed be to done at your hotel or at a bank, not on the (now small) black market. The star-class hotels have banking facilities at their reception counters. Ensure you are given a receipt and some change is useful, in particular Rs100 bills.

Tipping

Once virtually unknown in Nepal, this custom is spreading through the tourism services. Tipping hotel and restaurant staff is not necessary but if the service was good, a 5% tip or the small change will be appreciated. Tipping trekking crews is now normal and the companies offer guidelines.

POST AND TELECOMMUNICATIONS

The Nepalese postal system is slow. Letters to or from Europe, USA and Australasia usually take around two weeks but can take up to a month and surface mail three to six months. The best addresses to have mail sent to are the star-class hotels, American Express or the communication centres in Thamel, which also have faxes. The Poste Restante service in the GPO consists of large boxes for each letter of the alphabet that contain hundreds of letters and anybody can look through them although it's rare for ordinary letters to go missing.

Kathmandu is blessed with a good telephone system and international calls and faxes can be sent and received with ease. The international dialling code for Nepal is 977 followed by 1 for Kathmandu.

Several communications agencies in Kathmandu now offer an e-mail service.

TV, NEWSPAPERS AND MAGAZINES

Kathmandu has TV news in English at 9.15pm followed by the BBC TV World Service. Satellite TV on the Star TV network from Hong Kong is available in larger hotels.

The local English-language dailies are the *Rising Nepal* and the (rather better) *Kathmandu Post*. The *Rising Nepal* is still obsessed with the comings and goings at the royal palace, international news is usually confined to a few columns. The paper gives a rosy and vague outline of what the government is currently up to and also includes odd titbits, like the state of the New Zealand economy. The *International Herald Tribune*, *USA Today*, and the *Asian Wall Street Journal* are sold everywhere as are magazines including *Time*, *Newsweek*, *Far Eastern Economic Review*, *Business Week*, *The Economist*, *Stern* and *Der Spiegel*. There's a plethora of Nepali magazines, many advertising tourist orientated services and interests. One that is worth looking out

---

(**Opposite**) Many villages in the Everest region are built around a *gompa* (Tibetan Buddhist monastery). The interior of the temple at Pangboche Gompa is shown. Built 450 years ago it's the oldest in the region; and it housed a curious relic, said to be the scalp of the Yeti, but this was stolen in 1991.

for is *Himal*, a quarterly Himalayan development and environmental discussion magazine. The British Council has a reading room with a variety of magazines and papers.

HOLIDAYS AND FESTIVALS

Government office and business hours are 10am to 5pm. On Saturday government offices (including the trekking permit office) and banks are closed but you can still change money in larger hotels. Everything reopens on Sunday except the embassies. Souvenir shopping and sightseeing are possible every day although all museums are closed on Tuesday.

Nepal is a land of colourful festivals and these are celebrated with fervour, especially by the less well-off masses. Dates are generally determined by the lunar calendar so fall on a different day each year. The following will be of particular interest to visitors:

• **Dasain** (Durga Puja) is a 10-day October festival, the most important of the Hindu year, and commemorates the victory of good Lord Rama over Ravana, the demon king of Lanka. Rama, an incarnation of Vishnu, is venerated by Hindus as the paragon of all virtues, so the victory symbolises the ultimate triumph of good over evil. This is a time of family reunion and consequently results in total chaos as everybody heads home. On days eight and nine there's a mass slaughter of buffaloes, goats and chickens. Vehicles are blessed by having their wheels doused in blood. Government offices are closed for at least three days.

• **Tihar** (Deepavali) is the five-day Festival of Light that takes place in late October or early November. Amongst the symbolism is an acknowledgement of the value of brothers and sisters, dogs and cows. Children go from house to house singing and dancing and are given a little food or money. At the height of the festival on the third day people light their homes with candles to welcome Lakshmi, the goddess of wealth.

Sherpa festivals

• **Mani Rimdu** is the popular three-day Sherpa festival held at Tengboche in November and at Thame in May. Monks perform ceremonies and dances, both serious and fun. It is a major social occasion.

(**Opposite**) Temple bells above the doors of one of the many Hindu temples in Kathmandu. Devotees ring the bells to attract the deities' attention. Official statistics state that 89.5% of the country's population is Hindu, 5.3% Buddhist (many of them in the Everest region), 2.7% Muslim, 2.4% animist and 0.04% Christian.

• **Losar** Tibetan New Year is celebrated during mid-February. It is a time to receive new clothes (making them is a winter job) and put up new prayer flags.

• **Orsho** is a rite to protect the crops and takes place at the beginning of April.

• **Ch-rim**, to rid the land of evil spirits, occurs twice a year. The rite is enacted first after potato planting, then again after the harvest when the livestock returns from the summer pastures.

• **Dumji** is an important five-day festival that takes place during the monsoon, over the anniversary of the Khumbu's patron saint, Lama Sange Dorje. The gods are requested to subdue the evil spirits of the village. A group of eight families (different each year) lays on the feast. There are separate festivals in Namche, Thame and Khumjung.

• **Buddha's birthday** falls in May and the **Dalai Lama's birthday**, particularly celebrated by Tibetan refugees, is on 6th July.

FOOD

Despite the ethnic mosaic the local cuisine is not particularly inspiring (unless you stay with well-off Nepalese friends). Standard Nepalese fare, *dal bhat*, consists of rice, lentils and a few vegetables. It can become monotonous but is certainly cheap and filling – your plate is topped up until you've had enough. In the Khumbu, potatoes form a major part of the diet of the Sherpas.

In response to trekkers' requests the restaurants of Kathmandu (and along some trekking routes) experimented with foreign dishes with surprising success. There's now an incredible variety of non-Nepalese cuisines at these places. Authenticity is not a strong point but you can eat passably Mexican, Italian or Thai food. There are excellent restaurants in Kathmandu specialising in tandoori and other styles of Indian food. 'Buff' (buffalo) steaks are a feature on many menus, beef being outlawed in this Hindu kingdom, although some restaurants manage to import it. The range of Tibetan food includes *momos* (meat or vegetables encased in dough and steamed or fried), and meat soup known as *thupka*.

The cakes and pies can be a real delight. These vary from restaurant to restaurant but many are wholesome and just as Mum would make them. The vast choice includes apple pie, apple strudel, cheese cakes, chocolate cakes, lemon meringue pies, cinnamon rolls and banana cream pie.

DRINK

All water should be treated (see p240) before it is safe to drink. Plastic bottles of mineral water are available but from an environmental point of view drinks such as Coke are better since the glass bottles they come in are returnable. Several types of beer are brewed here, some under licence from foreign companies (Tuborg and San Miguel). *Chang* is locally brewed beer produced by villagers.

Not a prickly soup

One evening I stopped for the night at a recently-constructed lodge. The family were obviously very new to the tourist business and by the looks of things all their money had gone into building the little lodge with its windows of plastic sheeting. By the fire in the kitchen I was handed an extensive menu but it was clear that they had few ingredients. I ordered a simple meal: vegetable soup and fried rice. There was a hurried discussion as they set to work and I went out to watch the sunset. After a while they announced that dinner was ready. The soup was served with an anxious glance. It was very good, thick, green and tasty, and the rice was good, too.

Next day as I settled the bill I noticed that I'd been charged Rs5 (not the Rs15 on the menu) for the soup. I queried this and the owner looked worried and crossed it out. Surprised, I said that I was happy to pay as I'd enjoyed the soup. I asked what was in it and he indicated a bundle of weeds in a basket. These turned out to be stinging nettles, and he showed me the bamboo tongs used to pick them. They're very much the poor person's vegetable and obviously not what he thought rich Western trekkers should be eating.

THINGS TO BUY

In Kathmandu and at a few of the larger centres along trekking routes, shops selling souvenirs and handicrafts abound. They offer Newari art, Tibetan *thangkas* (paintings of religious symbols and figures, done on cloth), jewellery, bronze Buddhas and Hindu deities. Boys wander around the streets of Thamel pestering you to buy khukri knives, chess sets and Tiger Balm. Carpets come in a great variety, many with modern designs in vegetable-dyed pastel shades. Luxuriously thick, they are made mainly in Kathmandu from a blend of New Zealand and Tibetan wool. When buying jewellery finding quality silver is not easy and you should beware of glass 'rubies' and dyed concrete-dust turquoise'.

Hand-knitted jerseys/sweaters and clothing are made in distinctive styles of the regional cultures and are popular with travellers. In Kathmandu, embroidered T-shirts are a speciality. There's a wide range of motifs to choose from and they look good on fleece jackets too.

Bargaining

Throughout Asia, bargaining is a part of life, although trekking exposes you to few situations that require bargaining. Most lodges have a menu with fixed prices that really are fixed – where you eat or stay is your choice. Buying at markets or from a farmer or hiring a porter may require some negotiation. As a foreigner (incredibly wealthy in comparison to most Nepalese) you start at a disadvantage and this will be utilised. Bargaining need not be aggressive – it's better to treat it as a game with smiles and jokes. After a price has been agreed it must be honoured. Once the transaction is complete that is the end of the matter, all is forgiven and forgotten. Harbouring resentment comes across as a small-minded Western attitude.

SECURITY

Kathmandu is safer than most Western cities. Violent crime is virtually unknown, and it is safe to take taxis, cycle and walk the streets and alleys at night, although women may be safer in a group. Despite the relaxed atmosphere in hotels, staff are honest, rooms have barred windows and managers are security-conscious, keeping an eye on who goes in or out. In the cheaper hotels other travellers are a greater risk, if anything. The better hotels have security boxes for valuables and all will store luggage safely while you trek.

Around town adept pick-pockets work crowded local buses. The usual ploy is to distract you with conversation or by pretending to be interested in your watch. Pick-pockets have a field day at busy festivals, as the queues of foreigners outside the American Express office the following day testify. Keep your travellers' cheques and money in a pouch or money belt and never let your camera and other valuables out of your sight.

The trekking regions were once crime-free but as the population is exposed to the wider ways of the world, occasional cases of theft now occur. Violent attacks are almost unheard of in the Solu-Khumbu although the tents of trekking groups are occasionally slit during the night and valuables disappear. The trekking crews are trustworthy, although if you lend gear, you will have to ask for it back. In the crowded lodges during high season occasionally the odd thing goes missing, generally a camera or valuable trekking equipment, but in a quiet lodge things are absolutely safe.

You are incredibly wealthy by local standards so don't flaunt your gear or openly display large quantities of money and camera equipment. You should show that you value and care for all your belongings.

PART 3: KATHMANDU

The city

Nepal's capital, Kathmandu (population 508,000), is a fascinating city which rose to prominence in mediaeval times. You should allow a few days at the beginning or end of your trek to see the sights and explore its narrow alleys. In any case all trekkers to the Everest region must pause in Kathmandu for at least a night or two to get their trekking permits.

ARRIVAL AND DEPARTURE

By air
Arrival Tribhuvan International Airport is a 20-minute drive from the centre of Kathmandu. There's a bank in the immigration hall (ensure you're given a receipt) and 30-day visas are available for US$25.

Downstairs is the luggage carousel. Customs don't generally offer problems for tourists (although valuable items like video cameras may be noted in your passport for re-export).

Through customs is the quiet main hall where the tourist information booth gives out free copies of *Travellers' Nepal* (in which the star-class hotels advertise heavily) and a free map of Kathmandu, both well worth picking up. The hotel reservation counter deals with star-class hotels, making reservations and organising a free taxi service. The pre-paid taxi counter organises transport into town for Rs200 for the whole car or Rs100 per seat if you're travelling alone. You can do this yourself perfectly easily if you're prepared to bargain with the taxi drivers outside, and it should cost around Rs150 for the whole taxi. Plans to restart the government-run airport bus service (which used to cost Rs15) have not, as yet, come to anything. The pre-paid taxi desk operates a coach for Rs70, when they can get enough passengers together.

Outside the building is a chaotic scene similar to any Third World airport forecourt. Boys eagerly try whisking away your luggage to one taxi, while taxi drivers pull you to another offering discount hotel rooms. Travellers usually head for Thamel or Freak Street for budget accommodation. Taxi-drivers recommend the marginally more expensive Thamel hotels (where they can get commission) but it's easy enough to find your own hotel when you get to either of these places.

The several routes to town pass through narrow streets lined with crumbling red brick houses. You know you've arrived in Thamel when, after driving by a few roundabouts, you see the Department of Immigration on the right and the road ahead narrows to a jumbled mass of vehicles. This is as good a place as any to get out. Alternatively, ask for the Kathmandu Guest House, to land yourself in the centre of it all.

Departure If you leave Nepal by air, a departure tax of Rs700 (Rs600 for India and SAARC countries) is payable in local currency only, as you check in at the airport. In the bank here you can reconvert up to 15% of the remaining rupees for which you have exchange receipts.

By land

Most buses (except buses for the Everest region) terminate at the new main bus station which is in the north of the city. If you're coming into Kathmandu by bus it's worth asking the driver to drop you off as near Thamel as possible. From the bus station, however, there are frequent shuttle buses (Rs2) which pass by the northern end of Thamel on their way to the old bus station near the clock tower.

If you're arriving on a blue and white Sajha bus, note that they arrive and depart from just outside the GPO.

ORIENTATION

Greater Kathmandu, which includes Patan as well as Kathmandu itself, lies at about 1400m/4593ft above sea level. The Bagmati River runs between these two cities. The airport is 6km to the east, near the Hindu temple complex of Pashupatinath, with the Buddhist stupa at Baudha 2km north of Pashupatinath. The other major Buddhist shrine, Swayambhunath, is visible on a hill in west Kathmandu. The third city in the Valley, Bhaktapur, is 14km to the east.

Within Kathmandu, most hotels and guest houses and the Department of Immigration (for trekking permits) are to be found in Thamel, north of the historic centre of the city, Durbar Square. Freak Street, the hippy centre in the '60s and '70s which still offers some cheap accommodation, is just off Durbar Square. Some of the top hotels and the international airline offices are along Durbar Marg which runs south from the modern royal palace.

WHERE TO STAY

Hotel areas

Thamel is the popular travellers' centre. With over 150 hotels of varying standards and budgets, finding one that suits is rarely a problem. Close to the Department of Immigration (for trekking permits), Durbar Marg (for airline offices) and a 15-minute walk to Durbar Square, it's well located. **Freak Street**, just off Durbar Square, was the infamous hippy hangout until the drugs scene was knocked on the head. Now, with a dozen or so hotels, it's quieter, cheaper and seedier than Thamel.

Away from the intense tourist scene are other small hotels scattered throughout Kathmandu. Swayambhunath and Bodhnath are where many of the Westerners studying Buddhism stay.

Costs

Prices given below and on p74 are for the high season (Oct-Nov/ Mar-Apr) for single/double/triple rooms, with common (com) or attached (att) bathrooms as indicated. You may be able to get a discount of anything up to 50% outside the high season, depending on the length of stay.

Many hotel owners quote their prices in US dollars; rupees are quite acceptable, though. Given the high rate of inflation, this is a sensible idea – US$ are used below, too. The dollar/pound exchange rate hovers around US$1.50:£1. Hotels are [keyed] to the map on p75.

Recommendations

• Budget guest houses (US$5/£3 or less) There are around 40 places to choose from in this price bracket, and in some you'll also get an attached bathroom for this price. Try to get a room that faces away from the roads – Kathmandu is plagued by noisy dogs.

Well-run by a friendly Tibetan family is the **Hotel Potala** [12] (☎ 416680), more of a guest house than a hotel. All rooms are doubles with shared bath and cost from US$2-5. Nearby, the **Memorable Guest House** [31] (☎ 243683) is another cheerful cheapie with rooms for US$2/4 (com). There's a good range of rooms from US$4-12 at **Earth House** [28] (☎ 418197), and a roof-top terrace. Also efficiently run is the **Marco Polo Guest House** [50] (☎ 227914) with rooms for US$3/4 (com) and US$5/7 (att). The rooms at the back are quietest.

Other recommendations in this price range in Thamel include the **Buddhist Guest House** [15] (☎ 224189), the spotless **Kathmandu Guest Home** [16], the friendly **Rainbow Guest House** [41] (☎ 410182), the **Pooja Guest House** [22] (☎ 416657) - popular with overlanders, the **Mont Blanc Guest House** [24] (☎ 222447) which is good value, as is the **Guest Palace Guest House** [28] (☎ 225593).

The **Kathmandu Peace Guest House** [53] (☎ 415239) is, as the name suggests, located in a peaceful area – a short walk north-west of Thamel in Paknajol. Rooms are US$3/4 (com) and US$5/8-15 (att), and there are even mountain views from here.

• **Cheap hotels in Thamel** With rooms from US$5/10 (att), the **Hotel Jagat** [68] (☎ 227701) is good value, although it's on the southern outskirts of Thamel. An excellent choice is the friendly Tibetan-run **Mustang Holiday Inn** [88] (☎ 226538), not to be confused with the Mustang Guest House. Rooms are US$8-20/US$10-30 (att). **Hotel Utse** [114] (☎ 226946) is nearby and similar, priced from US$13/20 (att); next door the **Hotel Norling** [109] (☎ 240734) offers stiff competition at US$10/18 (att). In the heart of Thamel is the **Hotel Garuda** [113] (☎ 416340), with clean rooms from US$13/17 (att).

The best known of the cheap hotels in Kathmandu must be the long-running **Kathmandu Guest House** [82] (☎ 413632), a landmark in the city. Popular with expeditions it's often fully-booked in the high season. They have a few rooms from US$6-8/8-10 (com) but most accommodation here is US$17/20 (att) in the new wing.

• **Moderately-priced hotels** There are numerous reasonable hotels in the US$15-30/£10-15 price range. Most have attached restaurants. All rooms have attached bathrooms with hot water. The **Hotel Karma** [116] (☎ 417897) is a friendly place that's recommended; rooms cost from $15/20 (att). Also good, and at the same price, there's **Hotel Buddha** [120] (☎ 413366) nearby, and **Hotel Moonlight** [119] (☎ 419452), situated in Paknajol. There's free snooker and billiards here.

Unlike virtually all the other hotels in the city, the **Hotel Vajra** (☎ 272719, fax 1-271695) is not a concrete block but built in brick and wood in the classic Newari style. Situated between Thamel and Swayambhunath, it was conceived and paid for by a Texas billionaire. There's a restaurant, a well-stocked library, and a roof-top bar with views over the city. Room prices are US$14/16 for singles/doubles with wash-basins, and from US$33/38 with attached bathroom.

• **Expensive hotels** The centrally-located, five-star **Hotel Yak & Yeti** (☎ 413999, fax 1-227 782) is probably the best place to stay, with rooms from US$150/160 to US$450. Rich Nepalis, however, consider the **Soaltee Holiday Inn** (☎ 272550, fax 272205), in the west of the city, to be the best hotel in Nepal. It's similarly priced.

On Durbar Marg is the **Hotel de l'Annapurna** (☎ 221711, fax 225236) with rooms from US$125/135-300, a large pool and casino. The **Hotel Malla** [140] (☎ 410320) is very pleasant, just north of Thamel with rooms from US$100/110.

Thamel Accommodation In ascending order by price for singles/doubles with common (c) or attached (a) bathroom. Prices in US$ but payable in rupees.

01 **Chitwan Tulsi** $1.50/2 (c)
02 **MK GH** (212866) dbl: $2 (c), $3 (a)
03 **Norling GH** (221534) $1.50/3 (a)
04 **H. Aroma** (222229) $1.50/3 (c), $2/4 (a)
05 **Green Land GH** (244553) $1.50/3 (c)
06 **Htl Mercy Palace** $2/2, $3 dbl (a)
07 **Pheasant Lodge** (417415) $2/2.50 (c)
08 **Cosy Corner** (417799) $2/2.50(c) $5 (a)
09 **Fishtail Home** $2.50 dbl (c), $3 dbl (a)
10 **Machhapuchhare Guest House** (410875) $2/2.50 (c)
11 **Continental GH** (221446) $2/3 (a)
12 **Hotel Potala** (416680) $2/3 (c)
13 **Friendly GH** (414033) $2/3 (c)
14 **Kunal's** (411050) $2/3 (c), $4 dbl (a)
15 **Buddhist GH** (224189) $2/3 (c), $4 (a)
16 **Kathmandu Guest Home** $2/3 c, $3/5 a
17 **Hotel Silk Rd** (212224) $2/3 (c), $4/6 a
18 **Hotel Star** (411004) $2/3 (c) $6/8(a)
19 **Dolpo GH** (224367) $2/3 (c), $6/8 (a)
20 **Everest GH** $2/3 (c), $4 (a)
21 **Namaste GH** $2 (c), $3/4 (a)
22 **Pooja GH** (416657) $2/3 (c), 3/4 (a)
23 **Yak Lodge** (224318) dbl: $3.50c $4.50 a
24 **Mt Blanc GH** (222447) $2/3 c, $3/5a
25 **White Lotus GH** (224563) $2/3c $4/5 a
26 **Htl Florid** (416155) $3 (c), $5 (a)
27 **My Mom's House** $2/3 (c), $4/5 (a)
28 **Guest Palace GH** (225593) $2/3c, $5 a
29 **Souvenir GH** (416416) $2/3 (c), $4/7 (a)
30 **Hokkaido GH** $2.50/3 (c)
31 **Memorable GH** (243683) $2/4 (c)
32 **Skala** (223155) $2/4 (c), $3/5 (a)
33 **Ajanta GH** (411023) $2/3 (c) $4/6 (a)
34 **Gurkha Soldier GH** (230666) $3/4 (c)
35 **King's Land GH** (417129) $3/4 (c)
36 **Blue Sky GH** $3/4 (c)
37 **Mini Om GH** (229288) $3/4 (c)
38 **Polo GH** (212256) $3/4c, $4/5a
39 **Centre GH** (223109) $3/4 (c), $5 dbl (a)
40 **Namaskar GH** (410182) $4/5 (a)
41 **Rainbow GH** (410182) $3/4 c, $4/5 (a)
42 **Fuji GH** (229234) $4 s (c) $5/6 (a)
43 **Gorkha** (214243) $3/5 (c), $6 (a)
44 **Hotel Oshin** (417157) $3/5 (c), $3/6 (a)
45 **Tibet Home** (224986) $4/6 (a)
46 **LP GH** (412715) $3/4 (c), $5/6 (a)
47 **Tourist GH** (418305) $4 (c), $6 dbl (a)
48 **A-One GH** (229302) $4 (c), $6 (a)
49 **Tibet Peace GH** (415026) $3/4c, $4/7a

50 **Marco Polo** (227914) $3/4 (c) $5/7 (a)
51 **Tara GH** (220634) $3/4 (c), $5/8 (a)
52 **Htl Puska** (225027) $3/5(c),$6/8(a)
53 **Ktm Peace GH** (415239) $3/4c, $5/8a
54 **Holy Lodge** (416265) $3.50/5c, $8/12a
55 **Hotel Angel** (227916) $3/4 (c), $6/10 (a)
56 **Shangri-La Guest House** (227388) dbl: $5 (c), $10 (a)
57 **Earth House** (418197) $4/6c, $6/12a
58 **Valentine** $4/6 (c), $8 dbl (a)
59 **Deutsch Home** (415010) $4/5c, $7/10a
60 **Shiddartha Guest House** (227119) $5(c), $7/10/12 (a)
61 **Hotel Shakti** (410121) $4/6c, $6/12a
62 **Htl Iceland** (416686) $4/6c, $11/14a
63 **Lhasa GH** (226147) $5/6 (c), $7/10
64 **Hotel Horizon** (220904) $6-20 dbl (a)
65 **Down Town GH** (224189) $5/7 (a)
66 **Thahity GH** $5/8 (a)
67 **Mustang GH** (419789) $5/8c, $9/12a
68 **Htl Jagat** (227701) $5/10 (a)
69 **Htl Mt Fuji** (413794) $6/8 (a)
70 **Htl Eyeball** (226048) $6/10 (a)
71 **Acme GH** (414811) $6/8 (c), 14/18 (a)
72 **Holyland GH** (411588) $6/10 (a)
73 **Hotel Namche Nepal** (417067) $5/6 (c), $6/7 (a)
74 **Universal GH** c$5/10 (a) opening soon
75 **Hotel Mughal Durbar** (222176) c$6/10 (a) opening soon
76 **Damaru GH** (244063) $4/6c, $6/12a
77 **Green Peace Ktm GH** $4/6 (c), $10/12a
78 **My Home**(231788) $5/8 (c), $7/10 (a)
79 **Capital GH** (414150) $5/8 (c), $9/15 (a)
80 **New Tibet Rest House** (225319) $6/9 (c), $8/12 (a)
81 **Hotel White Lotus** (226342) $6/10 (c), $10/14 (a)
82 **Kathmandu Guest House** (413632) $6/8 (c), $17/20 (a)
83 **Sagarmatha GH** (410214) $6/10c, $14/20a
84 **Potala Tourist Home** (410303) $6/10 (c) $10/15 (a)
85 **Wayfarer's Inn** (413471) $7/10 (c), $10/15 (a)
86 **Shakya GH** (410266) $7/10c, $10/12a
87 **Htl Nana** (418633) $8/10 (a)
88 **Mustang Holiday Inn** (226538) $8-20/10-30 (a)

89 Potala GH (220467) $8-10/15-20 (a)
90 Pilgrims Htl (416910) $8/10 (c), $15a
91 New Tibet Cottage (226577) $8c, $15a
92 Yeti Guest Home (419789)
$8/12 (c), $12/16 (a)
93 Thorong Peak Guest House (224656)
$8/12 (c), $14/18 (a)
94 Tibet GH (214383) $9/10c, $13/15a
95 Newa GH (415781) $8/15 (a)
96 Prince GH (414456) $10/15 (a)
97 Htl Himal Home c$10/15 (a) open soon
98 Hotel Shree Tibet (419902) $10/15 (a)
99 Khangsar GH (216788) $10/15a
100 Lovers' Nest (220541) $10/15 (a)
101 Sherpa GH (221546) $8 (c) $10/15 (a)
102 Hotel Lily (413184) $10/15 (a)
103 Hotel Bikram (417111) $10/15 (a)
104 Htl Greeting Palace (417212) $10/15a
105 Hotel New Gajur (226623) $10/16 (a)
106 Hotel Pisang (220097) $12/15 (a)
107 Hotel The Earth (228890) $12/15 (a)
108 Htl Yeti (414858) $8/10 (c), $12/16 (a)
109 Hotel Norling (240734) $10/18 (a)
110 Hotel Sonna (418399) $11/18 (a)
111 Imperial GH (229339) $12/15 (a)
112 Htl Blue Diamond (226320) $12/15 (a)
113 Hotel Garuda (416340) $13/17 (a)

114 Hotel Utse (226946) $13/20 (a)
115 Htl Gauri Shankar (417181) $14/19 a
116 Hotel Karma (417897) $15/20 (a)
117 Htl Tashi Dhargey (415378) $15/20 a
118 Hotel Tilicho (410132) $15/20 (a)
119 Htl Moonlight (419452) $15/20 (a)
120 Hotel Buddha (413366) $15/20 (a)
121 Htl MM Internatl (411847) $15/20 (a)
122 Hotel Mona (412380) $15/20 (a)
123 Hotel Excelsior (410853) $15/22 (a)
124 International GH (410533) $16/19
125 Hotel Mandap (413321) $18/24 (a)
126 Htl Tashi Dhele (217446) $18/25 (a)
127 Hotel Shikhar (415588) $18/26 (a)
128 Hotel Tridevi (416742) $20/25 (a)
129 Hotel Rimal (410317) $20/25 (a)
130 Hotel Tayoma (211149) $15/30a
131 Trans Himalayan G(214683)$20/25a
132 Hotel Tenki (414483) $25/35 (a)
133 Tibet Holiday Inn (411453) $20/35 (a)
134 Nirvana Garden H (222668) $30/40 a
135 Hotel Thamel (417643) $30/40 (a)
136 Htl Norbu Linka (414799) $30/45 (a)
137 Hotel Manang (410993) $35/50 (a)
138 Htl Marshyangdi (414105) $50/60 (a)
139 Htl Vaishali 4* opening 1996
140 Hotel Malla (410320) $100/110

WHERE TO EAT

There's an almost inexhaustible number of places for eating and drinking in Thamel. Considering that few main courses are over US$3/£2, and many cost around half this, the restaurants are all good value.

• **Breakfast** The **Pumpernickel Bakery** does a roaring trade in cinnamon rolls, bagels and other pastries and cakes, all served in its pleasant garden. **Helena's**, nearby, is equally good. **Mike's Breakfast** and the **Northfield Cafe** (Mike's more convenient branch in Thamel) have become Kathmandu institutions but are now quite expensive. You breakfast on authentic American fare (hash browns, pancakes and syrup, fresh coffee with free refills etc) in a garden, serenaded by classical music. The breakfast special is Rs130.

• **Western** For 'Western' food on a budget try **Lips Cafe** at My Mom's Home which offers chicken fried rice for Rs25. **Neighbours' Restaurant** in the Tourist Guest House does a filling egg curry rice for Rs27. Nepal's answer to McDonald's is **Nirula's** on Durbar Marg. Beef-burgers are out of the question, mutton Maha-burgers being the alternative.

Many places have steaks on the menu, usually (but not always) buffalo steak. The **Everest Steak House** is excellent, with a wide range of steaks, from Rs130 – right up to Rs600 for chateaubriand! **The Third Eye** is also good and, in the back room you can recline on the cushions while you eat. **KC's** is as much a Thamel institution as the Kathmandu Guest House. The food's good but prices are distinctly up-market – a sizzling steak costs Rs195. Another Kathmandu institution recommended for its food is the **Rum Doodle** (see Nightlife below).

Helena's is a popular place, main dishes are Rs80-140, there's good cappuccino and a wide range of cakes and pies. Nearby, the **Clay Oven** has outdoor seating in a small garden. Main dishes here range from Rs55 to Rs125. The **Road House Cafe** is a rather self-consciously cool terrace-diner with a have-a-go-at-anything menu. The food's quite good and there's a live band some nights.

There are numerous pizza places around Thamel; several also show videos in the afternoons and evenings to pull the customers in. **Fire & Ice Pizzeria & Ice Cream Parlour**, opposite the Department of Immigration, is streets ahead of the rest. Italian-run, some of the best pizzas on the subcontinent (Rs150-250) are now turned out here. It's very popular but closed on Sunday.

G's Terrace is another Western-Nepali joint venture and authentic but expensive Bavarian cuisine is served in this pleasant roof-top restaurant. **Old Vienna Inn** serves Austrian cuisine for similar prices. You can buy delicious salami rolls (Rs42) to take away both here and in their **Delicatessen Center** on Kantipath.

Simply Shutters Bistrot (☎ 226015) is a recommended place for a special occasion. The menu is sensibly limited to a few choices on a set menu (Rs340) and the quality of the food is high. The restaurant is closed on Tuesday; reservations are essential.

• **Nepali & Newari** There's a cheap Nepali place (no name), serving daal bhat for Rs30, by the entrance to the Acme Guest House, and another, (**Nepali Foods Restaurant**), near the Tourist Guest House. The **Nepalese Kitchen** has a range of superior daal bhat specials (Rs80-165) and live music several times a week.

Thamel House Restaurant (☎ 410388) is set in a renovated 100-year-old Newar house. It's an interesting place for a celebratory dinner; main dishes range from Rs80-130 and the nine-course set meal costs Rs450.

• **Tibetan** restaurants are amongst the cheapest places to eat in Thamel. The **Tibetan Restaurant** in the same building as the Lovers' Nest Guest House is excellent value and is run by very friendly

Tibetans. You can get a plate of ten momos here for Rs15; buff chowmein costs Rs20. **Tibet's Kitchen** in the Sherpa Guest House is recommended and also good value.

• **Chinese & Thai** Most restaurants have spring rolls and chowmein on their menus although what appears on your plate is usually unmemorable. The **New China Town Restaurant** is recommended – there's a Chinese chef; main dishes here range from chicken fried rice (Rs55) to prawn in black bean sauce (Rs150).

Now in larger premises in Lazimpat, **HimThai** still has a pleasant garden setting and a good reputation. Prices have risen, though; and most main dishes are around Rs160.

• **Israeli** Catering to the large number of Israeli visitors that the country is now attracting, **Aburami** opened in 1992. Hummus with chapattis costs Rs48, Israeli salad with chapattis is Rs94, and they do some of the best chips (Rs36) in town. It's a popular place and they put on special meals to celebrate Jewish festivals.

• **Japanese** There are a number of Japanese restaurants here and some of the dishes are surprisingly authentic. **Fuji**, pleasantly located just off Kantipath, is good. Assorted tempura costs Rs180 and set meals range from Rs230-550. **Koto**, on Durbar Marg, is slightly better value.

• **Indian** The **Shalimar Restaurant** does chicken masala that's good value at Rs35; chicken tikka costs Rs75 and the chef is from India. There's Kashmiri food, including rogan josh, at the newly-opened **Hotel Mughal Darbar**. On Durbar Marg, the **Amber Restaurant** is popular with local people. The top Indian restaurant is the Hotel de l'Annapurna's **ghar-e-kebab** (☎ 221711).

• **Vegetarian** Most restaurants have some dishes for vegetarians who are sick of daal bhat but there are also places that specialise in Western-style vegetarian food. In Thamel, the best places are **New Nirmala** and **Skala**. On Freak St, **Paradise Vegetarian Restaurant** is a great place to eat. If it's Indian vegetarian food you're after, try the excellent **Foodsmen Maharaja Restaurant** near Hotel My Home. The owner, a Sikh, supervises the production of delicious Punjabi cuisine. A cheese paratha is Rs18, egg curry Rs35.

NIGHTLIFE

Rum Doodle Restaurant & 40,0001ft Bar is a Kathmandu institution, with yeti prints on its walls inscribed by the members of many mountaineering expeditions. As well as a wide range of drinks (hot buttered rum at Rs70, for example) the food here is good; main dishes are Rs100-150.

The **Tom & Jerry Pub** is noisy and popular, an old favourite. There's a rooftop terrace, pool tables and satellite TV. **Pub Maya**, **Maya Cocktail Bar** and **Ground Round** are all similar. Particular tastes of music are catered for at the **Reggae Pub** (above Aburami Israeli Restaurant) and the **Blue Note Jazz Bar**. **Old Spam's Place** is the closest you'll get to a British pub in Kathmandu.

The Sherpa Hotel and Hotel d'Annapurna (both in Durbar Marg) and the Shankar Hotel (off Kantipath) put on **cultural shows**. The French Cultural Centre occasionally sponsors a play, jazz night or mime act and details are advertised. The top hotels all operate **casinos**. If you recently flew into Nepal you're entitled to Rs100-worth of free coupons at the Soaltee Holiday Inn casino. There's a shuttle bus (also free) that leaves Thamel and major hotels every hour, 8pm to 11pm.

HEALTH PRECAUTIONS IN KATHMANDU

Drinking water and restaurant hygiene

In Kathmandu the quality of the tap water is inconsistent and definitely not fit to drink without treatment. Many hotels can supply filtered water but unless the filter has been looked after it ceases to be effective. Treat water yourself or stick to bottled drinks.

In the past a meal at one of Kathmandu's exotic restaurants was almost guaranteed to make you ill. Much has changed and the better restaurants try to be serious about hygiene and a few are now confident enough to have open-plan kitchens. Most claim to wash salads in iodine and use boiled water for ice-cubes but many restaurants serve drinks without ice to save questions.

SERVICES

Banks

Larger hotels can change money at reception. In Thamel there are several authorised money-changers but their rates, like the hotels, are not as good as the banks. Rastriya Banija bank has an exchange counter at the Department of Immigration; in the shopping centre opposite is the Himalayan Bank; Nepal-Grindlays also has an exchange office in Thamel. In Kanti Path, east of Thamel, Nabil Bank offers some of the most competitive rates in the city; the main branch of Nepal-Grindlays is also here. The American Express office (☎ 226172, open Sunday to Friday 10.00-13.00 and 14.00-17.00) is by the Hotel Mayalu.

Bookshops & libraries

Kathmandu has some of the best bookshops on the sub-continent, including many small secondhand shops where you can trade in your novel for another. Most international news magazines are available.

The Kaiser Library, Kaiser Shamsher Rana's private collection, is worth visiting as much for the building as for the 30,000+ musty volumes. This Rana palace is now the Ministry of Education & Culture, just west of the modern royal palace.

The British Council Reading Room on Kanti Path is open to all and has the main UK newspapers, although they're all a week or more old.

Communications

The GPO is a 20-minute walk south of Thamel, on the corner of Kanti Path and Prithvi Path. This is where to go for Poste Restante mail. When sending a letter don't put it in a post-box but ask them to frank it or the stamps may be removed and resold. Sending mail is far more easily attended to by the numerous communication centres in Thamel which take letters to the GPO for franking each day.

The cheapest place to make an international phone-call (minimum three minutes) is at the Central Telegraph and Telephone Office, opposite the national stadium at the southern end of Kanti Path. Since this is a 30-40 minute walk from Thamel most people make their calls at one of the **communication centres** dotted around Thamel. They provide excellent services for a small charge above the normal rates, and most do not impose a three-minute minimum on phone calls. You can make international calls, send and receive faxes and mail, photocopy and even type a letter at some. The business centres in the big hotels are generally much more expensive for the same services.

Some places are now offering e-mail connections. Currently, the cheapest place is Global Communications (glocom@glopc.mos. com.np) in the shopping centre opposite the Department of Immigration. They charge Rs 60 per kb to send (Rs 30 if on disk) and Rs 20 to receive.

Embassies

Australia (☎ 411578), Bansbari
India (☎ 410900), Lainchaur
Israel (☎ 411811), Bishramalaya House, Lazimpat
New Zealand (Honorary Consul ☎ 412436), Dilli Bazaar
Sweden (☎ 220939), Khichapokhari
Thailand (☎ 420410), Bansbari
UK (☎ 411590), Lainchaur
USA (☎ 411179), Pani Pokhari

Medical clinics

CIWEC (☎ 228531, open Monday to Friday 09.00-12.00, 13.00-16.00) is an exceptionally competent clinic which has now moved to a more convenient location just off Durbar Marg, near the Hotel Yak & Yeti. Consultations cost US$35 or equivalent in any currency. **Nepal International Clinic** (☎ 412842, open Sunday to Friday 09.00-17.00) is also excellent and consultations cost US$30 or equivalent. It's opposite the Royal Palace, slightly east of Durbar Marg.

Cheaper clinics in Thamel include **Synergy** (☎ 413503), opposite Blue Note Jazz Bar; **Everest International** (☎ 411504) on the square north of Les Yeux; and **Himalaya International** (☎ 225455) near Hotel Utse.

Trekking equipment rental

There are perhaps 20 shops with a wide variety of equipment so you can afford to be selective and shop around. Large deposits are required: money of any sort or valid airline tickets but credit cards should not be trusted to anyone.

WHAT TO SEE

A virtual living museum, the Kathmandu Valley is crammed with sights and scenes and it's well worth setting aside several days to take some of them in. The most popular attractions are mentioned below. Aimless wandering through the narrow streets also has its rewards, though. Amongst the colourful confusion you'll come upon numerous temples, stupas and other holy places.

Swayambhunath

From this huge stupa on a hill in the west of the city, the all-seeing eyes of the Buddha overlook the entire Kathmandu valley. It's also known as the Monkey Temple and dotted around it are several other shrines and temples. There's a pilgrims' rest house, a Buddhist library and *gompa* (Buddhist temple) as well as a Hindu temple dedicated to the goddess of smallpox. Behind on a smaller hill is a favourite temple for children, dedicated to Saraswati, the goddess of learning. Walking (half an hour from Thamel) or cycling through the colourful streets is the most pleasant method of reaching the hill.

Pashupatinath

Beside the sacred Bagmati River, this is one of the most revered Hindu temples on the Indian subcontinent. Entry to the main temple is barred to non-Hindus but there are numerous other shrines in this large religious complex. Dedicated to Shiva, the destroyer and creator – stone *linga* fertility symbols are everywhere. Cremations take place on the banks of the river, providing a morbid tourist attraction. You'll see lots of *sadhus*, saffron-robed holy men, who perform various feats here (including rock-lifting – with their penises no less!). Pashupatinath is on the eastern outskirts of Kathmandu, easily reached by bike or taxi.

Bodhnath (Baudha)

One of the largest stupas in the world, Bodhnath is surrounded by a thriving Tibetan community. Prayer wheels line the mandala-shaped base. These must be turned clockwise, the direction in which you should walk around the stupa. There are lots of souvenir shops as well as Tibetan restaurants and a few guest houses. Close by are a variety of Tibetan gompas. When visiting you should leave a small donation.

Patan

Once a separate city-state, this ancient historical centre is now a southern suburb of Kathmandu. It's an architectural feast, at the centre of which is Durbar Square. Temples abound and it is best to explore on foot or by bicycle. The outskirts of the town are beautiful and semi-rural, the most desirable residential area for wealthy Nepalese and expatriate staff.

Bhaktapur

Compared with Kathmandu and Patan, the other cities in this mediaeval trio, time has stood still in Bhaktapur. Wandering round the narrow streets and temple-filled squares is fascinating and school-boys act as surprisingly knowledgeable guides. They'll want some baksheesh (Rs20 or so, though they'll try for more). Staying here overnight, especially during a festival is well worthwhile.

It's 14 km from Kathmandu and you can get here by taxi, mini-bus or trolley-bus. You can also cycle here although the pollution on the outskirts of the city is horrific. Hiring a mountain bike to combine with a steep ride to Nagarkot makes for an adventurous expedition.

Nagarkot

Perched on the eastern rim of the encircling hills, the Himalaya from the Annapurnas to Everest are visible from Nagarkot on a clear morning. It's a popular overnight excursion although the exploring possibilities on foot or by mountain bike warrant more time. There are plenty of cheap lodges, and buses from Bhaktapur leave every hour or so. A tourist mini-bus leaves outside the Kathmandu Immigration office at 1.30pm and early morning sunrise tours are easily arranged by travel agents or with a taxi driver. Close by is Dhulikhel, another favourite viewing spot. Just off the Arniko Highway this is also easily reached.

Dakshinkali

Sacrificial blood flows freely on Tuesdays and Saturdays for the goddess Kali at this temple. Like hungry hyenas tourists jostle to take red-splashed photos and a few turn vegetarian. It is 20km from Kathmandu, an uphill cycle ride. Alternatively, buses leave from Martyrs' Gate, just east of the GPO in Kathmandu.

SIGHTSEEING TOURS

One of the more competent operators is Gray Line. Bookings can be made through travel agents and hotel receptions. Half day guided tours cost around US$3/£2. Many travel agents also organise their own tours. To get the most from these ensure you will be accompanied by a qualified guide.

Mountain flight

Almost every morning during the high seasons, RNAC, Nepal Airways, Everest Air and Necon Air each operate a 'mountain flight' for close-up views of the Himalaya including Everest. It costs US$99 and departs only if the sky is clear. Tickets are refundable and bookings may be moved to the following day if the flight is cancelled.

Trek preparation in Kathmandu

KATHMANDU ENVIRONMENTAL EDUCATION PROJECT

The Kathmandu Environmental Education Project (KEEP) was set up to coordinate the activities of the multitude of organisations concerned with environmental affairs in the trekking industry and rationalise the courses on offer for Nepalese guides and sirdars. Under the umbrella of the King Mahendra Trust, their integrated approach includes educating trekkers on sound environmental practices and problems specific to Nepal. There's an interesting information centre near the Department of Immigration. It features displays, lectures and audio visual presentations and is staffed by dedicated and knowledgeable people, some of whom are trek leaders. It's a good place to meet other trekkers or put up a notice for trekking partners. Make a donation if you've learnt something from your visit: this is the only way worthwhile organisations like KEEP and the HRA can continue to function.

HIMALAYAN RESCUE ASSOCIATION (HRA)

The HRA was founded in 1973 with the primary aim of saving lives in the mountains by alerting trekkers to the dangers of altitude sickness. It's largely due to their unfailing efforts that the death toll from altitude sickness is now very low.

Their office is definitely worth visiting for advice and they also have forms here so you can register with your embassy. Unless you're trekking with an organised group, you're strongly advised to do this since your embassy's assistance is necessary if a helicopter rescue is required for you.

In addition to the Kathmandu information centre the HRA has two medical posts, one at Manang (in the Annapurna region) and the other in the Khumbu at Pheriche (see p169). They operate only during the peak trekking seasons, however, from early October to early December, and March to April.

ORGANISING A GUIDED TREK IN KATHMANDU

If you're planning to organise a trek with porters, tents and a cook along a standard route to the Khumbu it's worth pointing out that the better lodges here offer a competitive standard of service. As an alternative to the full organised trek you could hire a porter-guide or porter and use the lodges and their facilities. The expedition trekking style is, however, best suited to lightly-trekked routes, remote areas and for climbing trekking peaks.

Trekking companies in Nepal

All trekking agencies in Nepal must be owned by Nepalese nationals so foreign companies have to operate through them. They may have a Western trek leader as a company representative indirectly in charge. Despite the small offices, most trekking companies are well practised at organising treks. Many have been set up by sirdars who gained a particularly good name for themselves and had enough recommendations to secure steady business. Try to talk to another foreigner who's been on one of the treks organised by the company before signing up.

Trek personnel

A **sirdar** (trekking guide) is an organiser rather than a trained specialist of history and culture; guides as such don't exist for the trekking regions. He (virtually never she) will speak English and carries only his personal equipment. The older Sherpa sirdars are generally more knowledgeable about the region but few guides are expansive; displaying their culture is not a widely understood tourism concept.

The sirdar, who is often the leader as well when there is no foreign representative, hires and/or supervises the porters, the sherpas (who are not necessarily from the Sherpa clan, and distinguished by the lack of a capital 'S'), and is usually in charge of the money. It is therefore a powerful position and a good sirdar will ensure the trek functions in a trouble-free manner. A bad sirdar can cause endless problems. The **sherpas** are the sirdar's assistants, general helpers who erect and pack the tents, serve the meals, and help in any way they can. They ensure nobody gets lost and carry bags if the members tire. Most speak some English. The **cook** is another key figure, heading a small army of kitchen helpers.

A **porter** is a load-bearer, who generally speaks little or no English. The standard trekking company load is 30-35kg/66-77lbs but if you are doing the hiring then a more gentle 20-25kg/44-55lb will leave a spring your porter's step and flexibility about the stages.

Operating independently from the above personnel there is the **porter-guide**, usually someone who is not experienced enough to be a sirdar, but speaks some English and wants to try their luck at making more than the usual paltry wage. Since few people hire only a guide, they are willing to carry your backpack, leaving you with just a day pack. By asking around you may be able to find a porter-guide in Lukla; but they are scarce in Jiri.

Yaks and zopkios (see p153) are also load-bearers and are often used in the Khumbu instead of porters, especially by large groups. Yaks are normally used only above Namche while zopkios are to be found from Lukla and above. They carry double the load of a porter, 60-70kg/132-154lbs, for double the cost. Normally the minimum number you can hire is three, with a **yak driver** to look after them.

Costs At present the official minimum charge for a fully organised trek (all food, tents and crew) is US$20/£13.50 per person per day, for which you get a simple, often quite adequate level of service. US$30-40/£20-27 per person per day should provide a reasonable standard of service. The top companies charge around US$80-100/£53-67 a day for slightly better food and slicker service. The cost also depends on the number of people in the trekking group, and there are often discounts if there are more than a few people.

Ensure it is clear exactly what you are paying for and, more importantly, what is not included. All the wages for the crew must obviously be included, and all food plus tents, but are bus tickets, taxes and the National Park entrance fees additional? Decide also on the rates for extra days, for example if you decide to trek for longer, or if the flight is delayed.

HIRING GUIDES AND PORTERS

When looking for a porter/porter-guide, follow your instincts. A pleasant manner is more important than fancy clothes, and in fact for porters, the older and scruffier, the more reliable. Mutual respect is important so don't be afraid to show who's boss. They are being paid comparatively well and the working conditions are less demanding than a normal porter's job. By hiring somebody you take on the responsibility of an employer. One couple who had previously hiked a lot in the Rockies said, 'It was like having a child with you'. Others find the experience rewarding and at the very least it makes getting up the hills easier. Trekking personnel look after themselves in most situations, finding food and lodgings (and often assisting you in this task), but when it comes to snow conditions with the risk of frostbite and snow-blindness, they are notoriously naive. Usually it is you that will have to take preventative action and pay for hired boots and jackets and sunglasses for porters.

Hiring in Kathmandu Trekking companies are happy to arrange crew but be clear what the charges include. You normally pay a daily rate to the trekking company and then pay for the crew's food and lodging on the trail. A few guides are adept at running up huge bills so it's sensible to establish what they will be eating. Most will, however, prefer dal bhat, the standard cheap Nepali food. Setting a daily allowance for food is a good idea: perhaps Rs150 to Rs200 in the lower areas and Rs200 to Rs300 in the higher, more expensive, regions. An alternative arrangement to agreeing to pay for the crew's food is to pay a higher food-inclusive daily rate.

Since you will be spending a great deal of time together, talk to the guide beforehand, perhaps even go out for a meal with him and if you have real doubts, ask for someone else. With porters, if they are going to high altitudes, insist on knowing the arrangements for gear hire. No matter what's agreed, once you're up there the crew often lack the right gear.

The daily rates for guides are US$6-12/£4-8, the higher rates being the norm. Rates for porters are slightly less, normally around US$5-8/£3.50-5.50 but prices vary considerably between the many agencies. Some trekking companies exploit their employees mercilessly. The crew may often receive no more than standard wages but must hire cold weather gear themselves and pay for food which is progressively more expensive higher up.

Guides wanting work (or touts who have contacts) can often be found outside the Department of Immigration.

Hiring on the trail At Lukla, guides, porters and porter-guides are usually easy to find. At Jiri only porters are readily available. Lodge owners often know who is looking for work. Families with young children or a group of women trekking together may be able to hire female staff.

Porter-guides can be hired for Rs200-300 a day plus food, or for an all-inclusive rate of Rs300-500. Bargaining is often required. Bear in mind that for menial jobs in Kathmandu the wage is Rs800-1500 a month.

Note that if you hire through a trekking company all staff are fully insured while those hired independently on the trail are not. Also, many people have mentioned that with hiring locally the rates are often high and work out to be similar to what was obtainable in Kathmandu though a trekking company.

MONEY FOR THE TREK

Provided you're not planning to buy a ticket at a rural airport (payment in hard currency only), it's best to take your entire budget as cash in Nepalese rupees since the only bank in the region is at Namche. About a quarter of the total amount should be in medium and small denomination notes. The most frequently used notes are Rs100 but busy lodges can usually break down Rs1000 notes. For the Arun, Makalu and Rolwaling areas it's safest to have all the money you'll need for that section in denominations of 100 rupees and less.

LUGGAGE STORAGE

Most hotels will store whatever you want to leave behind. There's normally no charge if you'll be staying on your return. Things are quite secure; a few hotels also have safety deposit boxes.

GETTING TO THE KHUMBU

By air

Until recently, arranging air tickets to airports in the trekking regions (particularly Lukla) was a trick best left to travel agents or trekking companies. But at the end of 1991 the government allowed the formation of private air companies in order to provide much-needed competition for the inefficient state-run Royal Nepal Airlines Corporation (RNAC). Now, with several airlines flying planes and helicopters, tickets to Lukla are easy to arrange, except perhaps in peak season.

Schedules and costs Airlines quote their prices in US$ but tickets can be paid for in most hard currencies (ie not Nepalese rupees).

Royal Nepal Airlines (☎ 220757) flies between Kathmandu and Lukla (US$83, four flights each way in the high season) but there are also departures to Phaplu (US$77, Thu, Sun) and Tumlingtar (US$44, Mon, Wed, Fri) both returning the same day. Bhojpur (US$77, Mon, Fri) is an alternative to Tumlingtar rarely used by trekkers because it's more expensive and requires a short extra day's walk. If you can't get a direct flight to Tumlingtar another option would be to fly to Biratnagar (US$77, daily to/from Kathmandu) on the Terai and take a connection to Tumlingtar (US$33, daily to/from Biratnagar). Royal Nepal has several mountain-viewing flights (US$99) each day, weather permitting.

Nepal Airways (☎ 420421) has flights between Kathmandu and Lukla (US$83, daily), Tumlingtar (US$44, Sat, Sun) and Biratnagar (US$77, daily). **Everest Air** (☎ 222 290) has daily flights between Kathmandu and Phaplu (US$77, Wed, Fri), to and from Biratnagar (US$77, daily) and mountain-viewing flights (US$99, daily). They also operate helicopters on some of the routes flown by Asian Airlines (below). **Necon Air** (☎ 472 542) has flights to Biratnagar (US$77, daily) and mountain flights (US$99).

Asian Airlines operate helicopters between Kathmandu and Lukla (US$83), Phaplu (US$80), and Syangboche (US$120). Lukla to Syangboche costs US$35. Their office is in Thamel.

Note that since Nepalis pay subsidised prices on flights costs for flying your crew from Kathmandu are: Lukla Rs1500, Phaplu Rs1250 (helicopter), Syangboche Rs2000 (helicopter).

> ### Chartering a helicopter
> Want to fly a group to Tengboche for lunch, or transport all the expedition equipment and the members to Ama Dablam Base Camp? Anywhere it's possible to safely land a helicopter, there are several companies who are happy to oblige. Try Asian Airlines or Everest Air (for large helicopters), Himalayan Helicopters (☎ 231236) on Durbar Marg, or Dynasty Aviation (☎ 414626) in Lazimpat. Picking up in the mountains can be trickier than setting you down since the take-off payload drops considerably with altitude. The maximum from Syangboche (3900m/ 12,795ft), for example, is around 2300kg. The hourly rate is US$2000; the trip cost is quoted before departure.

Buying tickets in Kathmandu Travel agents charge the same as the airlines. Check the official price as some travel agents try to add a 'service charge'. RNAC tickets for Lukla can be bought directly at the RNAC head office (☎ 220757, near the GPO) but other tickets must be purchased at their domestic sales office (☎ 223453, Thapathali).

Buying tickets at a rural airport On some flights tourists are given priority over locals. The fare must still be paid in hard currency. US$ cash or travellers' cheques are best since the US$ is the most readily-known exchange rate, except at Lukla where they're used to tourists.

Transport Options

By bus

Most bus rides are long and uncomfortable but stops are made for meals. Roadside stalls sell biscuits, fruit, sweets and soft drinks. Restaurants serve little more than dal bhat and are not too hygienic. It's wise to be cautious, especially at the start of your holiday.

Buses for Jiri, Dolakha and Barabise still use the old central bus station near the clock tower, not the new bus station north of Thamel.

Jiri Between three and eight buses a day leave Kathmandu's old bus station for Jiri (Rs175 with rucksack, 10-12 hours) between 5.30am and 7.30am. Tickets for the first bus can be bought a day in advance; for subsequent buses you must buy your ticket on the day of departure.

From Jiri the last bus leaves at around mid-day. You may be able to get a lift back on privately-hired transport returning to Kathmandu, more comfortable than the buses. Ask around at the lodges in Jiri.

Dolakha There's only one direct bus a day which leaves around 5am from the old bus station in Kathmandu. Otherwise you can catch any bus heading to Jiri and get off at Charikot (Rs72). It takes less than an hour to walk down to Dolakha from there. For the return journey the daily direct bus leaves Dolakha at 5am.

Hille/Basantpur The road that goes north from Dharan to Dhankuta and Hille is in the process of being extended and now goes as far as Basantpur. Kathmandu to Hille takes around 24 hours although it'll take less time when the road is finished. At present it's one of Nepal's more uncomfortable night-bus journeys. It certainly gives an interesting insight to life in the hot Terai and given the right frame of mind the ride can even be fun. There's no direct bus to Hille/Basantpur so book to Dharan (Rs204, night buses only, leaving Kathmandu's new bus station from 4pm), then change for Hille. It's better to book a seat a day or two ahead, at the main bus station or through a travel agent, and ask for a seat near the front. Buses between Dharan and Hille leave in the mornings. An alternative route is to Itahari first, then Dharan and Hille.

For the return journey the last bus for Dharan leaves Hille at around 2pm. The Dharan-Kathmandu bus leaves at 4 pm but if you miss this catch a bus to Itahari and a connection to Kathmandu.

Barabise There are frequent buses leaving Kathmandu's old bus station between 5am and 4pm for Barabise (Rs30, seven hours). The buses generally stop at the office on the west bank in Barabise, which is where you get tickets for the return trip to Kathmandu.

Tourist vehicles

A mini-bus to Jiri is sometimes operated (tickets from travel agents). Otherwise it's possible to hire a taxi or mini-bus for around Rs5000.

AFTER THE TREK
Chitwan National Park

A visit to Nepal's best-known national park, situated on the low-lying Terai in the south of the country, is an interesting contrast to a few weeks in the mountains. Amongst the forests of sal trees you're likely to see one-horned rhinos, rhesus macaques, langur monkeys, a number of different deer including the Indian spotted deer (chital), crocodile and, with a great deal of luck you might even spot a tiger or leopard. Some of the game-viewing is done on elephants.

Accommodation in the park ranges from 5-star safari lodges such as Tiger Tops (US$250/£170 per person per night) to budget places in Sauruha for around US$2/£1.50. Elephant safaris (US$7/£4.50 per person per hour) can be arranged in Sauruha.

There are flights from Kathmandu to Meghauli (Everest Air US$72) for Tiger Tops. For Sauruha, Tadi Bazaar is the nearest bus stop, 8km away. There are direct buses from Kathmandu and Pokhara, taking 6 to 7 hours from both places.

White-water rafting

Nepal has some of the world's best commercially-viable 'ultimate' descents for kayaking and rafting. However, this doesn't mean you'll be shooting rapids all day. Rafting expeditions tend to be two to eleven days of peace and tranquillity in incredible settings spiced with two or three heart-stopping and exhilarating rapids each day. The nights are spent camping beside the rivers, either out in the wilds or close to rarely-visited villages. Rafting is now possible year round (on different parts of the rivers) but the best times are September to November and March to May. Water levels are lower during the latter season but trips are still a lot of fun.

All-inclusive costs range from US$15-60/£10-40 per day, and trips are easily arranged in Nepal upon arrival. To get yourself hooked see a couple of the advertised slide-shows in Kathmandu and talk to the experts. There are many rafting companies offering the popular two to three day Trisuli River trip. For the longer Sun Kosi River trips and other expeditions it's worth paying a bit more for a quality outfit. Ultimate Descents (☎/fax 411933) near Kathmandu Guest House is a recommended organisation.

Tibet

A visit to this still exotic corner of the world is highly recommended. The main drawback is that, from Nepal, you may only be able to visit as part of an organised tour. The regulations for foreign visitors seem to vary from year to year. In 1987 and 1988 Tibet was open for independent travel and more than a few intrepid souls set off to mountain bike from Kathmandu to Lhasa. Since then the Chinese, despite officially opening Tibet several times, have unofficially done their utmost to discourage individual travellers. In 1994 several cyclists made the Lhasa-Kathmandu trip, but in mid-1995 (during the 'celebrations' in Lhasa marking 30 years of Chinese rule) it was visas for groups only.

From Nepal, there are four-day and eight-day group tours, run every Saturday, from around US$800/£500. These are easily arranged in a week from many travel agents in Kathmandu, who can also obtain a Chinese visa for you. Trekking tours are expensive, but it's possible and rewarding to trek to the north side of Everest. One of the best all-round operators is Arniko Travels (☎ 421861, fax (+977) 1-414594), opposite the Chinese embassy in Baluwatar.

PART 4: THE EVEREST REGION

Mountaineering history

EVEREST

Meantime let us count our blessings – I mean those thousands of peaks, climbed and unclimbed, of every size, shape and order of difficulty, where each of us may find our own Mt Everest. HW Tilman *Mount Everest 1938*

The search for the world's highest mountain

In 1808 the Survey of India began the daunting task of mapping the whole of the subcontinent. One of the goals was to discover if the Himalaya was indeed the highest mountain range in the world, as had previously been suspected. Already challenging, the project was made even more difficult by the fact that Nepal and Tibet, wary of foreign intervention, were closed to outsiders.

By 1830 the survey had reached the border between India and Nepal. Unable to cross into Nepal, surveyors resolved to continue the project from the plains. A baseline the length of the range was marked and in 1847 surveying the northern peaks began, using trigonometrical calculations based on the heights and distances of known points. Conditions were terrible: malaria was rife and monsoon rain eroded the observation towers each year.

Until the mid-19th century it was thought that Kanchenjunga, in Sikkim, at about 28,000ft (8534m), was the highest peak in the range. In 1856 calculations published by the Survey of India revealed that a mountain on the border between Nepal and Tibet was higher. This mountain was designated 'Peak XV' and its height stated to be 29,002ft (8839m); Kanchenjunga was 28,156ft (8582m).

The accuracy of this first survey is astounding, considering the fact that the mountains were measured from survey points 108 miles to 150 miles away from the peaks. In their calculations surveyors had to take account of the earth's curvature and the changing air density, which bends light. It's a sad fact that a survey made from the same points would not be possible today. Dust and air pollution is now so bad that it's rare to be able to make out even the second foothills of the Himalaya from the plains. The present accepted height of Everest is just 26ft (8m) higher: 8848m/ 29,028ft, from an Indian survey taken in

Nepal in the 1950s. It's interesting to note that when National Geographic made their much lauded 1:50,000 map of Everest, instead of re-measuring the mountain they used its accepted height as a base for all the other altitudes on the map.

The naming of Everest

It was not until 1865 that Peak XV was named. The accepted method of naming peaks at the time was to use the local name if one could be found. The first map of the area, made in the 1700s, marked this peak as **Tschoumoulancma** but the Surveyor General, Andrew Waugh, chose to name Peak XV **Mount Everest** after his predecessor, Sir George Everest, who oversaw the great survey of India.

This appropriately grand appellation stuck in the West but Tibetans and Sherpas have always used some variation of the name used on the 18th century map. The Dalai Lama, giving permission for the 1921 Reconnaissance Expedition, called it **Chha-mo-lung-ma**, the name adopted by the Chinese (but transliterated as Qomolangma or Chomolungma). This is also the name that the Sherpas use. Difficult to translate directly, it is usually said to mean: 'Mother Goddess of the World'. Sherpas sometimes translate it as 'Home of the Goddess of the Wind' or 'Home of the God or Goddess that Looks After Mothers'. (Makalu is said to be the home of the deity who protects daughters).

The Nepalese name is an even more recent creation than the English designation. They call it **Sagarmatha**, which has been variously translated as: 'Forehead Touching the Sky', 'Head in the Sky', 'Head above All Others' or 'Churning Stick of the Ocean of Existence'.

The Dalai Lama permits the first Everest expedition

Once Everest had been identified as the world's highest mountain nearly three-quarters of a century were to go by before an expedition could be set up to reach the area. The main interest was originally from the British but Nepal and Tibet were suspicious of this colonial power's intentions. Nepal already had a British Resident living in Kathmandu, installed as a permanent observer after they had lost the 1814 war to the British, and one resident foreigner was more than enough. Tibet's capital Lhasa had been a closed city for more than a century but in 1904 Francis Younghusband led a British expedition which fought its way through Tibet, killing many Tibetans, ostensibly to negotiate trade links between the two countries. For more than a decade the Dalai Lama withheld his permission for a British party to make an attempt on Everest. However, eventually he yielded to British demands and the first expedition was mounted in 1921. It was organised by the Royal Geographical Society with climbers from the Alpine Club and was followed by further attempts in 1922 and 1924.

1921 Reconnaissance Expedition

The first expeditions were remarkable for a number of reasons. Many of the most promising young mountaineers had been lost in the battles of the First World War so the average age of members of the reconnaissance expedition was an almost geriatric 44. Although composed of experienced mountaineers, their experience was of European mountains half the height of Everest. Very little was known about the effects of altitude and their equipment and clothing, although the best available at the time, would seem totally inappropriate by modern standards. It was not a strong team and only six of the nine members reached the base of the mountain after the long walk from Sikkim.

A major figure in the first expeditions was George Mallory. With his mountaineering partner, Bullock, he first spent a tough month exploring the area to find the easiest access to the mountain, the hidden East Rongbuk Glacier. It was immediately obvious that summer, the monsoon period, was not the most favourable time for climbing. But despite this and their appalling equipment, three Sherpas and three climbers reached the North Col, 6990m/23,000ft. By the end of the expedition a thorough exploration of the Tibetan side of the Everest Massif had been made, and Mallory had even peered into the Western Cwm, as he named it, from the Lho La.

Frozen spaghetti on the 1922 Expedition

The 1922 expedition, led by Brigadier General Bruce, arrived before the monsoon and boasted a thirteen-member team (including a film crew) and rather superior food supplies. As well as champagne and caviare there were tins of Heinz spaghetti which, like most of the other foodstuffs, froze solid at the higher camps.

They may have been better fed but the team members were still woefully under-clothed. A famous picture of Mallory and Norton, high on the mountain, shows them dressed in wool trousers and jackets with little room for more than a jersey or two and long-johns under this. They sported medum brimmed hats and, aside from the goggles, ice-axes and rope, would not have looked out of place strolling in an English park on a winter's morning. A series of camps was established. Camp IV was set up on the North Col and the primitive Camp V at a height of over 7600m/25,000ft. Although experience showed that this was too low for a serious attempt on the summit, the first attempt was launched from here. Nevertheless, Mallory, Norton and Somervell reached a height of 8150m/26,800ft without oxygen, before descending, all slightly frostbitten.

The second attempt was by Finch, accompanied by Bruce's son. Spurred on by hot tea and the discovery that using oxygen at night aided warmth and sleep, they climbed to 8320m/27,300ft. For Bruce this must have been especially satisfying since this was his first climbing trip. It was also the first time that oxygen had been used on Everest and some members of the group were very much against it, maintaining that its use was most unsporting.

The third attempt ended prematurely, 200m below the North Col with a fatal avalanche. Nine Sherpas were caught and seven of them killed. The Everest toll had begun.

'Because it's there' - the 1924 Expedition

It is immaterial whether or not George Mallory coined the immortal phrase: 'Because it's there', when asked in 1923 why anyone would want to climb Everest; it's for his pioneering contribution towards its conquest that he should be remembered, and the fateful 1924 expedition was to be his last.

Team members were still inadequately clothed, without down clothing. Each climber was given a clothing allowance of £50 to kit himself out. Norton boasted wind-proof overalls and a leather, fur-lined motorcycle helmet plus the usual all-too-thin layers, hardly sufficient against temperatures as low as -40°C (-40°F).

Early storms battered the group forcing them to retreat to Rongbuk Monastery. Here they received the Lama's blessing which they'd imprudently not bothered to seek out when they'd first arrived in the area. The freak weather patterns held up stocks of oxygen sets, leading to a shortage at Camp IV on the col but despite this Camp V was established. Camp VI was set at an altitude of 8170m/26,800ft, with Norton and Somervell staying there overnight. They set off early the next morning but Somervell was overcome by a serious coughing attack. He had developed frostbite in his throat and almost choked on a lump of his own frostbitten flesh which he later coughed up, giving him much relief. Norton was forced to struggle on alone and, labouring up steep ground covered with powder snow, reached a record altitude of 8570m/28,126ft, a phenomenal achievement. One has to wonder, if Norton had had an oxygen set, how much further he would have been able to climb.

That evening, with Norton suffering from snow-blindness and Somervell also out of action, Mallory chose the young and relatively inexperienced Irvine to accompany him next day. Odell who was older and more acclimatised might, in fact, have been a better choice. Sherpas climbed with Mallory and Irvine up to Camp VI, returning to report that apart from the stove rolling off the mountain, all was well. Next morning the weather was not perfect, and it is assumed that Mallory and Irvine left late. Odell climbed from Camp V to Camp VI studying the geology of the rocks along the way, and through a brief hole in the clouds saw the two climbers ascend a step. Initially he was inclined to think it was the second step before the summit but later suffered doubts. This was around 1pm so the climbers were far behind their schedule: Mallory had intended to be at the second step by 8am. A snow storm blew up and then cleared two hours later leaving the ridge and the summit cone fully visible but there was no sign of Mallory or Irvine. The night was also clear and a watch was kept on the ridge to the summit. However, they were never to be seen again.

Their disappearance began endless conjecture as to whether or not they reached the summit before they died. Subsequent climbers have remarked that Odell's description of where he saw them fits the third and final step better than the second; climbers are still easily visible at that point. If this were the case Mallory and Irvine quite possibly made the summit. To the day he died Odell wasn't sure which step he saw them on but thought it likely that they attained the summit. Their bodies have still not been recovered. This is not surprising since later expeditions have tackled the final stage of Everest up the face, rather than along the ridge, which was the route they used. In 1975, however, the Japanese Women's Everest Expedition was followed a few days later by a Chinese group. As one of the Chinese passed a Japanese climber he made it clear that the body of a British climber had been found at 8100m/26,575ft. If this were indeed true, the body could only have been Mallory's or Irving's. But the mystery continues because the very next day the Chinese climber himself disappeared in an avalanche.

Telephones on Everest – The 1933 Expedition

It was not until 1933 that another attempt was made. This boasted technical innovations: radio and, from Camp III to Camp IV, a telephone line. It was a strong team but bad weather interrupted the process of setting up intermediate camps, putting the expedition behind schedule. Nevertheless, they equalled Norton's altitude record, climbing without supplementary oxygen on bad snow.

British institutions like the Royal Geographical Society and the Alpine Club considered Everest their own preserve, jealously guarding it from attempts by outsiders. They were not amused by the announcement, in 1933, by the wealthy adventurer, Maurice Wilson, that he would climb Everest alone. He bought a light aircraft and flew himself from Britain to India. Despite having no previous climbing experience he managed to get as far as the North Col before succumbing to the cold. His body was found by the next group of climbers.

(**Opposite**): Mt Everest (8848m/29,028ft) and the Khumbu Icefall seen from high on Pumori's slopes.

The 1935 Reconnaissance Expedition

Led by Eric Shipton, this was the first of several expeditions to be headed by this famous explorer-mountaineer. He was known for his ability to think quickly and he preferred to travel light, living off the land, which was a major departure from the normal expedition approach. Since eggs were the most accessible source of protein they regularly appeared on the expedition menu, and Shipton notes that 'though many of them were rather stale we consumed enormous quantities. Our record was 140 in a single day between four of us, and many times our combined party of seven put away more than a hundred.' (*Upon that Mountain*).

One of the Sherpas taken on was an enthusiastic nineteen-year-old named Tenzing Bhotia (later Norgay), who proved to be ambitious and strong. Amongst the other team members was Dan Bryant, a cheerful Kiwi. The expedition had instructions not to climb Everest but the monsoon broke late so there would, in fact, have been time for a serious attempt that season. It was, however, a surprisingly successful climbing expedition in other respects, with an impressive total of 26 peaks over 6095m/20,000ft climbed by the seven-man group, and all for a total cost of a mere £1500.

Monsoon stops play

The following year the 1936 Everest attempt, for which the 1935 expedition had been preparing the way, was unfortunately washed out by the early arrival of the monsoon. The 1938 low-budget expedition was led by HW Tilman (recounted in his *Mount Everest 1938*). Having learnt lessons about the monsoon from previous expeditions, they arrived early but to no avail. The monsoon broke three weeks earlier than it ever had previously. Still, they continued, even trying a different route but snow conditions for the last 1000m steadily worsened.

Nepal at last

In 1948 the Kingdom of Nepal for the first time opened its doors a crack but only to parties interested in scientific research. Tilman was not a scientist (he claimed that he 'had hitherto refused to mingle art with science') but he compromised his principles and squeezed in a year later. He was allocated the Langtang area, which to his delight was marked 'unsurveyed' on his map. Later he was lucky enough to be invited to visit Namche, walking in from Dharan via the Arun River. He made the first ascent by a foreigner of the now famous Kala Pattar.

(**Opposite**) **Top:** Trekking with porters can be an enlightening and entertaining cultural experience for both parties, as well as benefiting the local economy. **Bottom:** Dingboche: Yak ready-saddled for the trip to the Saturday market in Namche.

The 1951 Reconnaissance Expedition

After the Chinese invasion of Tibet the northern route to Everest was sealed off with the closure of the border. An expedition, led by Shipton, was dispatched to reconnoitre an alternative, southern route through newly-opened Nepal. Although Shipton had turned down many suitable applicants for the team in Britain, recalling New Zealander Dan Bryant on the 1935 Expedition, in a moment of weakness he accepted a request from the NZ Alpine Club for two unnamed climbers to join the team. They were George Lowe and Edmund Hillary. It was to be the first time that a party had climbed after the monsoon, the traditional season being in the 'lull before the storm'. They arrived in Namche at the end of September and climbed to the Western Cwm. In spite of the danger from the Khumbu Icefall it was clear that the southern route up Everest was indeed feasible.

1952 – the competition closes in

Time was running out for the British and what they chauvinistically considered their exclusive 'right' to the area. In 1950 the first 'eight-thousander' (8000m peak), Annapurna, had been conquered by the French. After the British 1951 Reconnaissance Expedition to the Khumbu, there came an unwelcome piece of news: the Swiss had been given permission to make an attempt on Everest in 1952 and the British would have to wait until the following year. A French attempt was scheduled for 1954. Surprisingly, the Swiss almost agreed to a joint Anglo-Swiss expedition (obviously wanting to make use of Shipton's wide experience of the mountain) but the details could not be worked out to everyone's satisfaction. The Swiss chose Tenzing Norgay as their sirdar. He held them in high esteem because it was with two of the Swiss expedition members that he had successfully climbed a peak in 1947, his first despite 12 years climbing with expeditions.

The trek to base camp took 23 days from the newly-opened airfield in Kathmandu. They established five camps between Gorak Shep and the head of the Western Cwm and conclusively proved that it was a feasible route. Tenzing and Lambert climbed to just below the south summit but could go no further. It was realised that an additional camp and further logistical support were needed for an attempt to succeed. Their second attempt after the monsoon was dogged by bad luck, bad planning and the ferocious high-altitude winter winds.

Preparations for the 1953 British Everest Expedition

The Swiss attempts gave the British a chance to prepare properly. Training included an expedition to Cho Oyu in 1952, led by Shipton. Although they failed to reach the summit (see p102), the expedition was of great value: as a result important refinements were made to oxygen sets and clothing.

In planning the 1953 expedition internal politics played a large part. Though Shipton had led many previous expeditions and had immense popularity with the public, some members of the Alpine Club committee felt that he might not be the right man to lead an expedition of such size and under such pressure. This would surely be the final chance for them to reach the summit first. Diplomatic to the last, Shipton agreed that he was indeed happiest climbing with the minimum of encumbering resources and it was decided that John Hunt, an army officer, should lead the expedition which would be run on military lines. Strangely, most of the committee had never met Hunt, and he had been turned down for the 1935 Everest expedition on health reasons.

'We knocked the bastard off!' - Success in 1953

The 1953 expedition was an all-out assault. It was decided that oxygen was to be used to the limit of its advantages, for aiding sleep and climbing – anything to conquer. With all this equipment the walk-in was on a grand scale: the first of two groups of porters numbered some 350 people. Since the only currency accepted in the hills at the time was silver coins it took several porters just to carry the wages. There were 13 climbers, with Tenzing Norgay added to the climbing ranks, plus a reporter and cameraman.

The team spent two weeks climbing in the Khumbu area to aid acclimatisation before tackling the Icefall. It was while forging a route through this monstrous obstacle that Hillary and Tenzing first got to know each other and Tenzing demonstrated that he could match the very competitive Hillary. Once the camps in the Western Cwm were established sickness took its toll, setting back the schedules. However, after a 13-day struggle, Camp VIII on the South Col was established. Evans and Bourdillon made the first summit attempt from this camp although it was too far away to allow a safe return if they did succeed. In the event snow conditions deteriorated and one of the oxygen sets caused problems, so the climbers settled for the south summit. This was less than 100m/328ft below the real summit, but at that altitude, even with oxygen, the climbers estimated it to be three hours away.

The second assault was better planned. A higher camp, Camp IX, was established and Hillary and Tenzing rested here for the night, drinking quantities of hot lemon and even eating a little. At 6.30am on 29 May, they began the climb. They reached the south summit by 9am, and the snow conditions past this first critical point were good. What is now known as the 'Hillary Step', a 13m/43ft barrier, was overcome by chimneying up a gap between a cornice and the rock wall, a dangerous but necessary move. The summit, only a short distance away, was reached at 11.30am. In the words of Hillary:

I looked at Tenzing and in spite of the balaclava, goggles and oxygen mask all encrusted with long icicles that concealed his face, there was no disguising his infectious grin of pure delight as he looked all around him. We shook hands and then Tenzing threw his arm around my shoulders and we thumped each other on the back until we were almost breathless.' *The Ascent of Everest* John Hunt

By evening they had struggled down to the South Col where Hillary told his team mate: 'Well, George, we knocked the bastard off', though this was not exactly what was printed in the press at the time!

Conquering the world's top ten peaks

The world's ten highest mountains were all climbed in a relatively short span of frenetic mountaineering activity between 1950 and 1960. The heights, and dates for the first climbs, are given below:

1 Everest/Sagarmatha/Chomolungma	8848m/29,028ft	29 May 53
2 K2 (Pakistan/China)	8611m/28,251ft	31 July 54
3 Kanchenjunga (Nepal/India)	8586m/28,169ft	25 May 55
4 Lhotse (Nepal/Tibet)	8501m/27,890ft	18 May 56
5 Makalu (Nepal/Tibet)	8463m/27,765ft	15 May 55
6 Cho Oyu (Nepal/Tibet)	8201m/26,906ft	19 Oct 54
7 Dhaulagiri (Nepal)	8167m/26,794ft	13 May 60
8 Manaslu (Nepal)	8156m/26,758ft	09 May 56
9 Nanga Parbat (Pakistan)	8126m/26,660ft	03 June 53
10 Annapurna (Nepal)	8091m/26,545ft	03 June 50

In comparison to these, the heights of the highest peaks in some Western countries are rather less impressive:

Britain: Ben Nevis	1343m/4406ft
Australia: Mt Kosciusko	2228m/7310ft
New Zealand: Mt Cook	3754m/12,316ft
Switzerland/Italy: Matterhorn	4478m/14,692ft
France/Italy: Mont Blanc	4808m/15,771ft
Canada: Mt Logan	5961m/19,524ft
USA: Mt McKinley	6194m/20,320ft

Chinese attempts on Everest

The pressure bubble burst with the success of the British expedition. It was some time before further attempts were considered as now the other unclimbed 'eight-thousanders' commanded attention. The Swiss climbed Everest after their conquest of Lhotse in 1956. In 1960 the Indians came close to success and at the same time the Chinese attempted the pre-war route via Tibet. It was a mammoth affair, mounted on a grander scale than any previous attempt. Success was announced but no photos could be produced and the expedition account, after being suitably embellished by the propaganda department, made entertaining reading but was inconsistent with the mountaineering thinking of the time. We join them on the second step on a four metre wall:

Each one made several attempts but fell back each time. They looked at each other for inspiration. Time was marching on mercilessly, and according to the weather-station forecast, it was the last day of the fine weather period... Then Liu Lien-man had an idea that the "courte echell" (short ladder) technique might help, so crouching down he offered his companion a leg-up. Ignoring the biting cold and the danger of freezing, Chu Ying-hua took off his high-altitude boots and his eider-down stockings to make the climb easier.... It had taken them five full hours to overcome this obstacle.... dusk came and an icy wind howled dolefully. The three members of the Communist Party of China, Wang Fu-chou, Chu Ying-hua and Liu Lien-man, discussed the situation and it was decided to leave Liu Lien-man behind and press on.' *Mountaineering in China* (People's Physical Culture Publishing House)

They claimed to have left a plaster bust of Chairman Mao Tse-tung near the summit. Athough the attempt was ridiculed by the Western media (this was during the Cold War) it's now considered that the expedition did succeed in reaching the summit. There were rumours of another Chinese attempt in 1966 in which 24 climbers died but Chinese officials refused to discuss the incident. In 1969 it was claimed that three surveyors reached the summit without oxygen or additional support; and in 1975 another Chinese team was said to have reached the summit. Proof of their success was found by Doug Scott and Dougal Haston of the 1975 British South-West Face Expedition. On the summit they came upon a red Chinese tripod.

Recent attempts on Everest

More than 300 mountaineers have now stood on the summit of Everest and it continues to attract attention. New routes are attempted, such as the south-west face and the west ridge from Lho La. Different mountaineering methods have been applied and in 1978 Reinhold Messner and Peter Habeler reached the summit without the use of oxygen. Messner went on to make a successful solo climb without oxygen in 1980 and has since soloed all 14 of the world's 'eight-thousanders'. Other summiteers have relied on bizarre methods to gain media attention. In 1970 an intrepid Japanese adventurer actually skied part of the way down and, in 1988, Frenchman Jean-Marc Boivin jumped off the summit with a paraglider!

Walt Unsworth's book, *Everest,* and Peter Gillman's similarly-titled book are highly recommended for more information on the history of climbs on the mountain.

CHO OYU (8201m/26,906ft)

The name Cho Oyu is almost certainly Tibetan in origin and is translit-erated in several ways. My favourite is Chomo Yu which means 'Goddess of Turquoise', the colour the mountain often assumes at sun-set when viewed from the Tibetan side.

The 1952 British attempt

In 1952, while the Swiss were attempting Everest, Eric Shipton led a British expedition to Cho Oyu. They failed to reach the top probably because Shipton was unwilling to build a supply line up the mountain on the Tibetan side. Tibet was now in the hands of the communist Chinese and Shipton was wary of doing anything that might jeopardise the planned 1953 Everest Expedition. In 1951 he'd been caught by the Tibetans on the wrong side of the border. Quite prepared to hand over everything he possessed (Rs1200) when they brandished their swords and demanded a ransom, he was soon amused to discover that his ever-faithful Sherpas had bargained the final sum down to a mere Rs7!

Herbert Tichy's style of mountaineering

An Austrian attempt on Cho Oyu was launched in 1954, led by Herbert Tichy. The decision to climb was made on the spur of the moment after a conversation with a Sherpa, before Tichy had even seen the peak. The team consisted of three Austrians and seven high-altitude Sherpas but their prospects did not look good. One of the Austrians had previously been shot through the lung, another suffered severely from sciatica and Tichy admitted to smoking a lot and drinking 'without reluctance'. In addition, the attempt was launched after the monsoon, without oxygen, with little equipment and less than Rs1000-worth of food. At that stage in the history of Himalayan mountaineering, success had occurred only on well-equipped pre-monsoon expeditions.

On the walk in, Tichy soon noticed that changes were afoot in the area: 'We followed in the tracks of other expeditions – notably Everest expeditions. They had rubbed off the bloom which I was still able to enjoy in the west of Nepal the year before: they had also spoilt the mar-ket (four eggs for a rupee instead of 10) and the villagers treated us with that mixture of interest and condescension people bestow on a travelling circus'(*Cho Oyu by Favour of the Gods*). Tichy's relaxed approach to climbing left much time for merry-making with friends in the Khumbu. On one such occasion he notes that the Sherpa porters had done full justice to the parting from their friends and their families and when we overtook our proud array we saw that some of our Sherpanis were so drunk that their male companions had to carry them and their loads as well. This predicament was taken as a great joke' (*Cho Oyu by Favour of the Gods*).

1954 – Austrian success

The walk up to Base Camp, slightly north of the Nangpa La (just inside Tibet), was accomplished with only 27 porters. Camp IV was established at 6980m/22,900ft, ten days from Base Camp but then disaster struck. In savage winds with the temperature below -35°C. Tichy made a desperate dive to save one of their tents and suffered frostbite on his fingers. The climb had to be temporarily abandoned. Nevertheless nine days later he and his companions set off again, spurred on by meeting a Swiss expedition that had just arrived with the similar intention of attempting Cho Oyu. A storm pinned the Austrians down for two days before they could return to Camp IV. However, on the following day, 19th October 1954, Tichy, Sepp Jochler and Pasang Lama made the summit.

For Pasang Lama the ascent was all the more remarkable, indeed a quite heroic achievement. Having returned to Namche to pick up more supplies, at Marulung (4150m/13,615ft), a day's walk from Namche, he heard of the Swiss plans and so raced, heavily loaded, in a day up to Base Camp. Then, even more remarkably, the next day he ascended with a load to Camp IV and on the following day climbed to the summit.

MAKALU (8475m/27,805ft)

British/American 1954 Expedition

In the line-up for attempts on Everest, the French had been allotted the year following the British. The same order was established for Makalu (8475m/27,805ft), with the British and Americans given permission for the spring of 1954 and the French scheduled to follow them. The French were naturally not keen to follow in the wake of a British success (as on Everest) and the results were anxiously awaited. With a strong team that included Hillary, it looked as if success on Makalu was likely. However, the summit was not reached.

1955 – French success

The French were spurred into action with an autumn reconnaissance and gear-testing trip. Chomo Lonzo (7790m/25,557ft), just inside Tibet, and Makalu II (7640m/25,065ft) were both climbed.

The 1955 attempt was a classic assault of the mountain, superbly organised, kitted with the best of equipment and conducted as if the pride of the country was at stake. They were prepared for the worst and ready to make repeated attempts. However, perfect weather allowed all the expedition members, as well as some of the Sherpas, to reach the summit of Makalu between 15 and 17 May.

LHOTSE (8501m/27,890ft)

Lhotse was so named by one of the British expeditions in the 1920s; no local name for it could be found. It is Tibetan for 'South Peak' and Lhotse Shar is the south-east peak of Everest.

The 1956 Swiss Expedition

In the spring of 1952 the Swiss had climbed to 250m/820ft below the summit of Everest before being forced back. In 1956 an expedition was mounted with permission for Lhotse (at that stage the highest unclimbed mountain) as well as Everest. It was a very well planned and provisioned expedition and the team worked well together. A cautious acclimatisation programme was followed, with many rest days at Tengboche and Pheriche. It's interesting to note that in an effort to make the route through the Icefall safer, explosives were used!

Success came on 18 May, when Ernst Reiss and Fritz Luchsinger, using oxygen, fought their way up the steep slopes in unsettled weather to the summit. The second goal was also attained and four climbers reached the summit of Everest on the same expedition.

The Sherpas

Years of living in their villages left me well aware that Sherpas are no more strangers to greed, pride, love of power, jealousy or pettiness than other mortals. They seem still, for all the close familiarity, a singularly appealing people. Stanley Stevens *Cultural Ecology and History in Highland Nepal* (University of California)

The mountaineering exploits of the Sherpas on foreign expeditions since the 1920s brought them clearly into the world spotlight. Sherpa Tenzing's conquest, with Hillary, of Everest in 1953 was a fitting tribute to the part played by Sherpas in the history of mountaineering not just in the Khumbu but in many parts of the Himalaya. Although the lure of Everest has brought crowds of foreigners to their land, they seem to have weathered the cultural invasion surprisingly well. Theirs is an ancient culture which Westerners have learnt to respect, indeed admire, for its tolerance, comradeship and many other positive values.

Origins

Shar-pa is Tibetan for 'Eastern People' and the first Sherpas were almost certainly migrants from 1300km away in Kham (north-east Tibet) possibly fleeing from Mongol incursions. It's thought that they tried settling in a number of places en route but were consistently driven on, crossing the Himalaya about 500 years ago over the Nangpa La. Migration occurred in several successive waves with large numbers of people arriving in the late 1800s and early 1900s and another major migration in the 1960s after the Chinese invasion of Tibet.

Settlements first appeared in the mid 1500s on both sides of the Lamjura Pass (Junbesi and north of Kenja), where Sherpas still live today. The Thame and Pangboche gompas were established later, possibly during the 1670s, although it's likely that the area had been populated previously. It's thought that the Khumbu was used for pastures by Rai shepherds before the Sherpas arrived; the Dudh Kosi is known as 'Khambu' by Rais today.

Agriculture

The crop with the highest yields in the Khumbu is the humble potato and about 75% of the cultivated area is planted with them. Growing enough, however, is not easy and most families have always supplemented their income, originally by trading with Tibet and now mainly through tourism. Their agricultural methods are quite sophisticated even though their tools may be primitive. Land holdings are scattered and several crop varieties used in order to minimise the risk of blight and other diseases. The soil is not naturally very fertile but large quantities of organic fertiliser (compost, human waste and animal manure) have worked well, according to soil scientists. Women and children do much of the work but the roles aren't rigidly defined. Up until the 1950s all ploughing was done by hand with four men to a plough but now animals are used. The men tend to the animals and are also occupied with trade, often leaving their wives to manage the entire affairs of the household.

The Sherpas of Pharak and Solu live at lower altitudes and the milder climate enables them to grow a wider range of crops. In Junbesi, many of the vegetables served to trekkers are grown locally. Apples thrive in this area and apple pies and jams are on every lodge menu. Yaks, naks (female yaks) and crossbreeds, are kept high in the mountains away from the villages. Their milk that was once made into butter and traded with Tibet to keep the monastery lamps burning is now sold to local cheese factories. Sherpa trade in this area is now mainly with passing trekkers.

Diet

As one might expect, potatoes are eaten at almost every meal, although the well-off also eat rice. Potatoes are usually boiled and once they've been peeled (the skin is never eaten) they're dipped in salt and a chilli sauce. Savoury pancakes, made from a mixture of buckwheat (the nonsweet variety) and grated potatoes, are eaten with butter and chillis. However, the great Sherpa favourite is shakpa, a thick soup made with whatever comes to hand (usually potatoes!), a few vegetables and sometimes chewy balls of wheat flour.

With potatoes being a staple, it's not surprising that the Sherpas are connoisseurs of the varieties that are suited to the Khumbu. Trekkers also consume huge quantities of potatoes, not because there are no alternatives on the menu but because they're surprisingly tasty. If you show an interest, the lodge owner may show you the different types. The highest yielding variety (commonly served to trekkers) is not considered quite as tasty as some of the older types.

The Sherpa diet is fairly healthy. Naks and dzums (a yak/cow crossbreed) provide dairy products and meat is occasionally eaten, dried or fresh. In the past the diet lacked only iodine, a deficiency of which causes goiters and cretinism. The situation was quickly solved by the first doctor at Kunde hospital. Now the majority of salt in Nepal, instead of coming from Tibet, is naturally iodised sea-salt from India.

A year in the Khumbu

Many trekkers have mistakenly come away with the impression that Sherpas don't seem to do anything in the Khumbu apart from looking after trekkers. This is not the case. The Sherpa calendar of activities is governed entirely by the seasons with a short cultivation period. It's most fortunate that the main trekking season occurs at the end of the harvest.

April-May After the fields have been prepared, the potatoes are planted, followed by barley and buckwheat. These are labour-intensive activities.

May-June Traditionally, this is a time of trading. The high passes to Tibet are open for a short while after the winter snows have melted and before the snows of the monsoon arrive. It's also the season of yak-shearing and calving.

June-July The fields are weeded: a laborious job that may have to be done several times.

June-September After calving, the yaks and naks are herded up to the high summer pastures to protect the crops and save the grass lower down for the spring. Summer is the time of butter, cheese and curd production.

September-October These are the busiest months. At the high pastures, hay is cut while in the villages the potatoes are dug up and the barley and buckwheat harvested and threshed. Once this is completed the cattle can return to the villages. It's also the breeding season for cattle and the beginning of the trekking season.

November-March The long and cold winter months are filled with spinning and weaving, collecting firewood and feeding the animals by hand. It's also a time for trading, not only with Tibet, but also Kathmandu and trips to the capital are also made to beat the cold and visit friends. Losar, the Tibetan New Year which usually occurs in February, is the main festival.

The Sherpa House

Unlike the Tibetan house, which is flat-roofed and built around a court-yard, the Sherpa house features a roof adapted for the monsoon rains and has no courtyard. Although it does bear a superficial resemblance to the Tibetan house, the Tibetan architectural style is reserved for gompas.

The size of a house is a sign of prosperity. In the Rolwaling there are still many single-storied houses whereas in wealthy Namche there are now even some four-storey hotel 'sky-scrapers'. However, the majority of Sherpa houses consist of two levels. The ground floor is for stabling cattle and is a storage area for grain, animal fodder, firewood and tools. It's also where the *chang* (home-brew made from rice or bar-ley) is fermented. The upper level of the house is usually an open liv-ing-room, sometimes with the kitchen partitioned off.

Roofs are made of slate or wood, though slates are now being replaced by corrugated iron sheets. Walls are usually stone with huge wooden beams running between them to support the floor. In some of the older houses, the beams can be up to 25 metres long which gives some idea of the size of the trees in the forests that once covered this area of the Himalaya.

The layout of the interior is dictated by tradition. The west wall is for a shrine with Buddha images, candles or butter lamps and pictures of the Dalai Lama and the King and Queen of Nepal. Beneath the sunny south-facing windows are long benches, often covered with thick Tibetan rugs. The south-east corner is for the master bed, usual-ly the only bed, in which the whole family sleeps. If there are visitors for the night, they sleep on the carpeted bench seats. The sunless north wall is windowless and lined with shelves displaying the valuable kitchen-ware. The long tea-churn for making salt-butter tea should always be near the stairway. Many tea-churns are cherished family heirlooms, passed down from generation to generation.

The Sherpa view of life

Most Sherpas are followers of the Nyingmapa ('Red Hat') sect of Tibetan Buddhism, the most ancient and least reformed of the four major Tibetan sects. It developed out of the tantric practices introduced by the Indian Padmasambhava (Guru Rinpoche or 'precious teacher') and is combined with older beliefs of the Sherpas: the Bon-po religion and animism. Spirits and demons (*lu*) inhabit the springs, trees and rocks, and there are detailed rites for protection and exorcism.

As Buddhists, Sherpas view life as an endless cycle of rebirth into a world of suffering. Escape (*nirvana*) is possible only by accumulat-ing a series of 'good' lives. The measure of good and evil is *sonam*. By carrying out virtuous deeds you gain merit but sinful acts reduce the total at a rather unequal rate. One sin is far more powerful than a few good deeds so constant work is required to keep ahead. If you fall far behind you may not even be born human again: monastery dogs are considered reincarnations of the not-so-studious monks. The meritorious who have finally escaped may return to assist their brethren as reincarnate head lamas, such as the Lama at Tengboche.

All forms of life are treated with respect since to kill something is regarded as one of the greatest demerits. However, Sherpas relish meat and to eat it is no sin as long as the consumer was not responsible for the animal's death. The Sherpas' approach to life is remarkably unpuritanical and considerably more liberated than that of the Hindu Nepali. There is no caste system and women (Sherpanis) are treated much more equally. In most cases it is the Sherpani, rather than the Sherpa who controls the family finances.

Prayers for the world

In addition to general good conduct, repeating *mantras* (prayer chants) is an important means to gain *sonam*. Most common is the mantra *Om Mani Padme Hum*, meaning 'hail to the jewel in the lotus', the jewel being the Buddha.

The more times a mantra can be repeated, the better, so Tibetan Buddhism has evolved many ingenious labour-saving methods to mass-produce these prayers. **Prayer wheels** are filled with a long paper roll inscribed with mantras that are activated by turning the wheel. They come in many forms, from the portable hand-held device so admired by tourists, to huge wheels that with a single turn repeat astronomical numbers of prayers. There are also water-powered prayer wheels and multicoloured fluttering **prayer flags**, printed with mantras, infuse the winds with prayers to travel the world. The mantra may be carved onto a **mani stone**, which benefits both the carver and the person who has paid for the work. Large numbers of these stones are piled up into the mani walls you see along the trails.

Note that you should always pass to the left of a mani wall and walk clockwise (the direction in which prayer wheels must always be turned) around Buddhist shrines and monuments.

Mountaineers, sirdars and porters

Sherpas are well known for their dedicated service to mountaineering expeditions, first as porters and sirdars and later also as participating climbers. The part they play in many expeditions has often been behind the scenes but it is nonetheless crucial for that. On the 1922 Everest attempt, six Sherpas climbed to Camp VI (8170m/26,800ft) from Camp V 800m below, merely to deliver thermos flasks of beef-tea to the sahibs after a storm.

Shipton, who always took Sherpas on his long and unbelievably wild treks in the Himalaya and Karakoram thoroughly admired them:

'One of the most delightful things about the Sherpas is their extraordinary sense of comradeship. During the six months we were together, I never detected any sign of dissension among our three....This quality of theirs is due largely, I imagine, to their robust sense of humour. It hardly ever failed. Each enjoyed jokes against himself as delightedly as those who he perpetrated. Two of them would conceal a heavy rock in the load of the third, and when, after an exhausting climb, this was discovered, all three would be convulsed with mirth....They were forever laughing and chatting together as though they had just met after a prolonged absence.' (*The Six Mountain Travel Books*)

Even today, Sherpa high-altitude porters still play a vital role in many expeditions, and the opportunity for mountaineering training has spawned local heroes. Sungdare Sherpa was one among many. He climbed many mountains, often at great speed (Cho Oyu, 8201m/26,905ft, in 18 hours), and had attained the summit of Everest five times before he died a premature death (not as a result of a mountaineering accident). The majority of Sherpas who work for expeditions do so for money, however, and consider the risks a trade-off for income. Ang Rita, nine times summiteer who has never used oxygen, says simply that expeditions keep paying him more and more so he can't refuse. Most admired now, apart from the mountaineers, are the sirdars and trekking company directors who have broken through Hindu caste barriers to become some of the most successful business-people in Nepal.

Coping with development

The Sherpas' liberal and positive outlook on life combined with the head-start they were given through the Himalayan Trust (see below) have enabled them to develop and adapt at a far quicker rate than most peoples in Nepal. Although community spirit is strong, individual endeavour and achievement through hard work are respected. There is little resistance to change that is obviously beneficial. If a new strain of potato, for example, proves to be an improvement on a previous type, it will be widely adopted.

Change in the Khumbu has been rapid but not overwhelming. Houses are bigger, smarter and less pictureque but their basic design and the style of construction are still close to time-honoured methods. Some men now wear jeans and while it's rare to see men, other than monks, in entirely traditional clothing, it's equally rare to see women in anything other than the practical *chuba*, the style of dress that has been worn for generations. The diet is generally healthier and more varied but an increase in sugar consumption has led to a greater incidence of tooth decay, especially among children. The worldliness of the Sherpas has undoubtedly increased with the steady stream of visitors but they are nonetheless still delightful people and can be highly entertaining hosts if you have time to spend with them.

National parks

SAGARMATHA NATIONAL PARK

Set up to control the environmental impact of the increasingly large numbers of tourists visiting the Khumbu, Sagarmatha National Park was officially gazetted in July 1976. For the first six years, the National Parks Service of New Zealand provided training, management and guidelines. In 1979 it was declared a World Heritage Site by UNESCO in recognition of its rich cultural heritage and magnificent scenery. The park's area is around 1200 square km encompassing the entire watershed of the Dudh Kosi with the boundary being a virtually impenetrable ring of mountains. The numbers of foreign visitors has been steadily increasing: from 5066 people in the 81/82 season to around10,000 now. The local Sherpa population numbers approximately 3500 and the national park staff, around 60. There are more than 200 government civil servants living in the park.

Policies

Initially, there was local resistance to the park owing to worries that the people might be forcibly resettled, as had happened when Rara Lake National Park (west Nepal) was created. To allay such fears village areas were excluded from the park. There have inevitably been clash-

---

The Himalayan Trust and Sir Edmund Hillary

The Himalayan Trust is a charity that has helped local people set up almost thirty schools, several hospitals and construct many bridges and runways in the Solu Khumbu. Thirty years on, the positive results are obvious and the region is far ahead along the development road compared with the rest of rural Nepal.Its phenomenal success is the result of sound principles and dedicated staff. Sir Edmund Hillary deserves the highest praise for his selfless efforts. Almost every Himalayan Trust school, bridge and hospital bears the stains of Hillary's sweat and he still returns to Nepal virtually every year to continue the work. Villagers soon saw him as the one person who could realise their local projects. It is the fact that these were projects initiated by the people themselves (rather than imposed by the government or a distant aid agency) that has been the key to their success. Development has happened at the village pace. Involvement of the local people in their projects has been another reason for their success. As far as possible, villagers must provide land and labour although the Trust provides the bulk of finance required for materials. This degree of local involvement ensures that bridges, hospitals and schools are well cared for. In addition, more than 50 scholarships are awarded each year for further education, with priority for girls.

es of interest between villagers and park management. Villagers are unhappy at not being able to farm new land or even work existing terraces that had previously been abandoned. The view of the park management is that as land becomes more valuable, every bit must be protected if possible. The relatively well-educated people of the Khumbu now have a slow rate of population growth and the land at present in use already generates a surplus of crops.

Many of the park's policies have been accepted by the villagers once they've been seen to show positive returns. The management of forest resources is a good example. Local forests were once protected by the collection of firewood in different section on a yearly rotation. The nationalisation of forests and the arrival of large expeditions turned firewood into a valuable cash crop, with devastating results. A complete ban was placed on the cutting down of trees when the park came into being: a move that is now respected as the most sensible course of action. As well as organising reforestation schemes, the National Park is involved in the construction of facilities for trekkers (toilets), controlling rubbish disposal and raising local environmental awareness.

Like all environmental organisations in Nepal, Sagarmatha National Park is forced to operate with limited financial resources, with little forthcoming from the government.

BARUN-MAKALU NATIONAL PARK

The boundaries of this new park encompass the area from close to the Arun river to Sagarmatha National Park and include the Hongu/Hinku or Mera Peak area. It's been formed to set up the systems of environmental protection that may become necessary if the planned 'Arun III' hydro-electric scheme goes ahead. This massive project would require an access road that would open up a previously isolated area.

Facilities for the trekker

ACCOMMODATION AND FOOD

The development of lodges

The hill peoples of Nepal have traditionally provided food and accommodation for the many traders passing through their villages on the trade routes that cross the country. These small family-run establishments were nothing like hotels in the Western sense of the word.

Guests were charged for food but not for their lodging, which was very basic. Not so long ago these teahouses were providing the same level of facilities for the first foreign trekkers: little more than dal bhat and a hard bed. As the flow of trekkers grew it was soon realised that these foreigners were prepared to pay more for better accommodation and a choice of food.

Development was slow at first. In 1985 Kenja, Junbesi, Kharikhola and Monjo were the only places below Namche that had proper lodges. In the 1990s, however, many new lodges have been built and teahouses upgraded. Double rooms have replaced dormitories, and showers and toilets have been built. Extensive menus are provided for meals according to Western tastes. (Nepalis have just two main meals a day, both comprising dal bhat). Chimneys have now been installed in many places, and smoky lodges are rare. Lodges are now run as businesses, very different from the old teahouses with their hosts eager for news of the world beyond the village.

Nepal now offers surprisingly well-developed mountain lodge systems in the Solu Khumbu, Annapurna and Langtang areas. This is, however, a developing country that is still one of the world's poorest so although the lodges may be not be as grand as those you might find in the European Alps neither are the prices. Each lodge is, for the most part, owned and managed by a single family. Supplies are purchased or grown locally where possible but most things are carried in by porters.

Hygiene
Eating in well established lodges is now probably safer than eating a cooked meal on an organised group trek. The concept of washing hands, basic cleanliness and boiling water has been learnt from courses in Kathmandu as well as at the insistence of trekkers. Kitchens may lack stainless steel sinks and running water but they are, nevertheless, cleaned frequently. The style of cooking (frying or boiling) renders much of the food safe and salads are not to be found. Hot drinks are safe but local drinks such as *chang* are not always so hygienically prepared.

Lodges on the main routes
Food A typical lodge in this area offers an extensive menu (vegetarian except in and around Namche) based on noodles, rice, flour, potatoes, eggs and the sparing use of vegetables. Breakfast offerings include muesli, a variety of porridges, pancakes and bread with jam or eggs. Most meal choices are carbohydrate-heavy: exactly what trekkers require. Apple pie, chocolate cake, pizza and toasted cheese and garlic sandwiches have found their way onto the menus of some resourceful lodge owners. All serve tea, coffee, hot chocolate, hot

lemon and Coke. Bottled beer can also be found along with *chang* (local beer), the respected Khukri rum and infamous *rakshi*. Porters and guides can locate this fire-water quicker than an Aussie can sniff out a beer!

Bathroom facilities These are not so developed but a primitive hot shower or a bucket of water are usually available. Toilets are usually just a hole in the ground to be squatted over. No spotlessly-white anti-septic auto-flush toilets here, so watch your ankles. The rural Nepalese have land that needs fertilising so before foreign trekkers took to the mountains there was no need for toilets.

Lodgings Sleeping arrangements vary. Older lodges have dormitories while most newer or larger places often boast simple double rooms with thin partitions that will not insulate you from a snoring neighbour. Ear plugs can be helpful. Beds in the newer lodges have reasonably thick foam mattresses but in simple lodges the mattress is barely thick enough to disguise the knots in the wood below. It's covered by a single clean sheet and there's a pillow that can be of granite consistency. Down jackets make great pillows.

There is virtually no chance of getting bedbugs or fleas if you use your own sleeping sheet and sleeping bag, especially since most lodges wash the sheets and air the mattresses frequently. Hotel blankets and quilts, however, having often been used by porters, can contain unwanted bed companions. Unless you expect star quality facilities, you may be pleasantly surprised and happy with both the food and accommodation along the main trekking routes.

Simple lodges

The lodges in Lobuche, Gorak Shep, half the lodges in Chukhung and Gokyo, and lodges in out-of-the-way places above Namche are all simple lodges. These are basic places where there may only be a couple of dormitories (occasionally rather cold) and the menus are less extensive although the food is usually good. There's little privacy in these lodges but with the friendliness of the owners and warm gear they're quite satisfactory.

Lodges now remain open all the year round, even at Gokyo, Lobuche (but not Gorak Shep) and Chukhung, so trekking options are no longer restricted during winter and the monsoon. They also never seem to suffer the problem of being full to the extent that trekkers are stranded without a bed. There always seems to be space somewhere; you'll never be turned away. There are, however, a few particularly busy places (Tengboche and Lobuche especially), that during October-November are filled almost to bursting. Sometimes this is because people on a group trek inconsiderately decide a lodge is more attractive and warmer than their tents. The national park has been reluctant to allow the building of new lodges or the expansion of old ones in this area. Elsewhere, supply-and-demand laws seem to work well.

> **Choosing a lodge**
> Most trekkers tend to head either for the biggest and best-looking lodge or for the one where other trekkers are staying. Lodge-owners are well aware of this and will sometimes try very hard to attract the first trekkers arriving in the village, occasionally even trying to seat them outside (on seats provided for this very purpose) in order to attract more. Overcrowding can be a problem in the most popular lodges. At dinner there may be 15 trekkers ordering eight different dishes, all to be cooked on two fires, although most lodges do seem to cope remarkably well.
>
> Look around at a few places before deciding where to stay. Except at the height of the season, you may find an empty lodge that is equally good as the one the other trekkers are crowding into. It's also worth trying out some of the smaller lodges and teashops, at least occasionally. This can be a rewarding cultural experience that gives you a better chance to see how the family lives. Expansion and competition with the big lodges is beyond the means of many of these small lodge-owners, their money going to support relatives and pay school fees.

Off the main routes

In general, wherever there is a village, accommodation can be found. There may not be a lodge as such but people will often invite you to stay. If this does not happen try asking around (not considered rude by the Nepalis) and something will turn up. Conditions can be extremely basic, however, very different from the lodges on the main trekking routes. In strongly Hindu areas, your presence may be considered as *jutho* (polluting) so you may have to eat alone and perhaps even sleep on the porch.

Wilderness areas and base camps offer no shelter other than the occasional overhanging rock. You should also be aware that on detailed maps the dots marked in *kharkas* (high-altitude pastures) are usually just roofless stone buildings occupied only in the summer. Even then they are often unable to offer food or shelter.

SHOPS, BANKS AND POST OFFICES

Most lodges also run a small shop offering bottled drinks, three or four types of biscuits, chocolate, Mars Bars and some sweets. Often tins of fruit or fish can be found, along with noodles, coffee, drinking chocolate, tea, muesli, porridge, milk powder, jam and cheap batteries.

Namche Shops are well stocked and sell film (slide and print), batteries of all sizes including camera batteries, torches, socks, postcards, Swiss chocolate and Tibetan souvenirs. There's also a wide range of new and used mountaineering equipment for rent and for sale.

Camping food If you're not choosy it's quite possible to assemble enough for a few nights' camping from the better shops in almost any village. The diet may be monotonous but it is light and cheap. In Namche there's a strange variety of expedition dried foods, usually little cheaper than in the West. Lobuche, Pheriche, Chukhung and Gokyo always have an interesting cheaper selection. Many of the locals are involved with expeditions and in little villages the weirdest collections of left-over expedition food can sometimes be found.

Banks and post offices There are banks for foreign exchange at Namche (reliable), Salleri and Khandbari. Post offices are also found in these three places, plus Junbesi. All are closed on Saturdays.

Minimum impact trekking

Take nothing but pictures, leave nothing but footprints (Motto of the Sierra Club)

It is undeniable that trekking has had a significant impact on the environment, the culture and the economy of the Solu Khumbu, with effects both negative and positive. The opinions of experts as to the extent of the damaging effects of trekking on this region vary. Awareness of the problems has been raised, however, and solutions are being effected far more rapidly than elsewhere in Nepal.

It was most fortunate for the people of the Solu Khumbu that the trekking industry started just as the vital trade links with Tibet were being severed by the Chinese. The industry has now developed into the single most important force in the economy and the Khumbu has become the richest area in rural Nepal. Many schools, hospitals and bridges, the obvious benefits of development, have been built.

The negative effects are also obvious. For most Nepalis, firewood is the only source of energy, indeed more than 90% of Nepal's energy is derived from this source. This has led to severe deforestation in parts of the country which in turn has led to soil erosion. Trekkers contribute to this problem by placing greater demands on the fuel supply. The amount of wood burnt by the average lodge in just one day to supply trekkers with apple pies and hot showers would keep a Nepalese family fed for up to two weeks. Litter, never a problem before packaged goods arrived in the Nepal, is now an eyesore, especially glass beer bottles and plastic mineral water bottles. Less apparent but probably even more important, are the negative effects of trekking tourism on the culture of the area. Impressionable younger Nepalis mistakenly develop a Utopian image of the West and lose confidence and pride in their own culture.

Awareness of the problem is the first step, and there are a number of simple, practical measures that trekkers can and should take in order to lessen their impact on a fragile land.

ENVIRONMENTAL CONCERNS

Pack it in, pack it out

In national parks in the West, visitors are encouraged to take out all their litter (and indeed anything they bring into the park with them) when they leave. However, in Nepal the situation is not so straightforward since many of the national parks contain villages and much of what you consume is purchased locally.

Litter

The most worrying and obvious litter problems in the Khumbu and Hinku (Mera Peak area) are directly related to the activities of trekking groups. Tinned food and bottled sauces are served at every meal. The members may be careful with their litter, putting it in the bins set up in the camp but what happens to this rubbish? Sometimes it is burnt, the leftovers sitting in the embers. Sometimes it is buried in the toilet, covered by little more than an inch of dirt. It may be dumped at the nearest village or simply left in the snow. The problem goes virtually unnoticed by group members because the kitchen crew are the last to leave a camp or lunch spot. Despite constant clean-up campaigns, litter left by groups is now considered by the park management to be a serious local problem. Park rules specifically state that all rubbish generated by trekking groups must now be packed out and not dumped in village garbage pits which were dug for the needs of the villagers.

The problem of litter generated by individual trekkers is not so serious. There is little non-burnable litter that is not recycled, apart from some glass bottles and plastic mineral water bottles. Flour, sugar and rice come in sacks, the cardboard from egg-boxes is reused, oil comes in tins that are prized for roofing and very little tinned food is on

---

Sagarmatha Pollution Control Committee (SPCC)
Set up with assistance from the World Wide Fund for Nature (WWF), the SPCC has placed rubbish bins throughout the Khumbu. These bins are emptied regularly and much of the rubbish carried to the incinerator at Lukla. Along with national park initiatives, setting up this system has helped to heighten local awareness of the tourist obsession with rubbish and other visual pollution. Although rubbish was already less of a problem here than in other trekking areas of Nepal, the Khumbu has, as a result, become almost spotless. Some groups, however, still leave litter at camping sites. The SPCC has information offices in Lukla and Namche.

menus. Most lodges now burn the burnables and the park staff have dug rubbish pits at many strategic sites and instructed the local people in their use (although one hopes this is not a permanent solution).

• **Don't use mineral water** Since mineral water is sold in non-returnable, non-biodegradable plastic bottles and is now widely available in Nepal the empty bottles are becoming a serious litter problem. Use iodine to purify water (see p240) instead of buying mineral water; you can then also be sure that the water really is safe.

• **Put litter in bins** There is absolutely no excuse for dropping any litter along the trails. Yet many trekkers are guilty of this, even if only for the odd sweet wrapper. However, one piece of paper, multiplied several thousand times becomes a significant problem. Tissues, film cartons and biscuit wrappers are all easily stuffed into a backpack pocket for disposal in a bin at a lodge. You could also help by picking up a few bits of the litter generated by other people.

• **Set an example** The concept of litter is a relatively new one for the Nepalis. Virtually everything that was discarded in the past was biodegradable so not a threat to the environment. Take-away meals have always been served on sal leaves which do not become a problem when thrown away beside the trail. Trekkers can help here by example.

Other pollution
Use toilet facilities provided Most lodges have toilets which individual trekkers should use. Group trekkers should ensure that the toilets that are dug in their camps are of a sufficient depth and are properly filled in when the campsite is left. Trekking organisations have been criticised for not doing this. With the large number of groups there are now so many holes that finding a new space to put a toilet tent can be a problem. This is particularly acute in Tengboche and Gokyo. Toilet blocks specifically for the use of trekking groups are now being constructed throughout the Khumbu.

• **Burn used toilet paper** Nepalis use the 'water method' rather than toilet paper so all the pink streamers beside the track are generated by trekkers. Used toilet paper is easily burnt or put in the bin provided for the purpose. It should not be dropped into the toilet since villages often use human waste, as well as cow dung, as fertiliser on the fields, mixing it with leaves. Tampons must be wrapped and put in rubbish bins.

• **Don't pollute water sources** In the West the provision of clean drinking water has reduced the incidence of diarrhoea-related diseases so that they are now negligible. Nepal still has a long way to go but efforts are being made to provide villages with water from uncontaminated sources. If bathing in streams don't use soap or shampoo. Do not defecate close to the trail or a stream. If there is no toilet ensure you are at least 20 metres away from any water source, burn used toilet paper and bury your waste.

Fuel conservation

The total consumption of firewood by trekkers may be less than 0.1% of all the firewood consumed each year in Nepal but its effect is highly concentrated in a narrow ribbon along the main trails. Not only is wood used directly by lodges but also by all the porters who carry supplies for the markets. It is true that these porters would, like other Nepalis, use firewood anyway but in their villages away from these busy main trails. Depletion of the remaining forest cover compounds the already serious erosion problems.

For villages on the Jiri to Namche trail there is no instant solution. Kerosene has to be imported and is not entirely practical for lodge use. The micro-hydroelectric schemes cannot, so far, generate enough electricity for cooking and the establishment of an extensive national electricity grid is beyond the means of Nepal. The concept of replanting trees is spreading but the returns are a long way off yet.

There is some good news, however: Namche now has the most advanced hydroelectric system in rural Nepal, a 600kw medium-size hydro scheme. The lodges and the local people of Namche and the surrounding villages are adapting to cooking on electricity. Electric cookers are being adopted because they are cheaper to run than wood-fired stoves. One hopes that this admirable project will serve as a pilot scheme for others.

• **Help conserve firewood** To help in a small way do not make open fires, use iodine to purify water instead of getting it boiled, co-ordinate meal times and limit hot showers to lodges where the water is heated in back boilers or solar panels.

Trekking companies deserve the harshest possible criticism for contravening park rules by allowing their porters to cook on open fires, although they do use kerosene for meals for the trekkers and main crew. If you're trekking with a group and see fires being lit for cooking you should make a complaint in the strongest terms.

Accelerated erosion

Erosion is a natural phenomenon that creates river deltas and shapes mountains. In some parts of the world, however, it may occur at an accelerated rate that has serious consequences. The Himalaya are a young range of mountains, still in the process of formation, and erosion has always been considerable here. In the last few decades the problem has been exacerbated by rapid deforestation. The natural ground cover is being stripped away for firewood or animal fodder allowing rain to erode the essential topsoil. The problem is very serious: Nepal's forests are disappearing at the rate of 3% per year. One hectare of cleared forest loses around 50 tons of soil annually and approximately 400,000 hectares are cleared each year in Nepal.

• **Don't damage plants and stick to the trails** In the alpine areas, above the tree line, plants battle to survive in a harsh environment. Trekkers can have a negative effect on these areas. Big boots and yak hooves disturb the topsoil and sliding down a slope can leave scars that never heal.

A plea to group members
Please make voluble complaints to trek leaders and trekking company directors if any of the environmental recommendations noted in this section are not carried out. The entire group's unburnable litter must be taken out right to the end of the trek. Kerosene must be provided by the company not just for the trekkers but for porters' use. They may not use any firewood either in the national park or en route to Mera Peak. The police of the area are lackadaisical and although the park staff have authority there are no penalties for contravening park rules. The trekking companies and sirdars do not yet care, seemingly motivated only by personal gain.

CULTURAL CONSIDERATIONS

One of the great attractions of Nepal for the first visitors was the fact that the cultures of the many different peoples living here had evolved independently of Western 'civilisation'. Day-to-day life for most people had remained virtually unchanged. Sudden outside influence, however, has brought profound cultural change, particularly in the areas popular with tourists.

Whilst trees can be replanted in areas that have been deforested and mountains can be climbed leaving scarcely a trace of the climb, it is impossible not to leave some impression of your country and culture while visiting a foreign country and interacting with its people. The media is another major purveyor of images of the West, particularly through the cinema, where a fantasy world of exaggerated wealth and violence is portrayed. In Nepal, the effects of these cross-cultural exchanges may well be far more serious and damaging than environmental concerns.

There is no denying that the West is a technologically advanced society but its superiority over less 'developed' cultures does not, necessarily, extend beyond this. A visit to a country like Nepal can be a very rewarding experience, especially if you have not travelled much outside the West. Many things are done differently here but this does not make the methods any less valid and in some cases they may be better. The Nepalese way of solving problems, for example, is to avoid confrontation which starkly contrasts with the head-on 'Rambo' style of the West. The incidence of murder, theft and rape (outside the family) in Nepal is negligible in comparison to most nations, although it is rising with contact with the outside world.

● **Dress decently** Dress standards are important despite the fact that they are overlooked by many trekkers. Whilst men may go around without a shirt in the West, this is considered indecent in Nepal. Women should not shorts or sleeveless tops. See p35 for further information.

● **Respect people's right to privacy** Ask people before you take their photograph and be considerate when looking for subjects. Some older people believe that if you photograph them their lifespan may be reduced.

● **Don't flaunt your wealth** By Nepali standards, even the poorest foreign trekker is unimaginably wealthy. Nepalis often ask how much you earn but you should qualify your answer by giving them some examples of the cost of living in your country. Don't leave valuables lying around as this is further evidence that you have so much money you can easily afford to replace them.

● **Respect religious customs** Pass to the left of mani-walls and chortens. Prayer wheels should be turned clockwise. Remove your boots before entering a gompa and leave a donation; there's often a metal box provided.

● **Respect traditions** There are a number of other customs and traditions that you should take care to respect. Not doing so is insulting to your hosts. The left hand, used for washing after defecating, is not considered clean so you should never touch anyone with it, offer them anything with it or eat with it. The head is considered the most sacred part of the body and you should never touch anyone on it. Avoid pointing the soles of your feet at a person's head. If you're sitting with your legs out-stretched and a Nepali needs to pass, he or she will never step over you. Move your legs out of the way.

● **Encourage pride in Nepali culture** Express an interest in what people are doing and try to explain that not everything is as rosy in the West as the Nepalis might believe. In restaurants don't consistently shy away from Nepalese food. Local people are being taught by insidious example that packaged sweets, biscuits, noodles and chocolate are more desirable than local equivalents but in most cases they are actually less nutritious.

ECONOMIC IMPACT

The initial effect of independent trekkers using local lodges was a sudden increase in prices for many commodities along the major trekking routes. The villagers, naturally enough, sought the best prices for their produce and the highest bidders were the trekkers. In the short term this created a problem because villagers were more willing to sell scarce commodities to trekkers. It should, however, also be considered as a stage in the long development process: demand encourages production where previously there was no advantage in producing more. If the commodity is not available locally and it must be carried in by a porter, this creates work in areas where there may be few employment opportunities.

Teahouse trekking stimulates the local economy. Money from individual trekkers enters the local economy via the shops and lodges but it can have an effect on the whole area. Porters carry in the additional goods, new buildings may need to be constructed requiring local resources and labour, staff are required at the lodges and local producers have a new market. Collectively these provide more jobs and can lead to a higher standard of living, not just among lodge-owners. This is immediately obvious from visiting areas frequented by trekkers and comparing them with villages without this stimulus. Namche probably has the highest per capita income in Nepal, ahead even of Kathmandu. It's often stressed that little of the money stays in the lodge-owners' pockets. This may be true but there are many others who benefit.

The economic impact of trekking groups is somewhat different. The main beneficiaries are the government (in the form of taxes) and the trekking company directors (profits). The secondary beneficiaries are the employees, who are rarely local people so their earnings do not stay

---

Environmental dilemmas

Making environmentally-friendly regulations for the trekking industry involves complex factors. Consider this classic example. Soft drinks, mineral water and beer are luxury items consumed mainly by trekkers. They are carried over great distances but in the process considerable value is added which benefits the local economy. There's a returnable deposit on soft drink (but not beer or mineral water) bottles so, close to Jiri, the bottles are collected. However, by the time an empty Coke bottle reaches Namche it is no longer economic to return it for the deposit so it is discarded. Safe disposal is possible, and the SPCC (see p116) has begun ferrying some bottles out of the area, but in practice glass tends to end up everywhere. A secondary problem is that soft drinks start to enter the local market with disastrous consequences for teeth, in a country that has few dentists. So, should bottled drinks be banned from the park, or banned from some areas, with the consequent loss of income to porters, shop-keepers and lodge-owners? The park warden believes that canned drinks are a lesser evil but these are currently more expensive and less widely available than bottled drinks.

in the area. In fact, locals receive virtually nothing. Camping fees are Rs5 per tent and since the bulk of provisions are carried in, little food is purchased locally. Only firewood is used, and rubbish left.

● **Don't bargain for food & lodging** These prices are fixed.

● **Don't give to beggars** Some trekkers, embarrassed at the disparity in material wealth between their country and Nepal, have given money to beggars and sweets and pens to children. They may have thought that they were helping but the opposite is probably true. As well as fostering an unhealthy dependency attitude, begging can in some places be more profitable than earning money by portering or working in the fields. Giving sweets to children not only encourages them to see Westerners (and hence the West) as bringers of all good things but also leads to tooth decay, until recently quite rare in Nepal.

On the trail you may encounter more creative forms of begging: teenagers asking for funds for their school. It's hard to judge how genuine many of the claims are but remember you don't have to give anything. You'll be shown a book with names and amounts donated; if the sums are unrealistically large, the solicitation probably isn't genuine.

The Minimum Impact Code

Developed by environmental groups in Nepal affiliated with the King Mahendra Trust for Nature Conservation, the Minimum Impact Code requests trekkers to:

'Conserve firewood Be self-sufficient in your fuel supply and make sure your trekking staff uses kerosene and has enough warm clothing. Make no open fires. Limit hot showers. If possible stay at lodges that use kerosene or fuel efficient wood stoves and space heaters.

Stop pollution Dispose of all trash properly. Paper products, cigarette butts, toilet paper, food scraps etc should be burned or buried. Bottles, plastics and other non-biodegradable items should be packed out or deposited in rubbish pits if available. Use toilet facilities provided. If none exist, make sure you are 20 metres away from any water source and carry a small shovel to bury wastes. Don't use soap or shampoo in any stream or hot spring. Supervise trekking staff to make sure they cover toilet pits and dispose of garbage properly.

Be a guest Do not damage, disturb or remove any plants, animals, animal products or religious artifacts. Respect Nepali customs in your dress and behaviour. Women should not wear shorts or revealing blouses and men should always wear a shirt. Avoid outward displays of physical affection. Ask permission to take photographs and respect people's right to privacy. Begging is a negative interaction that was started by well-meaning tourists – please do not give anything to beggars. Don't barter for food and lodging. Encourage young Nepalis to be proud of their culture.

Above all, remember that your vacation has a great impact on the natural environment and people who live off its resources. By assisting in these small ways, you will help the land and people of Nepal enormously.'

PART 5: TRAIL GUIDE AND MAPS

Using this guide

Itineraries

The routes described are not broken up into a rigid day-by-day schedule. Instead all the possible stopping points are listed, leaving it for you
to decide how far you want to walk each day. Be as flexible as possible when planning your itinerary and don't always try to stay at the
biggest and best lodges. Often the most memorable interactions with
local people occur in places not frequented by large numbers of trekkers. Example itineraries are given in Appendix A.

Accommodation and places to eat

The places to eat at and/or stay in at each village are indicated by symbols on the map. **Large lodges** 🏠 are the bigger and better establishments that will have a comprehensive menu, dormitories and even
a few double rooms. **Simple lodges/teahouses** 🏠 may not have a separate dining room and may have only one dormitory but they're certainly more homely than the fancy places. Some are in locations where
trekkers rarely stay, stopping at them only for tea or a meal. **Tea
shacks** ▽ are the simplest places. In the lower country they are often
just a few bamboo mats over a wooden frame and generally don't look
too hygienic. In the most basic there are no beds for guests, only room
on the floor.

If there's just one lodge or teahouse it'll be shown as an **outline**, a
few will be shown **half blacked-in** and if there are many lodges or teahouses they'll be shown with a **black symbol**.

Lodges are constantly being upgraded so it's difficult to recommend one place above another. It's really worth talking to other
trekkers for specific recommendations although standards of food vary
greatly even within a lodge depending on who's doing the cooking.

Walking times

The hills render measured distances in miles or kilometres virtually
meaningless; walking times are far more useful. These are given along
the side of the maps, with arrows indicating the villages they refer to.
While I have tried to be consistent as to the times quoted, there is
inevitably a high degree of variation. A range of times is given and they

should be treated as a rough guideline for planning the day's walking. The group pace is sedate with plenty of time for relaxation. Porters carry 30-35kg on group treks so the length of the trekking day is limited by this. Time must also be allowed for the kitchen crew who are the last to leave camp after cleaning up and must then race ahead to prepare the next meal. The need for adequate shelter for porters effectively prevents camping in unfrequented wild spots unless groups are well prepared. Groups may walk short days in order to stop in a camping place that is a traditional night stop. So the days are generally easy and lunch stops sometimes last half the afternoon. For people who are not used to exercise the pace is good but anyone who keeps fit by regularly playing sport will find the pace leisurely after the first few days.

Individual trekkers tend to cover more distance in a day than groups. Once at Namche the pace is solely dictated by the altitude gains and so involves rest days and half-day walks only.

Altitudes

These are given in metres on the maps and in the text they're also quoted in feet. Altitudes are approximate for villages since there are very few truly flat bits of ground on the entire trek. A village like Simigoan, for example, stretches up the hillside for several hundred metres.

Don't get too worried about the sometimes huge differences in altitudes between some villages. Trekking in Nepal involves crossing mammoth ridges all the time. Simply go at a pace that suits, stop frequently and you'll soon get used to walking uphill and downhill. There is in fact one absolutely flat stretch near Tumlingtar but, strangely, instead of being pleasant it's hell. You seem to be getting nowhere, the ground is hard and it actually seems tough walking.

Ridges are shown as **thick lines** on the trail maps that follow.

Village names

Most of the Sherpa villages have both a Nepali name and the traditional Sherpa name. A few even have a name exclusively used by trekkers. All the familiar names of a village are mentioned, with the one most commonly used by trekkers and guides repeated in the text.

Jiri to Namche

INTRODUCTION

Jiri to Namche takes most people seven to nine pleasant days walking, usually including a rest day at Junbesi and a shorter easy day or two. If you have more time available there are plenty of opportunities for side trips exploring little-visited villages and gompas. Several valleys are also worth more thorough exploration by well-equipped parties. For the extremely fit in a hurry, walking from Jiri to Namche in four days is possible. There are good lodges along the main route and since these are usually only a few hours apart it's no longer necessary to plan a detailed itinerary as suggested by some guidebooks. Simply follow your instincts and the advice of other trekkers rather than sticking to a rigid schedule.

The walk is strenuous, following a route that goes against the grain of the land; all the rivers and ridges flow north to south and the trail runs west to east. Following the standard route (not including side trips) by the time you reach Namche you will have climbed up almost exactly the height of Mt Everest, 8848m/29,028ft, and the corresponding descents to Namche total the height of Ama Dablam, 6828m/22,402ft.

Leaving Jiri there is an introductory hill, then three higher major ridges: an unnamed 2700m/8858ft pass, the Lamjura Pass 3530m/11,581ft and Trakshindo Pass 3071m/10,075ft. Once across the Dudh Kosi (river), the trail climbs high up the valley sides skirting steep rock faces before descending to recross the river several times before the final hill to Namche.

Kathmandu to Jiri

This part of the journey is made by bus, taxi or air (see p88). Asian Airlines can drop a small group (but not individuals) at Jiri while en route to Lukla or Phaplu.

Hiring a car and driver is the most comfortable alternative if you're not flying but you can go by bus for a fraction of the cost. From the old bus station in the centre of Kathmandu the first departure for Jiri is at around 5.30 am. Thieves are now working this route intensively so **take great care of your luggage**. These people are no mere opportunists, they are professionals – many trekkers have lost things from side-pockets, and occasionally even the odd whole rucksack goes missing. It's best to try to take your rucksack inside the bus; the ticket office is helpful and will often give you front seats or even a seat for your rucksack as well but other passengers may object to this. Most buses have a boot at the back that can be locked but since it's small you may have to put it on the roof. If you're in a group ensure that all the packs are stowed together on the roof and at the first chance for passengers to ride on the roof, go up and keep a close eye on them. There are also occasional pick-pockets at the bus station. Their favourite trick is to watch where you put the change after buying your ticket then hurry you onto the bus. The police have been unhelpful in all cases.

The first part of this 10 to 12 (and occasionally up to 16) hour bus journey is to Lamosangu (78km, 5 hours) along the Chinese-constructed Arniko Rajmarg or Kodari Highway that runs to the Tibetan border and Lhasa. Leaving Kathmandu you pass **Bhaktapur** where, until the early 1960s, the start of the trek to Everest began.

There is a steep climb out of the Kathmandu Valley and from **Dhulikhel**, at the crest of the hill, there are views on a clear day of the Himalaya from Manaslu to Everest. The road drops to **Dolalghat** (ghat means 'bridge') and crosses the Indrawati River. The Chinese road had progressed this far by 1967 so the first commercial treks to the Khumbu started from here.

After crossing the Sun Kosi ('Gold River'), the road follows the river into **Lamosangu** ('Long Bridge') stopping by the stalls by the bridge for dal bhat. One only needs to have a quick look around and sniff the air to realise that hygiene is not even marginal but there are biscuits, chocolate and soft drinks available.

From the bridge it's a further 110km to Jiri, marked by kilometre posts that start at 0km from the Lamosangu bridge. This road was part of a programme of Swiss aid as a model to demonstrate building techniques for mountain roads using appropriate technology. Rather than employing expensive machinery it was decided to maximise the use of local labour. Rocks were broken with hammers and a lot of sweat, and all the wire-netting was woven by hand, providing a vast amount of work. In addition to wages, food was sold in set quantities at subsidised prices to reduce the local impact of the hungry work force. The only heavy machinery used was a road roller. The result is a Swiss-quality road that will probably last longer with less maintenance than any other road in Nepal.

From Lamosangu it can be very pleasant to ride on the roof of the bus (theoretically illegal) but take a jacket or wind-cheater. At the top of the first major ridge is **Muldi** where there may be another stop before continuing to **Charikot** (km55) where trekkers are sometimes requested to register. The turn-off to the left here leads to **Dolakha**, a few kilometres away (see p206). On a cloudless day the massive twin-headed Gauri Sankar stands out.

The descent to the Tamba Kosi ('Copper River') is steep. At the bridge the driver takes a break for a cup of tea or two. If you are on the roof it's a good idea to start putting on warm clothes because it is still several hours and 38km to Jiri. You pass the plantations of a Swiss reforestation programme. After another pass the gradual descent to Jiri begins and at a stop at **Kot**, you might have to register at the police checkpost. **Jiri** is 10 minutes further on.

Note that in winter it's not unknown for a snowfall or sheet ice to block a high section of the road, which means a couple of extra days walking.

JIRI (1935m/6348ft)

Jiri nestles in a fertile valley and beyond the ugly materialism of the road it's a prosperous and tidy village. The people are mainly of the Jirel caste who originate, so the legend goes, from a Sherpa mother and a Sunuwar father. There are also some Sherpas and with the road (which linked Jiri in 1984) came the merchant castes, mainly Newars. There are many lodges but only a few that trekkers frequent. Most are four storeys high but look the same height as the three-storeyed buildings and inside the low doorways are headbangingly obvious.

Electricity comes from Lamosangu and it caused a few problems when it arrived. Many people had little concept of what it was and were rather surprised at the injury a mere piece of wire could cause. The fact that it costs something means that the farmers cannot afford it so it's used mainly by the local businesses and lodges. Since fire-wood (for cooking) is still cheap, apart from a couple of refrigerators and a hot water cylinder, electricity is only used for lighting.

With Jiri being the beginning or the end of a trek most people are anxious to be on their way and there is little to hold you here other than to inspect the various Swiss projects. Don't expect peaceful lie-ins in the morning. You'll be woken at the crack of dawn by bus horns announcing the departures to Kathmandu.

The SATA projects

Development with Swiss aid began in 1958 on a number of projects and in 1960 the hospital was set up. It's now staffed by two Nepalese doctors and offers a comparatively good service. This was followed by a public high school and a multi-purpose agricultural development station, that despite intensive efforts, has made only slow progress in introducing crop diversity and new farming techniques. Jiri is also the area base for a Swiss Technical School that started in 1983. All courses are free. The subjects offered are 'Junior Farm Technician', 'Construction Overseer' and 'Junior Mid-wife'; the competition for the limited places is intense.

Planning the first day's trek

Groups generally stay at Shivalaya for the first night. This is only half a day's walk from Jiri but the first morning is busy with the porters and their loads being sorted out. The short, easy day is also ideal for gently accustoming the legs to the rigours of trekking. The facilities at Shivalaya are quite good so less fit independent trekkers may also consider spending the night here. The next accommodation is in two simple lodges up the hill at Sangbadanda.

Fit walkers can comfortably make the numerous lodges at Deorali or, higher up the ridge, the Thodung Gompa or the cheese factory. Reaching Bhandar is possible but your legs may suffer the following day.

(Opposite) Top: Junbesi at the end of the monsoon season. **Bottom:** Development has brought suspension bridges, many of them in the Khumbu built by the Himalayan Trust.

JIRI TO SHIVALAYA – THE STANDARD ROUTE   [MAP 1]

There are two routes out of Jiri and they join each other after about ten minutes. From the bus park one route begins clearly as a jeep track (cum toilet); but above the school a smaller trail avoids that dirty area.

Chitre An hour out of Jiri is Chitre, a shanty of primitive tea-shacks. The surrounding area looks horribly bare with goats having eaten all the vegetation and the people look decidedly poor. This is probably one of the most impoverished areas on the whole route, although throughout Nepal there are many places similar to it. Around a bend lurks an unwelcome surprise – it's still a little way to the top of the small pass.

Small pass (2400m/7874ft) At the crest are a couple more tea-shacks and some new vistas. The path heads down; it's easy to follow and in about 10 minutes you pass a primary school. Around here is the usual spot for groups to have lunch. Another five minutes along the trail brings you to Mali.

(Opposite) Top: Most of the larger lodges now have energy-efficient stoves which incorporate a hot water system. **Bottom:** Whether you're taking off or landing at Lukla airstrip (see p148) the experience is always exhilarating.

Mali First there's a simple teahouse, then three lodges that look reasonable, one with a small shop in it. The facilities are basic and with it being so close to Jiri few trekkers ever stay here.

Leaving Mali the trail leads down, and down is the word. About one hour later a small stream is crossed, then past a couple of buildings is the long suspension bridge over the Khimti Khola to Shivalaya.

JIRI TO SHIVALAYA – THE ALTERNATIVE ROUTE   [Map 1]

This pleasant detour goes via Those, a bazaar town on the old route that was used before the road reached Jiri. There is still one simple lodge left in Those but walking to Shivalaya in a day is no problem.
    The trail from Jiri heads straight down the valley fairly close to the east bank of the Jiri Khola, then climbs and contours in and out of small gullies and around a main ridge. Here it meets the old main trekking route from Lamosangu to traverse in forest around the next ridge. After this it drops to Kattike and descends further to the Khimti Khola. Upstream a suspension bridge crosses to Those.

Those was the centre of an ancient iron mining and manufacturing industry that began to decline during the 1940s when Indian iron became readily available. Farming implements forged here were traded as far away as Tibet and this business was one of the first sources of wealth in Namche. A few iron products are still made here and it is worth the slight diversion. Shivalaya is a little over an hour upstream from Those.

Shivalaya (1800m/5905ft)
Sitting on the east bank of the khola, Shivalaya ('Shiva's home or temple') is not much more than a hamlet of eight lodges. They are all modest but pleasant. The settlement has an air of being new, and it is: the original Shivalaya was slightly downstream. When the road reached Jiri the main trekking route changed, so the villagers moved too.

SHIVALAYA TO BHANDAR   [MAP 2]

The trail out of Shivalaya is steep from the first step, and will get the sweat flowing. The gradient relents only after the next village.

Sangbadanda This is a mainly Sherpa settlement and has a couple of simple lodges with shops. Two minutes west is an important junction and a choice: the upper/left path leads to Thodung (see below); the right-hand trail is the slightly more direct and lower route to Deorali, about a couple of hours away depending on your hill speeds. Both trails are wide and easy to follow.

Side trip to Thodung This route is well worth the extra effort. The views are superb, especially on a clear morning when Gauri Sankar sparkles in the distance. In Thodung (3090m/10,137ft) there's one lodge set in the forest and it's known for its good food. The cheese factory here follows processes introduced by the Swiss, using similar technology to that in the small factories in the Alps. The idea was first introduced in the Langtang area after an FAO (United Nations Food and Agriculture Organisation) study. Now there are many similar government run factories and the trekking route passes close to three more en route to Namche.

Deorali (2705m/8875ft) means 'pass' in Nepali so this is a common village name. The actual village is slightly south where the water supply is better so again this is just a group of lodges. They are set in two neat rows with a mani wall (see p108), the first real sign of Buddhist Sherpa country, in the middle. You should always pass to the left of a mani wall or a wall of prayer wheels.

From some rocks immediately above the lodges there are superb views into the distance on a clear day; you can see much of the route ahead. Below, the hillside stretches down where the twin chortens of Bhandar are clearly visible. Take the left fork a couple of minutes below the pass; the descent is initially steep.

Bhandar (2200m/7218ft)

The Sherpa name for this area is Chyangma. Immediately above the chortens is a small gompa and below, a group of four lodges. The two main ones are **Ang Dawa Lodge** and **Buddha Lodge** but the others are also good.

A few of the lodges boast environmentally-friendly features that have become common in the better trekkers' lodges along the route. 'Green' showers are provided by running pipes through the cooking fire, then into a hot-water tank which is sometimes connected directly to the shower-room. This produces essentially free hot water, using energy that would otherwise go straight up the chimney. It's a simple though effective system that has taken off not because of the green revolution but because there are numerous advantages for the lodge owners (the only way change can be introduced in an economy that generates virtually no surplus cash). Lodge owners are asked to cook a variety of meals and sometimes in huge quantities and trekkers also request hot water for washing. Heating water takes a long time so an instant source of hot water is invaluable. The system is cheap enough for the lodges to afford but beyond the reach of ordinary villagers.

From the chortens the descent is gentle with about seven simple lodges or teahouses evenly spaced a few minutes apart down the hill. Past these is a flattish field with several houses around it, a regular camping spot for groups for their second night out of Jiri.

Asking directions

There's a certain art to asking the way on Nepal's trails. Naturally polite, the Nepalis don't like to cause offence by answering 'no' to a question like 'Is this the way to Namche?' So an affirmative reply to this question is just as likely to mean, Yes, I understand the question but I don't know the answer,' as it is to mean, 'Yes, it's the way to Namche'. You can try re-phrasing the question as: 'Which path is for Namche?' but rather than admitting they don't know, a Nepali may just take a guess at the answer. The solution is to ask again in a different way, and ask more than one person. If you ask the way at a junction and then walk away down the wrong trail locals will usually shout after you that you're going the wrong way.

BHANDAR TO KENJA   [MAPS 2-3]

From Bhandar to the covered wooden bridge, the trail is fairly easy to follow. Turn sharp left after crossing the bridge and keep left for a few minutes, dropping down to a group of buildings, a two-storey house and another with the second storey level with the track, reached in a few minutes more. Immediately after them are some stone steps. Follow these, **not** the trail that continues straight ahead. There's a similar trap at the next few houses: follow the path that sometimes resembles a stream descending to the left. Once across the next wooden bridge there are a few teahouses and a house by an obvious T junction; turn left here and follow the Likhu Khola to Kenja.

Kenja (1640m/5380ft)

This is a thriving 'lodge' town with a few good hotels and no bad ones. It's a mixed village, mainly Sherpa with some Chhetri (a caste immediately below the Brahmins, although concepts of caste are not always strongly adhered to in the hills). Kenja is slightly unusual in this respect because, apart from Jubing, the trek from Bhandar to the Khumbu is through exclusively Sherpa country. The mix here can be attributed to tourism. Once Kenja was nothing more than a couple of houses but people from up and down the valley were attracted by the rumours of fantastic wealth possible by setting up a lodge. By 1984 there were a couple of lodges and five houses but this has now grown to 10 lodges.

In mid-1989 Kenja was linked to an electricity supply as part of a Japanese aid project. There are 9 small generators and when they're all working (rarely) this generates 55kw which is enough power to provide electricity for cooking. Firewood is starting to become expensive but very few can afford the enormous cost of a stove. However, it was pleasing that the lodge owners I spoke to thought it entirely possible that within five years all lodge-owners would be cooking with electricity. Electricity would probably be a cheaper option than firewood by then. Stereos have already arrived here and one has to wonder how long it will be before there are video nights in Kenja.

In October you might see something that looks like a prickly pear dangling from leafy creepers. The local name is *iskus* and it must be cooked to be edible and tastes like a slightly sweet potato.

The side trail to Pike Peak (pronounced 'pee-kay'), the home of the benevolent spirit for this area, starts from the bridge over the Kenja Khola. The trail goes up the ridge to the south, then skirts the peak to a ridge heading north. It finally drops to the main trail after the Lamjura Pass but this is an incredibly long route with no facilities along the way.

KENJA TO JUNBESI   [MAPS 3-4]

From Kenja it's an altitude gain of 1900m to the top of the Lamjura Pass and for this reason many people recommend staying in Sete to break the climb. If you're reasonably fit, however, climbing over the pass in a single (tough) day from Kenja is quite possible. If you don't make it over the top there are some lodges where you can stay en route.

Sete (2575m/8448ft) This friendly Sherpa settlement is in two parts. First there are two lodges, one very spartan, then five minutes further on another three lodges with a few camping places. Sete is not a big village, with almost as many lodges as houses but it does have a small gompa.

Dagchu When you've got your breath back, it's around an hour from Sete to Dagchu, a recent village of six rather simple lodges atop the ridge. Out of the forested areas there are some good views. To the south-east (right) you can see the twin tops of Pike Peak, home of the local benevolent spirit. The trail to the pass continues up the ridge. Ignore all trails that lead off it. From some parts you can see the pass, well to the left of the ridge.

Goyem Another half an hour up brings you to Goyem with two groups of teahouse/lodges about five minutes apart. Apple juice, cider and apple brandy are all available here but the water supply is not clean so take particular care to purify water for drinking.

A minute out of Goyem is an important junction: continue up on the ridge through forest on a somewhat scrappy trail avoiding the good trail that begins contouring on the south side of the ridge. That is the direct, steep and rarely-used route to Salleri. The forest here is magnificent. Demand for firewood, however, grows with each new lodge built – a negative impact of the teahouse style of trekking. In spring the rhododendrons put on quite a show with whole hillsides covered in blossoms that from late February spread upwards reaching the crest of the pass by the end of April. The air is heady with their scent and with that of the many other flowering trees and shrubs.

Soon the trail becomes clearer and you reach a few **tea-shacks**. This is the point where the trail starts contouring to the north of the ridge. There are several junctions but each trail rejoins the main route a few minutes later. The last teahouse before the pass, usually has little water to spare but rarely closes since porters like to stop here for tea. The obviously-recent deforestation of the rhododendron trees just above is a horrifying sight.

Passing a few mani walls, it's around half an hour to the top of the pass. Unless the weather is perfect this section can be very cold and windy, and even in October snow can fall with the patches shielded by the sun not melting for several days. In winter there may be quite a bit of snow lying around making the track muddy and even icy – real down-jacket weather. The difference to the temperature that altitude makes is really driven home to you as you head up this pass.

Lamjura La (3530m/11,581ft) The prayer flags and chortens mark the gateway to the Solu (sometimes called Shorong) Sherpa area. It's common to suffer some altitude sickness, especially if you stay up here for a while to admire the view. This does not mean that you will not make it to the top of Kala Pattar, it's just a warning that ascending too fast has its consequences. You are in fact higher than Namche, where several nights are spent acclimatising.

It's possible to climb the hill to the north of the pass. At first there is no trail but head along the ridge slightly on the western side and soon a small but definite path begins. This contours under the peak before finally doubling back with a stiff climb to the summit. It is a very strenuous climb and even if you felt perfectly well on the pass, the extra 500m gain in altitude is often enough to induce a headache. Heading down from the pass, there are many paths weaving through the forest but luckily they all head to the same place: a few well-spaced restaurants an hour below the pass. Occasionally you may see monkeys in the forest here.

Tragobuk/Taktok (2860m/9383ft) Some of the houses here are beside a huge rock that's topped by a wind-powered prayer wheel. Continue straight through the long village and at junctions avoid trails that descend; these go to Salleri and not Junbesi. The scenic trail stays fairly high and rounds a major ridge and a large rock, with views of Junbesi and its distinctive yellow-roofed gompa. Take a look at the trail options immediately across the river from Junbesi while here.

A few minutes later at a sign-posted junction a trail leads off to **Serlo Monastery** where it is possible for a few people to stay.

JUNBESI (2700m/8858ft)

This is one of the most pleasant Sherpa villages en route to Namche and it boasts some particularly good family-run lodges offering delicious fresh bread, pizzas, apple juice and cider.

Although Salleri is the district headquarters, Junbesi has a primary school, high school and a health post. The high school has a particularly good reputation, largely due to the dedication of the headmaster. There's a staff of 14 at the health post many of whom roam the surrounding hills offering vaccinations and health education programmes but, unbelievably, no methods of contraception are available from them. School education in Junbesi became available in 1964 when Sir Edmund Hillary helped construct a school house. It was quickly expanded and in 1972 a middle school was added. Both were run by the Himalayan Trust until 1975 when Nepal nationalised the primary and middle schools. In 1983, a high school was created with Himalayan Trust assistance and now the three schools (under one roof) muster nearly 300 pupils. High schools in Nepal are still privately-run, supported by student fees. In a country where the majority of the population has no money to spend on education it takes hard work and dedication to attend a high school. The costs (Rs 2000-3000 for a year, including fees, books, bed and board) may not seem much but a village family, if they have any money at all, will need it to buy necessities and a little food around the lean time before harvest. Most of the pupils are boys and school fees, whether earned by father or son, will come from portering to Namche, low-paid agricultural work, or with luck a job as a porter-guide, or sherpa for a group, where a month or two's work will pay for a year's schooling. For the even luckier few the Himalayan Trust offers three scholarships a year for the high school.

Development on a pleasant scale is evident everywhere in Junbesi. Agriculture is diversifying and a few lodges provide the majority of their vegetable requirements from their own gardens. The brandies, wines, ciders and jams are made with local fruit, as are the apple pies. Soyabeans, wheat, corn, beans, potatoes and highly-prized barley are the traditional crops. However, the altitude and problems with irrigation prevent the growing of rice which must be carried in from Jiri. There's a small hydro electric scheme that provides lighting (with the odd hiccup).

In the centre of Junbesi is a **police check post** (often unmanned). Make sure you register here since it's for your own safety. If you go missing they'll have some idea of where to start searching.

A half-day trip to Thubten Choling

This is an active Buddhist monastery/nunnery with about 50 monks and over 200 nuns. Many are Tibetan; some are very recent arrivals. The murals were painted around 1970, a few years after the monastery was founded. The walk up is pleasant and, although it is little more than an hour away from Junbesi, with the friendly monks and beauty of the area do not count on being back for an early lunch.

From the monastery there's an **alternative route to Ringmo** over a 3476m/11,404ft pass. Unless you are confident about your route-finding ability, it is better to hire a lad from Junbesi who has been over before.

Other gompas

Around Junbesi are a scattering of gompas perched atop hills, good alternatives to visiting Thubten Choling. Rumbak, to the south above the track to Salleri, takes one and a half hours one way. Take something to eat and drink with you.

JUNBESI TO TRAKSHINDO   [MAP 5]

Leaving Junbesi The Junbesi Khola is crossed on a wooden bridge and from the other side, looking slightly downstream, you can see the hydro-electric plant. Note that after crossing the Junbesi Khola the main track divides twice. In each case take the upper/left path which should be signposted. The lower paths head to Phaplu and Salleri, a good half-day's walk away. The section around this huge ridge is one of the most pleasant walks so far. Although the trail climbs in places, it's not steep. The track is set high above the valley floor, at first through open forest. Later the view extends across the valley to picturesque villages surrounded by terraces and divided by sparse woodland.

Everest View Sherpa Lodge (3100m/10,170ft) This is an 'Everest View' lodge from which you can actually see Everest, the first point on the trek from Jiri where this is possible. Expanded in 1992 to provide dining with a view, it's perched on the end of a long grazing ridge that runs up to Numbur. Naks (female yaks) are milked in the summer and autumn months and the rich milk is used to make just under 1000kg of pure nak cheese (although everyone wrongly refers to it as yak cheese) every year. The lodge owner manages the production using old Swiss methods. Delicious curd is often available too.

Early morning is generally the best time to spot Everest. If there's a single cloud in the sky a corollary of Murphy's Law says it will obscure Everest first, and it does. For the energetic even better views can be had by climbing part of the ridge behind.

Sallung/Solung (2980m/9777ft) This hamlet also boasts magnificent views including a fraction of Everest and down the valley to the Phaplu airstrip. Sallung has four homely lodges. These and the Everest View Lodge are convenient places to stay if you visited Thubten Choling monastery in the morning and had a late lunch in Junbesi. Leaving Sallung, the clear trail wanders gently downwards. After a few gullies

1¼ – 2 HRS ——→   20-30 MIN   1 – 2½ HRS ——→   ¾ 1½H   20 MIN   1¼ – 2½ HRS

HALF DAY RETURN

THUBTEN CHOLING   TRAIL DIFFICULT TO FOLLOW   PASS 3476m   TO LUMDING KHARKA

RINGMO 2700m   Trakshindo La 3071m   TRAKSHINDO 2930m

RINGMO LODGE   TO NUNTALA

JUNBESI 2700m

Junbesi Khola

SALLUNG 2900m

Beni/Dudh Kund Khola

EVEREST VIEW SHERPA LODGE & CHEESE FACTORY 3000m

HALF DAY (JUNBESI – PHAPLU)

MAP 4 135   142 MAP 6

SCHOOL

CHIWANG GOMPA

Solu Khola

PHAPLU

N

MAP 5

SALLERI DISTRICT HQ

0   1km

3½ – 5 HRS (PHAPLU TO RINGMO)

you round another ridge for a change of view, the amazing knife-edge ridge of Karyolung whose ridge extends down to Ringmo and the Trakshindo La, the next pass.

The trail winds around ridges and streams to the old suspension bridge across the Beni/Dudh Kund Khola, whose waters originate from the glaciers in the impressive basin formed by Karyolung (6511m/ 21,361ft), Khatang (6853m/22,483ft) and Numbur (6959m/ 22,831ft). The twin peaks of Numbur and Khatang are the Shorong Yul Lha, where the Sherpa god for the Shorong area resides. It's possible to camp at the high grazing areas below their glaciers and stunning mountain faces; but this is virtually never attempted by trekkers.

Ringmo (2700m/8858ft) From the suspension bridge the trail climbs, steeply at first, to Ringmo and a major trail junction by the recently-built stupa. The south/right-hand trail heads to Phaplu and Salleri on a beautiful, wide path (see p187). Straight on is the route to the pass, Trakshindo La.

The spread-out settlement of Ringmo has two simple lodges, and two big lodges set among the apple trees. Apples, peaches and apricots are widely cultivated to such an extent that half the crop has to be made into delicious cider and fire-water brandies. This is also the main source of fruit for the famous Namche apple pies.

At the top of Ringmo are two 50-metre mani walls. After correctly passing to the left of both do **not** continue straight on unless you're going to Lumding Kharka. The correct route (often signposted) is to the right. This is the beginning of the ascent to the Trakshindo La.

Side route to Lumding Kharka The path that continues straight ahead from the Ringmo mani wall leads to high grazing pastures below Numbur and several isolated high routes into the Dudh Kosi. There are no lodges or even villages until the Dudh Kosi, a two- to four-day walk away (depending on which route you take). The Lumding La route offers some good and unusual views of Everest, Lhotse and Makalu. Interestingly it was used extensively by Tibetans who, because many yaks had died at Kharikhola in 1959, preferred this high route until the early 1970s. It was also the alternative route if the bridge across the Dudh Kosi below Jubing had been washed out. This was why the 1952 Swiss Everest Expedition were forced to use it. Two porters died of the cold which led to the Swiss providing the suspension bridge that now spans the Dudh Kosi.

Following the main route immediately right after the Ringmo mani walls, the trail divides after a few minutes at a well-signposted junction. The right fork goes to the Ringmo cheese factory and lodge (often closed in winter), at least ten minutes up (not the advertised five). The cheese and garlic sandwiches are potent enough to keep even the yaks away from you! The left/straight fork continues directly to the pass, less than an hour away.

Trakshindo La (3071m/10,075ft) The pass, marked by a white stupa, divides the Solu (Shorong) and the Pharak Sherpa areas. There's only a simple teahouse and a few tea-shacks where porters stop for a welcome glass of tea. It's less than half an hour down to the gompa at Trakshindo, on wide stone steps (or what's left of them).

Trakshindo (2930m/9612ft) There are two large but simple lodges and the shell of a house that serves as a kitchen-cum-dining room for groups. If you arrive in cloudy weather and stay here be sure to have a look outside upon waking: the views are amazing. Trekking peak fans will enjoy the impressive pyramid of Kusum Kangguru. In the coldest winter months you may wake up to snow here and ice on the trail. The **gompa**, established in 1946 by the Tengboche Lama, can be visited and is usually open sometime early in the morning or around sunset. For a group of people the monk will often open up specially and you should leave a donation.

Nuntala is visible from the gompa and when leaving, the path contours around immediately below the gompa fence and past a house or two before descending. The route down continues to contour, in and out of gullies with a steep descent or two. You pass some camping spots popular with porters heading for Namche.

NUNTALA TO SURKE   [MAP 6]

Nuntala/Manidingma (2350m/7710ft)
Primarily a Sherpa village with a few Rai inhabitants, Nuntala (see plan on p142) is pleasantly situated in a large valley. The bushes around and below the village are tea bushes. The views are better at the pass or gompa but the snowy tip of Karyolung can still just be seen, above a ridge to the north.

The wide paved street is lined with inns. Development here has been rapid since the first real lodge started operating around 1983. Environmentally-friendly water heating systems were installed in the fireplaces of some lodges in 1988 and electricity first lit the street lamps in July 1991. This mini hydro-electric scheme was set up privately by Pasang Sherpa, one of the many lodge owners, using a bank loan. The 'power house' is easily identified by the water pipe used to power the generator. If it's open take a look inside; Western concepts of a power station are of huge buildings and complex machinery but this system would fit in a Paris bathroom. It's all been well thought out

TO CHAUNRIKHARKA

Lumding Khola

MAP 7 151

STEPS TO LUKLA

SURKE 2300m

CHUTOK LA

Puiyan Khola PUIYAN

Khari La

MAP D 210 PANGKONGMA

1/2 – 2 1/4 HRS

2 – 3 1/2 HRS

3/4 – 1 1/4 HRS

N
MAP 6

BUPSA 2350m

KHARTE

Khari Khola

TO BUPSA

Deku Khola

Dudh Kosi

KHARIKHOLA 2050m (SEE PLAN BELOW)

MAP 5 139

SLIPPERY IF WET

JUBING 1700m

LANDSLIDE AREA

0   1 Km

(SEE BELOW)
NUNTALA 2350m

1 – 2 HRS   1/2 HR   1 – 2 1/2 HRS

NUNTALA

Danfay Lodge

Naulekh View Lodge

CAMP

Mountain Trekkers Lodge

Shangrila Guest House

Himalayan Trekkers Lodge

Reasonable Lodge

Sherpa Guest House

Thamserku Guesthouse

POWER HOUSE

Blue Heaven Lodge

Boudha Lodge

STUPA

Nuru Lodge

Star Bharunje

Riverside

Star Trekkers Lodge

5 Star Hotel

TAILORS

Lakpa Tensing Sherpa's Holiday Home

SHOP   Trekkers Inn

Namaste Lodge

Sunrise Lodge

KHARIKHOLA

for the needs of the village. By switching belts during the day the turbine is used to drive a circular saw or a flour milling machine. It had to be carried up here because an airlift by helicopter would have virtually doubled the total cost.

Leaving Nuntala there's a steep descent of at least a couple of hours to the suspension bridge across the Dudh Kosi. Early in the morning it can be very slippery with dew. There's a teahouse five minutes before the bridge but little else on the way.

Jubing (1700m/5577ft) Half an hour uphill from the bridge, this is the only non-Sherpa village past Sete. It's a pretty

> **The Dudh Kosi**
> The origin of this river is intimately tied to where you are heading; the Khumbu. Dudh is the Nepali word for milk and 'milky river' is an apt name for it. The colour is caused by powdered rock, a product of the massive forces involved as glaciers grind their way down valleys. Although rock is heavier than water the turbulence doesn't give the finely divided silt a chance to settle.

Rai village, especially attractive in winter when the Khumbu appears brown and dry. Here plants thrive in the tropical warmth of the low altitude with flowers and vegetables growing year round. It is a rice-growing area, although the higher reaches of the village can support only millet and maize, the monsoon crops, and wheat plus barley in the winter. There are four lodges, each spaced a few minutes apart. Being warm year-round it's good place to do a batch of washing – or at least a sock rinse.

Around 10 minutes out of Jubing is a small but distinct trail junction. Continue upwards, **don't** take the path that cuts left through paddies and can be seen contouring around the next ridge. Another 10 minutes up the hill is a group of three double-storeyed houses and another trail divide. Both forks head for Kharikhola, the left path is slightly longer in distance but not in time and is a little more gentle on the legs. The right fork is the 'Nepalese way' (the shortest distance no matter how steep) and is always used by porters. It heads over a small pass which offers good views up the valley. Khumbui Yul Lha is prominent, and with a map it is easy to figure out roughly where Namche, Khumjung and Kunde are, although they cannot actually be seen. The high snow and rock peak in the distance is Gyachung Kang (7922m/25,990ft), not Cho Oyu as guides will tell you.

KHARIKHOLA/KHATI THENGA (2050m/6726ft)

This is a large spread-out village with houses dotted among the countless terraces. Among the Sherpas are a few Magars, there are thriving businesses, a boarding school and it's an agriculturally-productive area though not nearly as productive as Jubing. Not only is it at a higher altitude (and so significantly cooler) but it also gets less sun, the terraces being north facing. Despite higher-yield crops, with the rapidly rising population there can be food shortages in the weeks leading up to the harvest. This is an especially difficult time for villagers as there is little trade from trekkers in the summer.

Kharikhola is developing into a focal point for the surrounding villages. This was started with the founding by Hillary and the Himalayan Trust of a school and health post. The school grew rapidly, developing into a high school with an excellent reputation that has drawn pupils from villages several days' walk away. Now tailors and merchants have set up shop. Electricity arrived in 1989, a private scheme organised by one of the lodge owners.

The many lodges strung out along the main path for several kilometres are basically in three groups. Some are very tidy and freshly painted but all are smaller and more homely compared to the Junbesi or Namche lodges. Groups often camp in the noisy centre of town, or by the lodge on the outskirts, closest to the khola. Lodges and shops are beginning to sell chocolate bars and film for trekkers.

If you spend the night make an early start next day, leaving well before the sun actually reaches Kharikhola or the going gets hot and sticky. The chorten at Bupsa can be seen from Kharikhola but once over the small bridge there are several false crests that can be rather demoralising on the slog up to Bupsa.

Bupsa/Gompa Danda/Bumshing (2350m/7710ft) Perched on top of the ridge, this is a very welcome refreshment stop after the long climb. There are three teahouses in a cluster and, a few minutes further on, a couple more well-spaced lodges. Below, along the ridge, is a small gompa you may be invited to visit, donations expected, of course.

Route to the Arun river, Tumlingtar and Hille Take the trail straight up the ridge behind the lodges in Bupsa (see p213).

Route to Namche The trail between Kharikhola and Chourikharka was considerably altered in the early 1980s, levelling several small climbs. Despite the quicker trail porters haven't changed the stopping places so for groups this day is easier than it once was. Old maps still mark the original route which climbed to Kharte, above Bupsa.

There's another trail that goes directly from Kharikhola to Surke but it's dangerous and therefore not recommended. It stays much closer to the Dudh Kosi and was used mainly by porters wanting to make a quick return down valley. Considered too steep for laden porters, it was never used for the journey up-river. Trekkers were never encouraged to go this way and now, since it has been neglected, it is very dangerous involving some tricky traverses where the track has fallen away.

Khari La The hills are not over yet: the trail continues steeply up, cutting into valleys and rounding ridges to the Khari La. From here, at 2850m/9350ft, Khumbui Yul Lha and Gyachung Kang are visible. This is not really a pass, the real Khari La being a little above on the route of the old trail.

Puiyan/Paiya/Chutok (2780m/9121ft) The surrounding area was once heavily forested but many trees were cut down to make charcoal. This practice was banned in 1992 to try to save the remaining forests lining the Dudh Kosi here. Three larger lodges and two simple ones make up the settlement. A little further on is one more lunch place and a few tea-shacks but once past these there are virtually no facilities until Surke, a couple of hours away.

Chutok La The new route passes 200m below the actual Chutok La, at 2780m/9121ft but the views of Khumbui Yul Lha and Gyachung Kang are still good, though better just around the corner. The steep rock peak is Gonglha, above Lukla and the bigger mountain is Kusum Kangguru. Part of Lukla airstrip can also be seen, but this is difficult to recognise: it's no use looking for a stretch of level ground.

Surke/Surkie/Bua (2300m/7546ft) Local legend says that this area was once a lake, and this would account for the fertile soil. Bua, the Sherpa name for the hamlet, means 'damp', no doubt from the lack of sun, but in fact it's a pleasant enough place. Just around the corner from Surke are the first good views of Nupla (5885m/19,308ft) which forms part of the spectacular Kongde ridge that rears up above the Bhote Kosi by Namche.

Route to Lukla About 10 minutes out of Surke are some stone steps heading up; these lead to Lukla in about an hour. Although the trail starts off well-defined it breaks up into many confusing paths. Note that it's not necessary to visit Lukla; and if you wish to do so in order to confirm an air ticket note that this can be done only a few days in advance. Note also that opening hours are very limited (see Lukla below).

Direct route to Namche This continues straight ahead. A little further on is an impressive waterfall, so high and close that it defies most camera lenses, although over the bridge and up the hill there's a more complete view. The trail traverses some impressively steep hillside. In the past, in tough country like this, the trails tended to be precarious and narrow but to cater for tourists this has been blasted out to a safe width. Stone steps and a few cunningly-constructed stone shelters herald Mushe, still a few minutes away.

Mushe/Nangbug

This is a pleasant place with three lodges; since it is overshadowed by Lukla few people stay here. Many vegetables are grown in the area especially for the hotels in Lukla and Namche.

Chourikharka/Dungde (2760m/9055ft)

Meaning 'yak-herding area', Chourikharka is often mis-spelt Chaunikharka, although if you listen hard to a local person saying the name, the quietest of n's can often be heard. Dungde, the Sherpa name, means *dingma* or flat farming area: a more accurate name now. The village begins at the top of the short steep climb to the kani and has three well-spaced lodges.

Route from Chourikharka to Lukla Thankfully Lukla is not visible from here but there are numerous small trails up. First head for the school, then from there a path leads up to join the main trail. The Hillary school was constructed in 1964 and has expanded to provide education to the final grade 10. There is also a health post founded by the Himalayan Trust. Alternatively walk to Chaplung and take the main trail.

Direct route to Namche If you're bypassing Lukla, the route description continues on p149.

Trekking from Lukla

LUKLA (2850m/9350ft)

Lukla means sheep corral, which is all it was before the airstrip was built. Now it's more like a tourist pen operated by a mish-mash of peoples: many Sherpas but also Rais, Brahmins and Chhetris. The sole industry is tourism but with an average of eight flights a day during the busy season, it's now quite a large industry. Development of the Syangboche airstrip may, however, change this.

For the children of the local people, Lukla boasts one of the few schools in the area that was not initiated by the Himalayan Trust. It's only a primary school so the middle and high school children must go to Chourikharka or to boarding school in Kathmandu.

Lukla now has a three-phase 15kw electricity system but charges are high so only the lodges can afford to be connected. Demand from the lodges outstrips supply although it's not used for cooking. This would require a supply of about 50kw more, necessitating the building

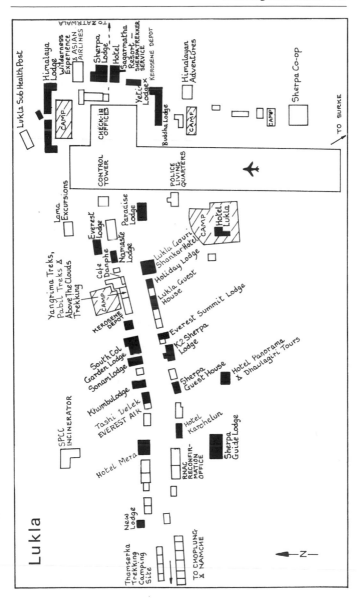

Lukla

of a small dam. There's enough electricity, however, to power a few stereos in some lodges – a gentle re-introduction to the 'real' world after a long trek.

Lodges

There's a wide variety of lodges. The most expensive and luxurious is the **Sagarmatha Resort** where rooms with attached bathroom cost around US$20/£13.50 a night. At the other end of the market are basic lodges for the porters and guides hanging around for another job and, of course, there's everything in between. The large number of lodges is due to the long queues that used to form for a flight out in the height of the season. Despite the numerous comfortable places to stay here, many trekking companies still provide accommodation in tents and members who want a bed in a lodge must pay for it themselves.

Services

Airlines RNAC, Asian Airlines and Everest Air all have offices in Lukla. Nepal Airways has an office but currently no flights. RNAC's office is open for reconfirmation only between 3pm and 5pm however this may change with the added competition provided by the other airlines. The other offices are usually staffed from 10am to 5pm. If you don't have a ticket and the offices are closed talk to your lodge owner who may be able to help.

The helicopters operate as many flights as are needed, although they often put on an extra flight only when three-quarters of the seats are sold. So although tickets may be slightly more difficult to come by at the busiest times, you still have a good chance of getting out of Lukla quickly.

Leaving Lukla

We woke at 6am to rain and thick cloud, so rolled over for more sleep. No chance of a helicopter today we thought. At 6.45am the lodge owner just about pounded the door down. It was still raining but she insisted we get up and pack immediately. While having a quick breakfast and still not really believing that she could be right that there would be flights today, we noticed that the cloud, although still thick, had lifted slightly and the rain was slackening off. Just a few minutes later we heard the distinctive chop-chop-chop of a helicopter which suddenly ducked under the clouds and onto the airstrip. In fifteen minutes, and to our complete surprise, we were airborne.

Other services Since national park rules prohibit trekking companies from using firewood, a **kerosene depot** has been opened here. There's also a **Health Post**, set up with French aid and often staffed by a French doctor and two assistants. There's no bank or post office.

Avoiding altitude sickness

All the scheduled flights arrive before lunch so it's quite possible to have a snack, then hit the trail and stay at Phakding or Monjo for the first night. Nevertheless some sensible planning is required to lessen the risk of altitude sickness occurring later. Doctors recommend taking 4-5 days to reach 3000m/9843ft and a minimum of 2-3 days. Since Lukla is at 2850m/9350ft you are already close to that altitude limit and Namche, at 3450m/11,319ft, is well above it. Yet most trekkers who fly in, trek to Namche in just over a day. These people are twice as likely to experience troublesome AMS, and form the majority of serious cases. The reasonable rates of ascent from Namche are widely publicised but this recommendation for the days below Namche has been totally ignored. Caution at this point will undoubtedly lessen the impact of problems experienced later.

A dizzying thought is the fact that you will have to ascend around 4800m/15,748ft, with a modest 2400m/7874ft of descents in total, to ascend Kala Pattar.

Lukla airstrip

The airstrip was constructed by local Sherpas with Hillary's supervision. It took a month and cost US$2650. Being quite short, it could safely handle planes with only about 8 passengers but it's subsequently been extended several times.

It's a tricky place to land a plane because everything is down to the judgment of the pilot with no radio beacons for guidance. He appears to aim into the lower end of the runway, pulling up at the last minute. This looks rather alarming from the passenger compartment as you dive into the mountains, then onto the runway hurtling towards the rock wall at the end of the airstrip. The landing is rough and bouncy since little is done to maintain the airstrip. Not surprisingly there've been some accidents. The last was in July 1991 when a plane came in for a heavy landing and the undercarriage snapped but nobody was seriously injured.

Helicopters, rather than landing vertically, use the same approach as the planes, coming in at speed and lifting the nose up at the last minute. They rely on downdraft to stop themnot only against the runway but often also against the rock wall at the end of the runway. The reason they take off and land along the runway is that it's easier than landing vertically.

Taking off by plane is no less exciting. With the propellers on fine pitch and the brakes locked the pilot pushes the throttles to maximum, only releasing the brakes as the locked wheels begin to slide. With a glorious rush the plane bounces into the air.

LUKLA TO NAMCHE   [MAP 7]

Chaplung/Chablung/Lomdza (2660m/8727ft) Marked by a cluster of buildings by the turn-off to Lukla, there are four hotels spaced a few minutes apart. The turn-off, if you're coming down from Namche, is marked by a group of houses. It's also signposted by Lukla hotel owners who have a vested interest in ensuring that you don't take a wrong turn. An elegant bridge crosses the Kusum Khola and offers impressive views of Kusum Kangguru. This mountain is revered by local people; its name means the 'White (or Pure) Mountain House of the Three Gods'. From certain angles three individual peaks can be seen. There are tea shops and a lodge at this sunny spot.

Ghat/Nynyung is the next settlement, just around the corner. Ghat means 'bridge' in Nepali and the bridge here was once important because it was one of the alternatives to the bridge at Jubing that was often washed away. With the advent of steel cabled suspension bridges it has lost its importance. The route to Namche does not cross the bridge but instead follows a trail lined with a number of teahouses a few minutes apart. Up a small hill is a lodge and then you pass some prayer wheels including a very large one.

Phakding 2640m/8661ft

A short half day's walk from Lukla, Phakding is the first overnight spot for groups who've flown in to Lukla. Since it's also the normal overnight stop for groups from Jiri, in the high season sirdars often send one of the crew to race ahead and reserve their favourite spot. There are other suitable villages to camp at (Chumoa/Monjo) but porters and most trekking companies don't like to change their routine. The large numbers of people stopping here accounts for the extraordinary number of lodges at Phakding. The first is the **Alpine Club Lodge**, a favourite group camping spot, and 10 minutes further up is Phakding proper where there are four lodges and campsites followed by another three or four by the bridge.

The Dudh Kosi is crossed here to the west bank on a big suspension bridge with an interesting history. By the Alpine Club Lodge is a rather perilous suspension bridge meant to replace the insecure wooden bridge further up; but the wooden bridge continued to be more popular because the route to the suspension bridge bypassed many lodges and involved a stiff climb. So eventually a second suspension bridge was constructed to replace the wooden bridge.

Just beyond Phakding the river bank has been ravaged by erosion, the area by-passed by a high detour. Between Phakding and Monjo, a leisurely couple of hours' walk, are several simple tea-shacks. **Toktok** has a single inn and **Bemkar** a simple lodge and many tea-shacks.

Route map key

Large lodges 🏠   Simple lodges/teahouses 🏠   Tea shack ☕

There may be just one 🏠   a few 🏠   or many 🏠   lodges/teahouses

Trail ╴╴╴   Pass ✕   Ridge ╱   Peak ▲   Trekking peak △

NAMCHE 3450m

Bhote Kosi

Imja Khola

WITH VIEWS OF EVEREST

NEW BRIDGE

THAOG

Sagarmatha National Park
Jorsale Entrance

MONJO 2815m

CHUMOA

BEMKAR

TOKTOK

Sherpa Lodge

Sherpa Garden

PHAKDING 2640m

Hotel 5 Star Water

CAMP

Sunrise Lodge

Riverside Lodge

CAMP

Khumbu Alpine Camp

Clubroom

Sherpa Guide Lodge

Dudh Kosi

GHAT

Kusum Khola

ND Lodge

Namoste Lodge

Apple Pie Restaurant & Lodge

VIEWS OF KUSUM KANGGURU

Tashi Tuki Lodge

Dudh Kosi

PHAKDING

Himalayan Trekkers

Phakding Guest House

Khumbu Travellers Lodge

CHOPLUNG 2660m

SeeYou Lodge

CHAUNRIKHARKA 2760m

Himalayan Trekkers

SCHOOL

Alpine Club Lodge

CAMP

LUKLA 2850m

N

MAP 7

0   1km

MAP 6 142

TO SURKE

TO ZATRWALA & MERA

159 MAP 8

1¾ – 2¾ HRS

1¼ – 2¼ HRS

NAMCHE – LUKLA   4 – 7 HRS

¾ – 1¼ HRS

¾ – 1½ HRS

40 MIN

FROM SURKE 1½ – 2¼ HR

Many of the villages around here lie out of view above the trail, on the old route. Older maps show the trail crossing a bridge to the east bank at Bemkar. The washed-out remains of this bridge can be seen and instead there's a shaky temporary bridge 20 minutes further up-river.

Chumoa is a town that has moved with the times. Old Chumoa lies just south of the temporary bridge, so to catch the trekking business a couple of lodges (one quite simple) have moved north to join the aging **Chumoa Lodge Hatago**. This was one of the first high standard lodges between Lamosangu (before the days of the road to Jiri) and Namche and was really a place to be looked forward to after the basic places on the long walk in.

Monjo (2815m/9235ft) There are three more lodges here and a few simple inns and tea-shacks. Signs welcoming donations herald a monastery situated a hundred metres or so off the main trail. A minute later you reach the gateway to the Sagarmatha National Park.

Sagarmatha National Park (Jorsale entrance)

At the guarded entrance to the park your national park permit will be checked. If you don't already have a permit you can get one here.

From this point on no firewood is allowed to be cut so all groups must use kerosene for themselves and also for the porters. Implied also is the universal 'Pack it in, pack it out' national park principle, a rule that most trekking companies flagrantly flaunt. The rules for rubbish are that whoever provides the goods or supplies should dispose of whatever rubbish they generate. This means that groups should pack out their rubbish, or at the very least dispose of it properly but many don't. For individual trekkers the locals, who also get the benefits of business, are responsible for disposal of the rubbish. In practice this is a surprisingly small quantity of rubbish since egg cartons and sacks for rice are recycled, empty noodle and biscuit packets are burnt. Glass bottles, however, are a problem and the solution may be to ban them.

Rubbish is better managed in the Khumbu than anywhere else in Nepal. There are two rubbish removal projects, one organised by the national park and the other by the Sagarmatha Pollution Control Committee, partly funded by the World Wide Fund for Nature (WWF). In fact the locals have seen the tourism benefits in keeping their villages tidy and free of rubbish and generally do a good job. Groups are by far the worst offenders when it comes to rubbish.

Leaving the park entrance the path drops steeply to the long suspension bridge, built in 1995, across the Dudh Kosi. In the past yaks have taken the higher trail that stays on the east bank.

In September 1977 a huge avalanche peeled off Ama Dablam into a glacial lake. Not surprisingly the lake burst and sent a great wave of water down the valley. A number of bridges which were normally unaffected by monsoon floods were wiped out as well as some sections of the trail. The route is still in a semi-repaired state and the next bridge is of the permanently-temporary kind. Its design is interesting since it's constructed to withstand minor floods. The foundations of a bridge often survive floods but the top of the bridge is usually destroyed by trees carried down on the high river. To guard against this a slight modification has been made, with a long middle section resting between shorter-than-normal cantilevers. With this design, usually only the middle section is destroyed in a flood.

Bridge over the Dudh Kosi Some boulder hopping and a couple of short climbs bring you to this long Swiss-built suspension bridge constructed in 1989 across the Dudh Kosi, the gateway to the Khumbu. Apparently designed with catastrophes in mind, it is indestructibly high above the river. After the steep concrete steps the path is broad and pleasant, having been widened and tidied up to lessen erosion. It is still quite a hill, especially hard on the legs if you flew in to Lukla and the rapid gain in altitude may induce a headache. Part of the way up is a welcome tea-shack, and from the ridge extending to the rear of it are views of Everest, Lhotse and Nuptse. As you near Namche, with occasional views of the town ahead and above, you reach a junction. The best route is upwards, along the trail that resembles a small stream.

Of Yaks and Naks

The first thing to get straight about yaks is that there's no such thing as yak's cheese. The yak is the male animal; the female is known as a nak. The yak is found over a large area of central Asia, from Mongolia to Nepal. It's well-known for its shaggy coat and its ability to survive high in the mountains. In fact, it has evolved into an exclusively high-altitude animal – it cannot survive long below 3000m/9843ft. Wild yaks, still found in isolated parts of Tibet, are huge, often 1.8m at the shoulder. They can weigh close to a ton with horns almost a metre long. The yaks in Nepal are smaller, weighing no more than 400kg but are incredibly tough. They can survive sleeping out in temperatures as low as -40°C/F and are very resistant to disease, unlike the lowland cattle and buffaloes.

There are more than a dozen types of yak crossbreeds, bred to get the best characteristics out of the animals used. Most common is the *zopkio*, a sterile cross between a yak and a lowland cow. Getting the animals to mate is not easy. For an amusing conversation, ask an expert how it's done. Unlike the yak, the zopkio is able to survive below 3000m. This became important to the Sherpas when tourist groups started flying in to Lukla, which is just below the limit for their yaks. The zopkio is less temperamental than the yak but cannot cope with extreme cold or rough tracks. The yak, on the other hand, is the only pack animal capable of crossing the Nangpa La (the glaciated trading pass between the Khumbu and Tibet). Differentiating between yaks and zopkios is easy. Yaks horns have a distinctive double curve and their hair is longer and shaggier than that of crossbreeds. The other common cross is between a Tibetan bull called a *lang* and a nak. This produces a *dimzo* (or *zhum*), prized for its milk, and popular in Solu and Pharak.

NAMCHE/NAUCHE (3450m/11,319ft)

Welcome to the Namche bowl, the Zermatt of the Khumbu. This thriving village has grown up around a magnificent spring, the only water supply. Since all routes upwards pass through here and it's an essential acclimatisation stop, the facilities are well-developed and the village bustles with trekkers most of the year.

Called Nauchi by all Sherpas, the village is more widely known as Namche ('Namchi'), a century-old Nepali mispronunciation. It's also long been referred to as Namche Bazaar, inaccurate since at the time all trading was conducted in private homes; the weekly market started only in 1965. The Sherpa name, Nauchi, is in fact only a short form of an older name, thought to be Nakmuche or Nakuche, meaning 'big dark forest', unfortunately now an inappropriate name.

Acclimatisation

It is important for all trekkers to spend at least **two nights acclimatising** here and if fresh from Lukla you would be foolish not to spend three nights in Namche, especially if you have spent only one night on the trail between arriving at Lukla and coming to Namche. Even if you do adhere to this advice, however, it's not unusual to suffer mild altitude sickness at Namche and many people have trouble sleeping. If AMS symptoms do occur or are worse on the second night then staying three nights is a good policy; you will only invite further trouble higher up if your body is not given a chance to cope adequately here. A sound alternative is to spend the third night at Phunki Tenga which is slightly lower and may give your body a chance to recuperate. The fact that the next night will be spent 600m higher should not matter if you have already spent two nights at Namche. See p239 for more information on AMS.

If you have plenty of time, an extra night's stop in Thame or Khumjung would be rewarding and further aid acclimatisation. Since these villages are at an equivalent altitude to Tengboche they are also excellent alternatives to spending two nights there.

Lodges

In and around Namche there are about 20 lodges. The most popular are the group in the centre of town simply because of their location, but all the lodges are good and a number are run by locally renowned sirdars and high altitude climbers.

As is common further up there is a two-tier pricing system. The bed charge is nominal if you eat breakfast and dinner at the lodge. If, however you are in a group with your own cook or wish to eat at other lodge restaurants then the bed charges climb to cover this loss. The menus tend to be extensive and one of the Namche specialities is yak

Namche

KEY

1 Potala Mountaineering/View Lodge
2 Khumbu Lodge & Nepal Airways
3 Thawa Lodge
4 Mountaineering Equipment
5 International Mountaineering
6 Namaste View Lodge
7 Thamserku View Lodge
8 Trekkers' Inn
9 Health Post
10 SPCC
11 Asian Airlines; Mountaineering Shop
12 Tibetan Medical Store
13 Rastriya Banjya Bank
14 Footrest Lodge
15 AG Lodge

16 Sherpa Trekkers' Lodge
17 Buddha Lodge/Tailor
18 District Border Admin Office
19 Kala Pattar Lodge
20 Lucky Mountaineering
21 Tailor
22 Hotel Khumbila
23 Saturday Market
24 Sherpa Guide Lodge
25 Dental Clinic
26 Post Office
27 The Third Pole Lodge
28 Kerosene Depot & Everest Air
29 Paradise Guest House
30 Himalayan Lodge

steaks. Sufficiently tenderised and with a fried egg on top, they are delicious. With the installation of electric ovens new varieties of cakes and pies are appearing on menus.

Services

Although Namche feels important it isn't the district headquarters: that is to the south at Salleri. However, with a customs post, the National Park headquarters, an army post and other facilities for trekkers there are still rather too many government officials.

The **bank** is useful but it's dark and cold as death with dusty leather-bound ledgers and untidy piles of papers everywhere. It's open for changing money from 10am to around 2.30pm but closed on Saturday. The **post office**, open from 10am to 4pm, daily except Saturday, is really just a filing cabinet and a box. For your own safety you should register at the **police checkpost**, which is up the hill.

The **dental clinic** is the latest addition to the Khumbu's already superior facilities. It was initiated by Brian Hollander and funded by the American Himalayan Foundation and money raised by the 1991 Everest Marathon. It's run by a Sherpani who trained for three years in Canada; another Sherpa will join her after completing his training. It's usually filled with local people and obviously doing a good job repair-

---

Electricity

An innovative 28kw electricity system was installed in Namche in 1983, courtesy of UNESCO. It was locally managed and used two grids – one for evening lighting for the village and another during the day for cookers in three of the lodges. This scheme has now been superseded by the most advanced medium scale hydro project in the country.

The new system was set up with grant assistance totalling 124 million rupees from the Austrian government and 14 million rupees from the Nepal Electricity Authority (NEA). An Austrian non-governmental organisation (NGO) carried out the installation and gave technical assistance. The 600kw unit supplies around 500 households in Thame Cho, Namche, Khumjung, Kunde and the villages in between. The project was officially opened on 9 October 1995 although it had been running for sometime before.

The generators are housed in a traditionally decorated building below Thame. The two small turbines are fed by an artificial filter pool near Thame which collects glacier run-off from up valley. A 600mm diameter pipe, one km long, drops 200m to provide head. A Sherpa technician is being trained in Austria to help maintain the plant. Luckily, underground cabling for the villages proved cheaper than overhead wires but unsightly overhead cables run from the plant to the villages.

Since a bright light bulb uses around 0.1kw and a stove uses 1-3kw the scheme provides enough power for all village lighting and most cooking, including power for stoves in all of the lodges. Costs are reasonable too. For a private house a maximum of 1kw costs Rs350 a month or Rs450 for a 3kw maximum. Lodges use a meter system and for a large lodge during the busy months the bill may be Rs5000-10,000 a month.

ing the damage caused by the candy-culture for which trekkers are partly to blame. Visitors or foreign patients are welcome but running costs are high. Donations are appreciated.

The Saturday market

At this popular weekly gathering, Sherpas meet friends, catch up with the gossip, and of course trade supplies. Surprisingly, this famous market does not date back centuries but only to 1965 when it was started by an army officer to cater for the increasing number of civil servants the village was attracting. Tough, sheepskin-clad Tibetans sell tsampa, dried meat and perhaps a few souvenirs, while throngs of lowland porters offer food and goods arduously carried up to Namche. Most things originate from the road-head at Jiri, but there are also suntalas and rice from the Hinku, vegetables from Solu and eggs from Salleri. Some lodge owners from up valley can often be seen with wads of rupees collecting yak-loads of goods; others by-pass the market by employing their own porters.

Being one of the tourist highlights, the market determines many group schedules. Crowds gather early in the morning and thin out by late morning when all the trails out of Namche become busy. Sherpas from the closer villages wander home, groups trek up to Tengboche and the several hundred unburdened porters race down to warmer climes having delivered or sold their goods.

Traders from the beginning

Although the Saturday market was started only relatively recently, the Sherpas have long been traders, acting as middlemen between the Tibetans and the Rais. Traditionally Rais bartered maize, millet, buffalo skins and rice for Tibetan rock salt and wool. A wide variety of other goods were also traded. Iron farm implements forged in Those were prized in Tibet until cheap Indian steel became available. Solu supplied butter, stored in stomachs, for the thousands of butter-burning candles in the massive Tibetan monastic institutions, and a special soot used for making ink for the Buddhist printing centre of Shigatse.

This trade flourished until the Chinese invaded Tibet in 1959. The Tibetans were forbidden to cross the border, although the Nepalese Sherpas were not directly stopped, merely discouraged by bad treatment and occasional confiscation of their goods. For the Sherpas tourism conveniently filled this gap and is now more significant for them than trade with Tibet ever was. In 1990 the Chinese began to allow Tibetans to cross the border for trading purposes, giving them exit permits for only seven days (ie not enough time to visit the Dalai Lama in India). In 1992 these were extended to allow visits outside Tibet lasting up to 25 days.

Excursions

There are several possible day trips. Visits to the picturesque Khumjung and Kunde villages can be combined with the pleasant walk to the Everest View Hotel. A longer scenic trek is to Thame, with its gompa on the hill and the hydro power station below. Closer and well worth visiting is the National Park Headquarters at Choi Gang. This is also easily visited the morning that you leave for Tengboche but note that the Park Headquaters are closed on Saturdays. Less strenuous is the trek to Namche Gompa which is better visited early in the morning or late afternoon; it is, of course, open for tourists most of the day. A donation is expected. Other equally popular activities are clothes washing, apple pie feasting, chocolate bingeing and chang sampling.

Choi Gang and the National Park Headquarters

With Choi (or cho/tsho) meaning lake and Gang meaning hill dropping into a valley or flats, the name commemorates the fact that there was once a lake here. Nepali speakers have mistransliterated the name as Chorken or Chorkang, which in Nepalese translates to 'Thieves' Den'.

Long ago it was the main trading area before Namche and Thame took over. Deserted until the 70s, it's now the Sagarmatha National Park Headquarters.

Information Centre Built with New Zealand aid, the main building houses modest displays on the history and points of interest in the park. It's open from 8am to 4pm daily except Saturdays and public holidays.

There are superb views from the helicopter landing pad behind the information centre. Previously this was a favourite camping spot offering from-the-tent views of Everest, the Nuptse-Lhotse wall, Tengboche and Ama Dablam. Even the addition of a toilet in the foreground cannot detract from the magnificent views. With binoculars considerable segments of the route to Dingboche can be seen.

While walking up also note the pine trees surrounding the park building. These were planted in 1976 but are still small. Whereas in New Zealand, for example, commercial pine matures in 25 years, here it will be a hundred years before the trees look healthily large.

The Sherpa Cultural Centre, beside the Hotel Sherwi Khangba, is also well worth visiting. As this is a privately-run display, there is no entry charge. (In Nepal, a charge may be made only at museums and galleries run by the government). Donations are, of course, very welcome.

Lodges Several companies have bases at Choi Gang and there are three or four pleasant hotels. The latest addition is a huge traditional style building with double rooms and dormitories, the Hotel Sherwi Khangba (Sherpa's Old House). The concept is a little different from most other lodges – it has a library, evening slide shows and educational plus historical photos. It's an ideal place for groups to book, but marginally more expensive than normal Namche lodges.

AROUND NAMCHE

Syangboche (3900m/12,795ft)

Directly above Namche, although out of view, is Syangboche. In the past only the small single-engined Pilatus Porter planes could land here but helicopter services have changed that. Now the area is developing rapidly with the increasing number of flights. There are two good lodges and doubtless by the time you read this there will be more. If flying out you don't have to stay here – walking up from Namche or across from Khumjung in the morning is quite possible too.

If you have flown here without coming from altitude you are likely to suffer some altitude sickness, even if you descend to Namche to stay there. Don't forget there can be a delay of a day or so before you feel the full effects of the altitude. Descent to Phunki Tenga (3250m/10,633ft), although at a lower altitude, is not as safe as Namche since to escape from there requires climbing. It would be foolish not to stay at least three nights at Namche and a night at Phunki Tenga before attempting to trek higher. If you experience troublesome altitude sickness you may have to descend below Namche.

The Everest View Hotel This is an upmarket hotel for the rich to fly into and view Everest in absolute comfort. Luckily the views are excellent even from the beds because with the dangerously rapid gain in altitude this is where many people spend their time. Additional oxygen is provided and there are now also two small pressurised rooms to aid acclimatisation. When this 12-room hotel was first built there were teething problems and it was closed for several years. It is now open year-round and sometimes even full during the high season, mainly with Japanese on package tours. The cost is around US$200/£135 a night. The hotel is pleasantly designed, a low key affair that provides welcome employment for the locals, who never cease to be amazed by the outrageous costs. One job is the transportation of water from Khumjung, when the hotel supply runs out.

Khumjung (3790m/12,434ft)

This is a picturesque village with many beautiful houses. The direct impact of tourism is low (few trekkers stay here) but every family has some involvement with the trekking industry and hence the apparent wealth. Khumjung's gompa is at the top end of town amid a pleasant stand of protected trees. The other major building is the school on the flats. This was the first built by Hillary and friends. It has subsequently been expanded several times and is now a large high school.

There are a few lodges here. In the centre of Khumjung, below the gompa, is **Nima Lodge**. The others are at the end of town where there are fantastic views of Kangtaiga, Thamserku and Ama Dablam.

Leaving Khumjung The track to the Everest View Hotel begins by the chorten at the end of town and heads up the hill. The trails to Sanasa and Gokyo are initially the same, dividing by a house a few minutes down from the stupa.

Kunde (3840m/12,598ft)

Although Kunde virtually adjoins Khumjung the two villages are actually quite separate communities. The Kunde villagers have traditionally been associated with the Pangboche Gompa, while people from Khumjung go to Thame, despite the fact they have their own gompa.

Kunde is well-known for its excellent hospital. Built in 1966 as a Himalayan Trust project, it's staffed by a volunteer doctor from New Zealand or Canada. It offers exceptional services for a 'bush' hospital: there's even an X-ray machine. It's also one of the few places in rural Nepal where contraception and pregnancy testing are readily and reliably available. Most patients are local people who have developed a great respect for the hospital. Patients are asked to pay according to

---

(Opposite) Top: From the small pass between Namche and Khumjung numerous peaks are visible, including the very tip of Everest. **Bottom:** The calculators come out at the Saturday market in Namche (see p157).

their means – from a few rupees for a destitute porter to US$10-20 (or rupee equivalent) for a foreign trekker. You are most welcome to have a look around but donations are appreciated. It's open from 9am to 5pm (closed on Saturdays except for emergencies).

NAMCHE TO THAME   [MAP 8: p159]

Thame is a pleasant village with a beautiful gompa, about three hours' walk from Namche. Since it's 350m higher than Namche, groups often stay the night here as part of an acclimatisation programme before trekking to Gokyo – a very sensible idea. Even a day-trip, however, can help acclimatisation and it's an interesting place to visit.

Head up to the gompa and continue traversing up on the same trail which soon rounds the ridge enclosing Namche. Soon you come to a forest, a favourite area for local women to collect *soluk* (leaves and vegetation that are mixed with dung used to make fertiliser), singing as they work. It's also a good region to spot pheasant, especially the danphe, the colourful national bird of Nepal.

Phurte is the first village you come to and it has a forestry nursery funded by the Himalayan Trust. The fields between Samde and Phurte are known as *gunsas*; they are owned by villages at higher altitudes and used by them to provide crops earlier in the season. The gunsas here belong to Thame Cho residents but several sons with their families have moved down here permanently, establishing a small village.

Between Phurte and Thamo, visible high above the main track is a gompa. This is **Laudo**, a small monastic establishment built around 1970 as an arm of Kopan Monastery (near Bodhnath in Kathmandu). Laudo Monastery is often used by meditation groups.

> **Unfinished business**
> Since we were heading up to Laudo we offered to drop off the mail. Arriving at the monastery we talked to one of the lamas and asked if we could have an audience with the head lama and give him his letters personally. 'Certainly', he replied, 'he's here'. The only other person we could see in the room was a child playing on the floor. We asked again and with a look of confusion the lama repeated that he was already here. He motioned the child over and told us that the head lama had died a few years ago; this child was his reincarnation, in effect the same person. We talked to him for a while and then added the letters we'd brought to a large sack of unopened mail in the corner.
> (Kit Steer, New Zealand)

(Opposite) : The popular Buddhist prayer chant 'Om Mani Padme Hum' is carved onto thousands of flat stones and slates that are known as mani stones (see p108). As with any Buddhist shrine or monument, keep to the left when passing a wall of mani stones. **Top:** Khumjung village, near Namche.

Thamo/Thammu/Dramo The offices of the Nepal Electric Authority are here. Officials are observing and helping with the Thame hydroelectric scheme. The remains of the previous project can be seen on the opposite bank of the river, destroyed before completion in 1985 when a glacial lake burst. The wall of water engulfed many bridges and washed away farm land. The Himalaya is a young mountain range so sudden natural occurrences like this are frequent.

Immediately after the last houses of the village you can climb the stone stairs for the scenic new route or continue straight ahead across a temporary bridge to Thame and the Austrian hydroelectric project.

Thame (3800m/12,467ft) is part of the group of villages called Thame Cho (Thame Og (lower), Thame Teng (upper) and Yulajung) and is an area noted for its potatoes. There are a few lodges among the houses by the fields. These villages have traditional trading links with Tibet and just before or after the Namche Saturday market, Tibetans camp here and in Thame Teng. Thame has two gompas, the most frequently visited being a 15 minute walk up the track that begins on the ridge to the north and heads west. **Thame Gompa** was established on the advice of Lama Sange Dorje, fifth reincarnate Lama of Rongphu/Rongbuk, who played an important part in the spiritual history of the Khumbu. It's said that some of the books here are over 300 years old.

TO DOLE · TO THARE

DOLE NATIONAL
PARK CHECKPOST
3680 m

MAP 14

167 MAP 10

KHUMBU LODGE
NAMASTE LODGE

KhumbuiYul Lha
5761 m

PHORTSE

TENGA
3675m

SCHOOL

PHORTSE
3800 m

DEBOCHE
3770m

WATER MONG
3973 m

Imja Khola

Bhote Kosi

PHUNKITENGA
13250m

TENGBOCHE
3860m

Phunki Khola

KUNDE
3840m

KHUMJUNG
3790m

CHORTEN

SANASA
3600m

HOSPITAL

KYANGJUMA

MAP 8

EVEREST VIEW
HOTEL

NO NAME
LODGE

SYANGBOCHE

Dudh Kosi

N

NAMCHE
3450m

NATIONAL
PARK HQ

MAP 9

0   1 Km

NAMCHE – DEB   1¼ – 2 HRS →   ½ – ¾ HR →   1½ – 2¼ HRS →   ¼ HR →

Thame hydroelectric project This Austrian project is designed to provide power for Thame Cho, Namche, Khumjung, Kunde and the villages in between. The 600kw output will provide enough power for village lighting and for all the lodges to cook on, a welcome attempt to counter the tourism-related problem of firewood-use. Other applications have been considered, such as pumping water to houses. In Namche, all water is carried from the one spring.

The generators are housed in a traditionally decorated building below Thame. The two small turbines are fed by a pool, near the village, which collects glacier runoff from up the valley. A 600mm diameter pipe, one km long, drops 200m to provide the head. A Sherpa technician is being trained in Austria to maintain the plant.

To Lobuche and Kala Pattar

In this galaxy, which included a host of unnamed peaks, neither the lesser or the greater seemed designed for the use of climbers. – HW Tilman *Nepal Himalaya.*

NAMCHE TO TENGBOCHE   [MAP 9]

Leaving for Tengboche The trail that traverses from Choi Gang to Kyangjuma is wide and set high above the river. It's a beautiful walk except on Saturdays after the market, when it's crowded with groups of trekkers and yak caravans that kick up the dust. Tengboche is consequently also worth avoiding on Saturday nights.

Kyangjuma (3600m/11,811ft) This is the first set of teahouses you come to, about 1-1 1/2 hours from the National Park HQ. There are a couple of lodges with friendly owners and Tibetan souvenirs line the path. The trekking groups often stop here to buy things and their porters look on first in amazement at the prices paid and then in horror as they realise the extra weight they'll be expected to carry.

Route to Gokyo or Pangboche via Phortse A few minutes' out of Kyangjuma and just before Sanasa is a small junction with some writing on a rock by it. The upper trail climbs in a couple minutes to the main trail from Khumjung to Mong (see p180).

Sanasa (3600m/11,811ft) is five minutes beyond Kyangjuma. There's another small cluster of teahouses and more Tibetan souvenirs to tempt you. Often, Himalayan thar (goats) and pheasants may be seen just out of Sanasa but it takes keen eyes to spot them. After rounding a ridge the descent to the beautifully situated old suspension bridge begins. There are a few teashacks along the way.

Phunki/Phongi Tenga (3250m/10,663ft) This is around the corner from the bridge and, despite being a popular lunch spot, is quite small. If the altitude at Namche was troubling you this is the lowest place north of Namche to stay the night.

The walk up the hill to Tengboche is very pleasant. You pass through a blend of forest and shrub on a wide trail with many shortcuts leading from it. It's also one of the better places for spotting pheasant, thar and deer. They seem quite undisturbed by all the noise of passing trekkers. The end of the climb is heralded by a *kani*, an arched entrance with ceiling paintings of deities and forms of Buddha. Its function is to cleanse people of the many feared spirits before entering the sacred area.

TENGBOCHE (3860m/12,664ft)

This is a great cultural and religious centre for the people of the Khumbu region. The newly-reconstructed gompa is famous as the setting for the Mani Rimdu dance festival in late October or early November. Tengboche (sometimes spelt 'Thyangboche') is a favoured overnight stop for the majority of trekkers. Being an acclimatisation stop, many trekkers, groups included, stay two nights so in the high season it is very busy. If it snows groups often abandon their tents and take over the lodges. Good alternatives to a second night here are Pangboche, Khumjung and Deboche.

Behind the National Park Lodge is a ridge pointing to Khumbui Yul Lha that affords superb views. Look especially for the spectacular high trail from Pangboche to Phortse on the opposite side of the valley. Beware, however, of trampling the small pine saplings.

Rubbish and human waste are big problems here. Each group used to construct a toilet (tent) leaving hundreds of unsightly half-filled holes. Toilet blocks constructed by the park to solve this problem are now becoming dilapidated but it is park policy that all groups should use them. Your trekking crew might need a hint, and porters instructed to use this facility. There are also rubbish bins provided.

Lodges

There are only four lodges: the NZ-built **Tashi Delek Lodge**, the **Ama Dablam Lodge** above, the new **Gompa Lodge** and the **National Park Lodge** on the ridge behind the monastery buildings. All are owned by the gompa and are rented out.

Tengboche Gompa

This justly famous gompa is spectacularly situated under the mighty Kangtaiga ('horse saddle') and Tramserku mountains, in a commanding position with superb views up and down the surrounding valleys. You can see the Everest View Hotel and the National Park HQ down the valley. With these as markers it's easy to work out where hidden Namche and Khumjung are, and the path that brought you up here.

The gompa serves as a spiritual and social centre for the people of the area. Nearby is the monastery and young boys are sent here from all over the Khumbu to study Buddhism. For the period of study they must remain celibate but they may (and most do) get married when they have graduated.

Although the area has long been considered revered ground, the gompa was established only in the 1920s, by Lama Gulu at the request of the Abbot of Rongbuk. In 1934 a disastrous earthquake struck the area, in which the lama died and considerable damage was caused to the gompa. Rebuilt and headed by the present lama, Nawang Tenzing Zangbu, the gompa's move into the 20th century with the connection to an electricity supply was not an auspicious one. Less than a year later, on 19 January 1989, a heater overturned burning the magnificent gompa to the ground. Not all was lost since the majority of what could be removed, including the priceless book collection, was rescued. The construction of the grand new gompa was considerably aided by the Himalayan Trust and donations from wealthy locals. The library has now been put on micro-film, and the hydroelectric system has been revived.

Sherpa Cultural Centre
This was started by a number of Sherpas who have taken an active interest in the preservation of their culture for future generations. It's not intended as a dusty museum, more an archive for the storage of important documents and a place for Sherpas to meet and learn more about their culture.

Excursions from Tengboche
Behind the National Park Lodge is a ridge extending towards Khumbui Yul Lha that offers great views and is a good place for spotting wildlife. You can see the spectacular high trail from Pangboche to Phortse on the opposite side of the valley from here. Take care not to step on the recently planted saplings along the trail as you come down from the ridge in the half-light.

The forests above and below Tengboche are protected and are still considered to be owned by the monastery. It can be very pleasant to wander through the trees and there is quite a reasonable chance of seeing deer and pheasant. The rhododendrons are spectacular in the spring. For a longer, half-day trip, the rock peak above Tengboche, often called Hamugon, offers better views of the awesome Thamserku-Kangtaiga glacier. It's an easy but breathless scramble to the top of the first peak. Listen to your body though, while ascending.

TENGBOCHE TO PHERICHE/DINGBOCHE   [MAP 10]

Leaving Tengboche The route takes the gully between the fields where groups camp. In ten minutes you reach the small **Lhotse Lodge** and if there are many groups in Tengboche, some use this camping spot. Water from the stream here may be cleaner than the supply in Tengboche.

Deboche (3770m/12,369ft) is five minutes further on and there are superb views of Khumbui Yul Lha which looks formidable from here. There's a large new lodge that should now have solar-heated water and behind a barrier of trees is the nunnery with 12 nuns.

After passing a few other hamlets you cross a spectacular little gorge on a short suspension bridge. This is the junction for the trail to Phortse (see p185). Turn right for Pheriche.

About 20 minutes later the trail passes through a cleft in some rocks, with a mani wall virtually in the middle. Just after, the trail divides and is usually signposted, the upper trail heading to Upper Pangboche and the gompa, while the lower path takes a more gentle route through the fields to Lower Pangboche.

Pangboche (4000m/13,123ft)

This used to be the highest permanently occupied village until trekkers created a demand in winter for accommodation higher up the valley. There are simple lodges in both the upper and lower parts of this pleasant village, although few trekkers stay here. Coming down the valley from Pheriche/Dingboche the turn-off to Upper Pangboche is by a small chorten, where the river widens and the first fields of Lower Pangboche can be seen. From Lower Pangboche there's another trail which starts from the corner of Namaste lodge and winds up to the gompa.

In **Pangboche Te Lim** (the upper village) the houses are clustered round the old gompa and there are three basic lodges here. The surrounding juniper trees have long been protected and are now very large. Legend has it that they were created by Lama Sange Dorje who tossed a handful of his hair into the air and it took root as juniper. Once the whole valley would have been thickly forested with trees this size.

The monastery is believed to be around 450 years old, which makes it the oldest Sherpa gompa. Many trekkers take the opportunity to have a look around; the lama (the 14th re-incarnate) or his wife are usually close by. It is customary to leave a donation. This gompa was home to one of the Khumbu's famous yeti scalps until it was stolen in 1991.

The lower village, **Pangboche Wa Lim** (3840m/12,598ft) was once just grass fields, which is what the name 'Pangboche' means. There's now a small settlement here with four developing lodges on the edge of the lower fields. Potatoes, radishes and a few vegetables are grown and there is often an abundance of wild mushrooms. Firewood collection in Pangboche is still well organised. Dead wood is collected from the opposite side of the valley from selected spots and when the supply thins another part of the forest is used. Yak dung, a valuable fertiliser, is now also used as fuel, something that started with the arrival of trekkers.

Route from Pangboche to Phortse The most direct route is a high and wild trail that begins from near the gompa. From the top of the gompa take the trail that contours west to two white chortens 100m away, then walk up to the bottom of Tashi Lodge and begin contouring. The path crosses fields and streams and is not always easy to follow but once away from signs of civilisation it is a well-used trail. It takes a couple of hours to reach Phortse.

Route from Pangboche to Pheriche and Dingboche There are several small *yersas* (yak herding areas) en route. The first you come to is **Shomare**, owned by the villagers of Pangboche and used for growing potatoes. There's a small teahouse here. **Orsho/Warsho** is the next *yersa* and it also has a single teahouse-cum-lodge. Both are occasionally closed.

Pheriche or Dingboche?
The villages are 45 minutes apart, separated by a ridge. Both have lodges and are at roughly the same altitude so it depends on your plans for the important acclimatisation day as to where you stay. If the climb to Nangkartshang Peak (or Gompa) appeals, or you plan simply to relax it really does not matter where you stay. If planning a day trip to Chukhung then it is more convenient to sleep at Dingboche. There's a trail to Lobuche from either village, and they are of equal distance.

To Mingbo and Ama Dablam Base Camp See p194.

Route from Lobuche Khola bridge to Pheriche The track to Pheriche turns off before the little bridge over the Lobuche Khola. There are several routes but the one indicated by a crude sign painted on a rock is the easiest to recognise. Despite its being marked on even the most recent maps, there is no trail immediately after the bridge. From here it takes 30-40 minutes to reach Pheriche.

Pheriche (4280m/14,042ft)

There are four lodges and a few houses spaced along the track that runs through the village. The lodge shops can be a good place to replenish camping supplies. Pheriche can get quite crowded during the high seasons.

Himalayan Rescue Association Medical Post This was built in 1976 by the Tokyo Medical College for research purposes. Now it's staffed by two Western volunteer doctors who are available for consultations and who also give daily lectures on altitude sickness that are well worth attending. It's open only during the peak trekking seasons (October to mid-December and March to May), when the donations and consultation fees are able to cover the running costs.

Half-day trip to Nangkartshang Peak For the amount of effort involved, this excursion from Pheriche or Dingboche offers some of the best views in this region, a perfect scenic lunch spot.

From Pheriche the path zigzags up directly behind the HRA building on the track heading to Dingboche. Some time before the steep descent, continue up the ridge past a stupa.

From Dingboche any track heading up to the ridge will do. Then, from the stupa is a small trail that follows the ridge up, and up, and up. The top is marked by prayer flags and you are brought up short by a sudden drop. The views here are magnificent with Numbur, Chukhung, Makalu and Ama Dablam visible. There are several origins given for the name Ama Dablam (Amai Dablang). One says that it refers to the necklace of turquoise or coral usually worn by married women. With a little imagination it's possible to visualise shoulders and a head, and the pendulous lump of blue ice (a glacier) is roughly in the right spot for a necklace.

The gompa is usually locked and the trail to it is difficult to follow. Nearby are some meditation caves.

Half-day trip to the Ama Dablam lakes Among the moraine below Ama Dablam are two lakes at 4700m. Sometimes there's a bridge across the Imja Khola at the base of Dingboche and a track to Duroo, a small yersa. The alternative is to cross the single wire over the creek at the top of Dingboche and climb the steep hillside, or head upriver to Shangtso and hook back on the trail heading up. The lakes are also a great place for lunch.

Half-day trip to Taboche Base Camp Opposite Pheriche is stunning Taboche. Atop the broad ridge are a couple of small rock peaks that can be climbed, or a hidden higher valley to explore. Cross the bridge to Pangboche and from Tsuro Teng follow small trails up. Don't forget to take lunch.

Route from Lobuche Khola bridge to Dingboche Leaving the trail to Pheriche, cross the bridge and it's a 30-40 minute walk to Dingboche.

Dingboche (4350m/14,271ft)
The houses of this village are dotted about the fields, land owned by people from Pangboche and Kunde. There are five lodges in all, two simple but pleasant ones at the beginning of the cultivated area, then one in the middle of the village and the last two just above this. The top three lodges are favoured by trekking groups and can become very crowded as members find them rather warmer than their mess-tents.

From Dingboche you can make the half-day trips described above or head to Chukhung (below). If you suffered mild AMS on the first night here it may be a better idea to trek slightly lower during the day. The bridge across the Lobuche Khola is the closest point that's easy to reach. Often this small drop in altitude can make a difference.

Tsampa

Dingboche is the barley-growing and tsampa-producing area of the Khumbu. Sherpas and Tibetans revere this grain above all others – only barley is considered pure enough for offerings to the deities. Dingboche has the right soil for barley and a reliable water-supply. It's also the closest village to Cho Polu, the mountain home of the barley god. Ritual offerings of barley are shaped to resemble it.

The process of making tsampa (barley flour) is quite complex. First the dark-coloured barley is dried in the sun, then mixed with white barley from Solu. The dark high-altitude barley is considered more nutritious than the white variety. The mixed grains are soaked in water and re-dried three times before being stored for a few days. Next the barley is roasted in sand in huge pans. The grain explodes like popcorn and immediately afterwards is ground up to produce a light fluffy flour. It can be eaten dry and washed down with *chang*, mixed with *solja* (salt-butter tea) to make a thick porridge or rolled into a doughy ball to be chewed. For trekkers, ordinary sweet tea is used for tsampa porridge, rather than *solja*.

DINGBOCHE TO CHUKHUNG   [MAP 11]

By the top lodges in Dingboche the track continues between the hill and the upper fences and is easy to follow through the low scrub. **Bibre** is above the main trail but below, beside the path is a solitary one-roomed house where an old woman from Dingboche sells cups of tea as well as biscuits and chocolate during the trekking seasons. From

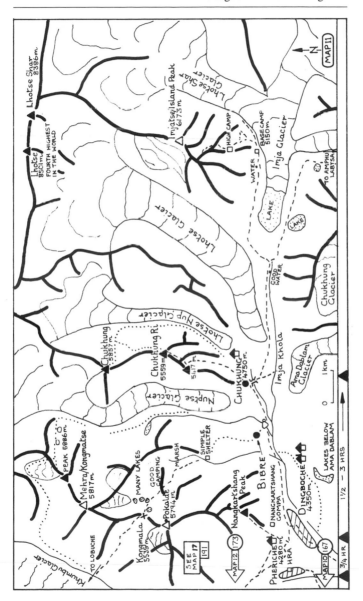

here Imjatse/Island Peak looks awesome, a triangle of almost sheer rock and incredibly steep snow faces, steep enough to bring a lump to climbers' throats. Yet strangely at Chukhung its magnificence fades.

Chukhung 4750m/15,584ft This is traditionally a Pangboche herding station (or *phu*) because of the rich and extensive grasslands in the valley. It's nestled under the terminal moraine of the Lhotse Glacier and is surrounded by recent and ancient moraine debris. The views here are fantastic, even from the base of the valley, and they get even better the higher you explore. Looking down valley, Numbur, Khatang and Karyolung rise majestically above Kongde while Taboche (Tagouche/Tawouche literally means 'horse's head' but can be loosely translated as 'big ego') and Cholatse ('Lake-pass Peak') are closer to the right. Ama Dablam is quite something to see from here and the fluted snow wall above Chukhung Glacier is stunning, especially at sunset.

There are three simple lodges, one of which usually remains open for the entire winter unless there's a heavy dump of snow. The *phu* makes a good base to explore the huge valley system with its many 'small' peaks that can be fun to climb.

Hiring equipment The lodges here stock ice-axes, crampons, ropes, karabiners, harnesses, ice-screws, snow stakes and a tent or two. In the high season these are constantly being rented out and you may have to wait a day or two.

Half-day trip to Chukhung Ri (5559m/18,238ft)
This is an understandably popular excursion from Chukhung, involving an ascent of a ridge similar to Kala Pattar. The top cannot be seen from Chukhung but the paths are obvious scars ascending the side of the big pile of grass and dirt. At the saddle there's a choice: a lower peak (5417m/17,772ft) to the south or a trickier ascent on rock to the high peak (5559m/18,238ft). The views are staggering from both with Makalu dominating amongst a ring of mountains. It is possible to do this as a day-trip from Dingboche but the altitude (rather than the time) creates a problem.

Other routes: Island Peak Base Camp see p231; **Amphu Labtsa** see p193; **Chukhung Peak** see p193; **Kongma La** see p191; **Peak 5886m** see p192.

PHERICHE/DINGBOCHE TO LOBUCHE [MAP 12]
Route from Pheriche to Tuglha Leaving Pheriche, the trail meanders up the open valley, beautiful when the weather's fine but muddy if snow or rain has recently fallen. It then cuts up a small but obvious valley. A smaller trail then branches off to the left and heads directly to

Guybanare Glacier

6870m

Pumori
7165m

BETTER
VIEWS
OF
EVEREST
c. 5700m

c. 5600m

BASE
CAMP

Kala
Pattar
5554m

175 MAP 13

MEMORIALS

Khangri Shar Glacier

GORAKSHEP
5170m

Khangri Nup Glacier

ROUGH
GROUND

Khumbu Glacier

Lobuche Glacier

TO THE
CHO LA

Lobuche
6105m

GOOD
CAMPING

5368m

PEAK
5886m

Lobuche
4940m

SEE
MAP 16
188

Mehra
Kongmatse
5817m

Lobuche Khola

DZONGLHA
4850m

TO LOBUCHE
BASE CAMP

MEMORIALS
4840m

Kongmala
5535m

SEE
MAP 17
191

Tshola
Tsho

TUGLHA
4600m

Pohalde
5794m

Cholatse
6440m

171 MAP 11

Tshola Glacier

PHULUNG KHARKA

GREAT
VIEW
Nangkartshang
Peak

Taboche
6367m

NANGKARTSHANG
GOMPA
TO CHUKHUNG

N

MAP 12

TABOCHE
BASE
CAMP

PHERICHE
4280m HRA POST

MAP 10
167

DINGBOCHE
4350m

0   1 km

2 - 4 HRS

1 - 2 HRS

1½ - 3 HRS

3/4 - 1½ HRS

½ - 1 HR

1½ - 2 HRS

the bridge over a few perpetually slippery boulders, while the main path heads up to join the trail directly from Dingboche just a minute before the bridge to Tuglha.

Route from Dingboche to Tuglha Climb the ridge behind Dingboche on one of the many trails to the plain. There are then several paths to follow, all leading to the bridge across to Tuglha.

Tuglha (4600m/15,092ft) The three lodges are primarily involved in making lunch for trekkers on the way up. Few people actually stay here, but if you didn't feel very well at Dingboche or Pheriche despite a rest day, you're less likely to get an altitude-induced headache if you stop here for the night rather than continue on to Lobuche.

The hill immediately beyond Tuglha is tough, especially if your pack is heavy. At the crest (4840m/15,879ft) are more than 20 memorials for Sherpas and a few foreign climbers who tragically didn't make it down again. From here the trail climbs gently and it's just over an hour to Lobuche. At this altitude, even in October there's ice on the streams; by December they may be frozen over.

Lobuche (4940m/16,207ft)
There are four lodges here: the upper two are known for their excellent food, the third one for its warm dormitory, and the last one is not known for anything in particular, probably the reason why it's quiet and pleasant. Groups have a wide area to camp in but more often than not members decide that the lodges are rather more attractive than their cold tents and move in. This may then create accommodation problems for individual trekkers. Nights here from October are invariably below 0°C and January temperatures are sometimes lower than -20°C/-3°F. Once the sun strikes Lobuche mornings are pleasant and often warm.

Lobuche is set on the slopes of a very pleasant ablation valley which, possibly because of the altitude, is very little explored off the path to Gorak Shep.

Supplies Lobuche is on the return route to Namche from Everest Base Camp so many expeditions sell off their surplus food to the lodges here. There's often an abundance of foreign delicacies, chocolate, energy snacks and dehydrated foods for sale.

Short excursions The small moraine towards Nuptse offers scenic sunset views if clouds have not rolled up the valley too far. The moraine immediately north of the *phu* is a stiff climb that's a little longer than it first looks but it also offers a few surprises: the Lobuche Glacier is close and spectacular. The grassy slopes behind Lobuche are also worth the climb. The sure-footed and energetic can attempt the three rock pinnacles, each harder than the last, for great views.

LOBUCHE TO KALA PATTAR   [MAP 13]

To Gorak Shep and Kala Pattar

Early in the season when it's still not really cold many groups leave Lobuche well before dawn to reach the top of Kala Pattar for sunrise. This is a rare and usually rewarding experience (once you've got over the shock of the early start). By December, however, the low night temperatures make starting with the sun a more reasonable proposition. The walk to Gorak Shep takes only about one and a half hours for the fit and fast, or up to three hours for the less fit. Kala Pattar is one to two hours beyond Gorak Shep. Even for the slow, the round trip should take less than eight hours.

From Lobuche the path is clear and pleasant at first, gently wandering up the ablation valley. Then it climbs, twisting and turning to thread its way onto the rough moraine of the Khangri Glacier. Here it's important not to lose the main track and you should beware of the ice-covered stream in the middle. The rough walking ends suddenly and the trail virtually falls into Gorak Shep.

Gorak Shep (5170m/16,962ft)

There are three simple lodges with abundant supplies of biscuits and tea, in addition to menus that include the most expensive Coke in

Nepal. The lodge-owners are friendly but if you intend staying here you must be confident that you won't suffer altitude problems and you need a very warm sleeping bag. On a November night the temperature **inside** a lodge could plummet as low as -20°C/-3°F. Even in September the inside temperature can drop below 0°C/32°F. The lodges are usually closed during January and February.

Ascending Kala Pattar

Kala Pattar, which means 'Black Rock' in Hindi, is the most popular viewpoint in the area for Everest and the Khumbu Icefall. The first foreign ascent was in 1950 by Tilman and Oscar Houston (father of the doctor, Charlie, AMS specialist) who rated it a 'subsidiary feature' without the extensive view of climbing access to Everest they sought. However, surrounded by glaciers and truly alpine terrain it offers breath-taking views.

Stop and look for the two trails up Kala Pattar before crossing the sand. The one that zigzags straight up leads to the slightly lower and easier peak at 5554m/18,222ft while the trail that traverses around gives the option of ascending this easier peak or the more northern peak (5600m/18,373ft). In snow use the longer but less steep route. Between where the two trails begin is a small spring with delicious water. It can be cold and windy on top of Kala Pattar at any time of the year so take your warmest clothes. In winter, especially in snow try to avoid getting your boots wet and beware of frostbite.

Two Glacier Rock 5529m/18,140ft

Less imposing but virtually as high is the hill marked 5529m on the National Geographic Everest map and 5527m on the Khumbu Himal map. The 360 degree panorama is not as impressive but you can see more of Everest. Pick up a trail of sorts at the northern end of Gorak Shep and head for the square cairn on the skyline. Over the other side is rough moraine and a small ridge, behind which, near the lake, is a flat spot often used as Pumori Base Camp.

Another view

For a better view of the Khumbu Icefall you can climb another of Pumori's spurs. Continue north-east of Gorak Shep past the memorials. Some of the ground is quite rough. Pumori was named by Mallory (in 1921) and this Tibetan name means 'Daughter Peak'.

Everest Base Camp

While this walk can be interesting, there are no views of Mt Everest and it's not a very popular excursion for trekkers. To visit Kala Pattar plus the Base Camp in a single day is extremely tough – beyond most people. If you're going to visit one or the other, then Kala Pattar is the better choice.

The trail is very rough (often only a line of yak shit) and easy to lose. It begins a few hundred metres north of the sandy flat of Gorak Shep, dropping down on a loose and sometimes dangerous moraine wall before heading towards the middle of the glacier. Some expeditions don't mind the occasional visitor (especially when from their home country) while others prefer no distractions. It takes between 1 1/2 and 3 hours each way.

HEADING DOWN

From Lobuche most trekkers reach Pangboche, Deboche or Tengboche in a day. Groups tend to make for Deboche or Tengboche (making it more crowded). It's possible to reach Namche in a tough single day – the Everest marathon is from Gorak Shep to Thamo and Namche.

Coming down the valley from Pheriche/Dingboche the turn off to Upper Pangboche and the gompa is by a small chorten, where the river widens and the first fields of Pangboche can be seen. After the first lodges in Lower Pangboche finding your way can be tricky: ask directions.

A good alternative to the standard Tengboche route down is to go via Phortse and Mong – see p180. Trekkers with more time can walk to Chukhung easily in a day via Dingboche or the Kongma La (see p191). To Gokyo via the Cho La is covered on p190.

If you're flying out you can either leave from Syangboche, less than an hour above Namche; to Lukla takes a day for the fit.

How the yak got its coat

According to an old Sherpa folk tale, the yak and the buffalo were brothers and lived on the plains in the shadow of the mountains. It was just before the monsoon when the ground was dry and hard and there was very little food to be found. High above in the mountains, the yak thought he could see some greenery. Was this some lush meadow? He decided to go and investigate. The buffalo insisted that he take his coat as it would be cold up in the mountains and, since it was summer, the buffalo wouldn't need it on the plains.

The yak set off and journeyed high into the mountains, glad of his brother's coat since it was very cold. The grass in the mountains was fresh and green and he ate hungrily as he travelled. The higher and further away from the plains he went the more delicious the grass seemed to be. Eventually he remembered his brother and decided to start for home. But he'd come so far and up so high that he was now completely lost. The yak never did get down to his brother so he kept his warm coat. This is why the yak has so much long hair and the buffalo has so little. The buffalo missed his brother and would often stare up into the mounains looking for him, so this is why the buffalo seems often to be looking up towards the mountains. The yak tried very hard to find the way down and this is why, to this day, the yak still wanders up and down.

To Gokyo

INTRODUCTION
Acclimatisation

Planning a sensible acclimatisation programme is essential if you're heading directly to Gokyo. The helicopter rescue pilots call it 'Death Valley' because many people go up too fast, unaware of the consequences. This is partly because the walking days are short, tempting trekkers to go on past their acclimatisation limits. The HRA advice is that a minimum of three nights must be spent at Namche, and en route to Gokyo, you should stay at Dole, then Machermo or Pangka. If you flew into Lukla, allowing even longer will mean less trouble later. There are many alternatives to spending all this time in Namche: visiting or staying at Thame, Khumjung/Kunde or Tengboche, and any these options, if planned carefully, will aid acclimatisation. See Appendix A for example itineraries.

The route

The first section out of Namche is a high open traverse; its highest point at almost 4000m/13,123ft. The trail then drops abruptly through forest almost to the level of the river before climbing again. You may see deer and pheasant in this area. The countryside opens out offering great vistas of mountains on both sides of the deep valley and back to the stunning mountain wall above Tengboche. The climb up to the ablation valley beside the Ngozumpa Glacier leads you into a different world of azure lakes and golden alpine pastures beneath sparkling mountains overlooking the longest glacier in Nepal.

Facilities

Phortse used to be the last permanently inhabited village with only high *kharkas* and *yersas* higher up the valley. Now strategically-placed lodges stay open even in the depths of winter to cater for trekkers, although note that some owners close their lodges for the Saturday market.

NAMCHE TO GOKYO [MAPS 14-15]

Route from Namche to Khumjung/Sanasa see p163.

Route from Khumjung This beautiful village is a sensible place to spend the night at the start of the Gokyo trek. By a house a few minutes after the large chorten at the end of the village is a junction. You

2½ HRS TO FIRST POND
½ HR.
1 – 1¾ HRS
3/4 – 1¼ HRS
1 – 1½ HRS

183 MAP 15

Na 4400m
Cholatse 6440m
MACHERMO 4410m
Taboche 6367m
THORE 4300m
LUZA 4360m
THARE 4390m
LHABARMA
DOLE 4040m
KONAR 4050m
167 MAP 10
DOLE NATIONAL PARK CHECKPOST 3680m
KhumbuiYulLha 5761m
PHORTSE TENGA 3675m
Khumbu Lodge
Namaste Lodge
SCHOOL
PHORTSE 3800m
Imja Khola
DEBOCHE
WATER
MONG 3973m
STEEP STONE STAIRS
TENGBOCHE 3860m
PHUNKI TENGA 3250m
Phunki Khola
KHUMJUNG 3790m
SANASA 3600m
KUNDE 3840m
KYANGJUMA
MAP 8 159
PHURTE
EVEREST VIEW HOTEL
NO NAME LODGE
SYANG-BOCHE
Dudh Kosi
NAMCHE 3450m
CHORKANG
NATIONAL PARK HQ
Bhote Kosi
MAP 7 151
N
MAP 14
0   1km
Thamserku 6608m

can continue directly to where the two trails to Mong cross the band of rock up a hair-raisingly steep stone staircase on a route that's little used. Alternatively you can descend to Sanasa, stop for tea and a look at the souvenirs and take the more popular lower path, although this still includes a staircase or two.

Route from Sanasa From Sanasa it's little more than 100m along the trail to Kyangjuma to a small junction beside a rock. This trail climbs in a few minutes to the main trail from Khumjung to Mong. Once through the rocks the trails cross the golden hillside gradually gaining height to a point overlooking Tengboche. Close to Mong is a small stream, in dry times the only water supplu for an hour in either direction.

Mong/Mohang (3973m/13,035ft) is marked by a chorten and is in effect a small pass. Ten years ago there was nothing up here. Now, villagers from Khumjung and Trashinga have established some pleasant simple lodges.

The descent is rather steep but with great views over to Phortse and the spectacular river gorge below, including an apparently-inaccessible natural rock-bridge.

Phortse Tenga (3675m/12,057ft) means 'Phortse Bridge' but the trail no longer descends to the river. Once a dirty place, the settlement has now been cleaned up. For the village of Phortse and the routes to it see p185.

Dole National Park Check Post (3680m/12,073ft) The staff here, stuck in this horribly cold and miserable spot, may want to see your receipt for the National Park entrance fee. A minute further on is an army post. They're here supposedly to protect the wildlife (especially the valuable musk deer) and the forests. The village of Dole is about an hour further on, up the long hill, through an area where you're likely to see colourful pheasant and shy deer. In rain or snow this trail can be slippery.

Dole (4040m/13,254ft)

The name means 'Many Stones' but despite this it's a pleasant *yersa* with three lodges, two side-by-side and the other across the little khola that divides the fields. Here the yaks and naks are brought up in mid-June to graze and fertilise the soil with their dung, producing a rich crop of hay. There are a few fields of potatoes and one lodge owner is experimenting with other vegetables.

After Dole the trail continues to climb, then flattens to a pleasant traverse with broad vistas. There's nowhere to stay or eat in **Lhabarma**.

Luza (4360m/14,304ft) is an hour or so from Dole and has several pleasant lodges. If you're feeling the altitude staying here rather than Machermo and spending the next night at Pangka or Machermo is a good idea.

Machermo (4410m/14,468ft) is a relaxing spot with superb views, especially of some little-known mountains. There's a big new lodge and a few smaller hotels.

Most people head directly from here to Gokyo but if acclimatisation is causing a problem it might be wiser to stay in Na (4400m/14,436ft, see p185) and explore the area, or rest at Pangka.

Pangka 4480m/14,698ft Two small but pleasant lodges opened here in 1994.

The trail climbs out of the yersa, then around a ridge. There are some more magnificent views and then the path leads to where the high moraine of the Ngozumpa Glacier meets rock walls. Follow the rock wall, crossing the wooden bridge over a stream that comes from the first lake/pond. To the right (east) is a milky stream, the beginnings of the Dudh Kosi. Do not attempt to cross this: head left of the bridge. A cold night, especially in winter, freezes the spray and sometimes even freezes the stream, diverting it onto the path which becomes treacherously slippery. There are hundreds of cairns to confuse matters.

The First Lake/Pond A sudden change of scenery introduces the first pond; it's really too small to be called a lake.

Longponga/The Second Lake (4720m/15,485ft) Groups occasionally camp in this tranquil place.

Gokyo (4750m/15,584ft)
On the shores of the third lake is the Gokyo yersa. Among the motley collection of huts are six trekkers' lodges not all of which have attached toilets. The fanciest and most popular lodge is the Gokyo Resort, a modified leftover of the film room built for the 1991 'Balloon Across Everest' expedition. Snapped up by an astute businessman, its level of service has encouraged the once sleepy lodges here to develop. Although Gokyo has several shops they are simpler than the expedition-stocked lodges of Lobuche and Pheriche; finding a variety of camping food is not so easy.

The sunset view from Gokyo Ri is only one of the many reasons for visiting Gokyo. Relaxing on the lodge patios overlooking the picturesque lake is considered reward enough by some but it's the potential for far-ranging exploration that sets it apart from Lobuche. Climbing to the top of the Renjo/Henjo La is exhilarating and walking up to the fifth lake and beyond can only be described as 'out of this world'. Many of the peaks around here require some steepish scrambling or bouldering. Recognise your limits and take account of the weather; otherwise enjoy!

Gokyo Ri (5340m/17,519ft) A stiff one and a half to three hour climb on an obvious track brings you to this viewpoint. The panorama stretches well into the distance, a blend of glaciers and grass, rock, snow and ice. Sunsets can be unforgettable here, as can be the descent afterwards, if you forgot to bring your torch/flashlight.

Henjo/Renjo La (5417m/17,772ft) The trek to the top of this pass can be a pleasant short day walk. In addition to some breathtaking new vistas, you end up in real alpine territory and pass beside a white glacier. Being so close to the mountains above the lake is exhilarating. Although it looks much further from Gokyo, it's only 2-3 hours to the top. A reasonable sense of balance and adventure is required as there are a few steep sections.

Begin by crossing the stream at the head of the lake, then follow the trail that contours, skirting the lake. At the head flats the views of Everest, Lhotse and, later, Makalu are interesting and quite photogenic. Cross the flats and stay to the right. There are some cairns once the rock scrambling begins but no real paths. The main thing is to gain altitude up small river gullies, eventually crossing the main stream that issues from high above.

At the first crest the view is quite unexpected and looks substantially different from the view from Gokyo. Again, stay to the right on the flat area. From here note the position of the pass above (it's marked by at least 10 large cairns) and pick your own route up. It's best to ascend following cairns over glacier-rounded slabs to the top of these then skirt south a short distance at a point that looks as if it could be tricky, to find the dusty steep track up. Alternatively, walk alongside the glacier on rough rock and later there is a steep loose scree slope to the dusty track. For the route over the other side see p195.

Donag/The Fourth Lake (4870m/15,977ft) A track leads up the valley but a more scenic way is to follow the crest of the moraine as far as possible. In about an hour you reach the fourth lake. This is large and beautiful, flanked on one side by sheer cliffs. The most exciting features, however, are the Nameless Teeth north of the lake.

The Nameless Teeth (5800m/19,029ft) It's well worth scrambling up to have a closer look at these tooth-like towers, and the views are fantastic. The climb can be made in a day-trip from Gokyo but with the altitude this is a trip only for the fit and acclimatised. The route up

TIBET

CHO OYU BASE CAMP
(NO FACILITIES)

Gyazumpa
Six Lakes

Ngozumpa
Fifth
Lake
4990m

Scoundrel's
View

Nameless
Teeth
5800m

Kangchung Peaks
6089m   6103m

Donag 4870m
Fourth Lake

Ngozumpa Glacier
(ROCK COVERED)

Small
Ridge

CHUGIMA/
CHOLA
5420m

Gokyo Ri
5340m

SPRING

Obvious
Saddle

TO RENJO LA
5417m

GOKYO
4750m

SEE
MAP
P24

MANY
TRAILS

DRAGNAG
4700m

188 MAP16

Longponga
Second Lake
4720m

Lake

First
Lake/Pond

NA
4400m

N

MAP15   0   1 Km

MAP 14 179

2½ HRS FROM MACHERMO   ½ HR   ¾ HR   1 – 1¼ HRS   1 – 1¾ HRS

PANG KA

CHO LA TO GOKYO   1 – 2½ HRS   LONG HALF DAY

steepens over large boulders, getting quite difficult. It looks as if there is no way on but it's possible to climb over the boulders to the point where you reach a drop to the next tooth, at around 5600m.

The views are simply incredible – the wall between Cho Oyu and Gyachung Kang defies description from this distance and the web of glaciers is fascinating. There's also the most extensive view of Everest you'll get anywhere in the Khumbu (without resorting to serious mountaineering). You can see part of the Geneva Spur (but not the Hillary Step), the South Col, the stunning Lhotse face and Nuptse. To the north is the famous North Ridge and the First, Second and Third Steps where Mallory and Irvine went missing. The perspective from this point, although not as close as from Kala Pattar, is more realistic than elsewhere.

Ngozumpa/The Fifth Lake (4990m/16,371ft) This jewel is about one and a half to three hours from Gokyo. Climbing the moraine, the pile of dirt to the east, to overlook the Ngozumpa Glacier also offers a 'Scoundrel's View' of Everest that is more extensive than from both Gokyo Ri and Kala Pattar. It's called a Scoundrel's View because no climbing is involved to reach this 5000m/16,404ft point)

Gyazumpa/The Six Lakes/Cho Oyu Base Camp The scenery up here is so spectacular it's overwhelming. It's a half-day trek from Gokyo but well worth camping here so that you can have more time to appreciate the views. For the really intrepid it is possible to climb close to the summit of point 5553m; or for going where you shouldn't, there is a steepish ice route to the Sumna Glacier.

Cold comfort

You can do some crazy things on the spur of the moment. Sitting in a lodge at Gokyo we rustled up a stove and a few foam pads (but no tent) and decided to camp up the valley.

As we prepared for bed, toasty warm after a good hot supper, it was a normal, for early December, -13°C. My sleeping-bag is so thick it could bring an Egyptian mummy to life, but I awoke to find my toes a little cold. Putting on socks and the hood of my jacket for good measure I inspected the thermometer. I thought of John in his much thinner three-season bag and shouted across 'Are you still alive?! It's -29°C!'

During the night we both put on more clothes but it seemed to continue to get colder. I checked the thermometer later. It was way off the scale, somewhere around -35°C. Luckily the morning was fine and the first rays of the sun were surprisingly warming. Herman, the third member of the party, had slept soundly through the night but woke up with a blue nose – the only part of him exposed to the freezing night air.

TO AND FROM PHORTSE [MAP 14: p179]

Route from Na to Phortse The quickest route down from Gokyo is via Dole and Machermo. However, rather than back-tracking, there's an alternative trail on the east valley wall directly to Phortse via Na.

Na/Nala (4400m/14,436ft) The tourist world of lycra and Ray-Bans has all but passed this place by. There are only two basic places where it's possible to stay and eat.

Leaving Na, aim for the small bridge. The trail is so faint that it can't be seen from the opposite side of the valley but it is there and it becomes clearer.

At **Thore (4300m/14,107ft)** tea and bikkies are served during the high season from the single building here (an ex-nak shed?). **Thare (4390m/14,403ft)** also boasts a quaint lone teahouse that is occasionally open. A short climb leads to the chorten at 4278m/14,035ft with magnificent views.

Konar (4050m/13,287ft) is deserted during the trekking season. In summer it's a large hay-growing area. Around the corner any of the trails leads to Phortse.

Phortse (3800m/12,467ft)

Pronounced 'Phurtse' or 'Phur-che' by the locals, 'phurte' means 'flight', and it's supposed to have gained its name when the Khumbu saint, Lama Sange Dorje, landed here after a trance-induced flight. It's a picturesque village, magnificently-situated and defended by steep hillsides. The area is famous for its buckwheat but potatoes are also grown in large numbers.

The forests to the south-west and the north are protected by a ban on wood cutting that was made over one hundred years ago by the lama who lived in the forest. In other areas, notably Namche, Khumjung and Kunde, when the government took over control of the forests and redefined the areas that could be cut, the pattern of use changed quickly. Here, the old lama's edict seems to have proved more effective. Phortse is reputed to be one of the most conservative villages in the Khumbu and there are only two lodges here so far.

Phortse to Na From the Khumbu Lodge at the top of the village head north (left) on a path that follows the walls but stays above the fields. There's another trail that starts from the middle level of the village but it's harder to follow.

Phortse to Phortse Tenga The trail starts behind the mani walls at the lower northern part of the village. It's a wide but sometimes slippery track passing through forest where there's a good chance of spotting pheasant. It continues down until you reach the wooden bridge. Close by is a protected stand of trees that is set aside exclusively for bridge repair.

Immediately after the bridge is a junction. Slightly to the right a path leads up to the main trail to the Dole checkpost (p180). The route to the left goes to some reasonable camping spots and Phortse Tenga (p180).

Phortse to Pangboche or Tengboche Walking without watching where you're going could be hazardous on this trail. If you're scared of heights and not happy walking along trails with steep drops beside them avoid this route.

The track starts from the top of the village on a gentle gradient with excellent views of Tengboche.

For the **gentle route to Deboche/Tengboche**, the turn-off for the bridge that crosses the gorge is immediately after the first small rock cleft. The path heads down steeply before continuing at a more gentle rate of descent. It's not always obvious, sometimes little more than an imaginary trail, and divides many times but it is not easy to become totally lost. Once close to the bridge the path heads up 100m or so to climb over bluffs below, crosses a stream, then drops to join the main Pangboche-Tengboche trail immediately above the bridge.

For Pangboche, at the first rock cleft continue straight on the main trail as it winds and climbs in and out of bluffs. It finishes in Upper Pangboche.

For Tengboche, direct from the southern corner of the village a trail drops to a small bridge for the steep climb to Tengboche.

From the bridge above Tengboche to Phortse The old path skirting around the bluffs immediately west of the bridge is now disused, for obvious reasons. You must now climb up about 100m on goat tracks until you reach a point where it's easy to cross the little creek to your left. Follow the tiny trail on the other side down to the fields. Work your way across, taking the upper paths where possible until you reach the main Pangboche-Phortse trail.

Sherpa names
Sherpas are often named according to the day of the week on which they were born. Dawa is Monday, Mingma Tuesday, Lhakpa Wednesday, Phurba Thursday, Pasang Friday, Pemba Saturday and Nima is Sunday. Another common name is Ang, meaning young.

Side trips and pass-hopping

PHAPLU TO RINGMO   [MAP 5: p139]
Phaplu
The short runway describes a gentle 'U' shape, a real 'Hillary job'. It was constructed to help build the Himalayan Trust hospital here. The hospital, now government-run, sits a few minutes' walk below the runway.

Lodges If you've just arrived in Phaplu and don't want to start trekking the same day or if you're waiting for a flight out, there are a number of places to stay. There are some trekkers' lodges just above the runway but it might be more interesting to spend the night in Salleri rather than Phaplu.

Salleri is a large rural town and is the district headquarters with a few simple local-style hotels. Few trekkers visit it so you'll be quite a novelty. The hydroelectric system is being expanded as part of the Swiss SATA project and carpet manufacturing has been started in an effort to introduce a local money-generating industry.

Route from Phaplu to Ringmo
From Phaplu you can either walk directly to Ringmo or make a very worthwhile detour to Junbesi. For Ringmo, take the wide trail beginning just above the end of the airstrip. There are a couple of basic places en route that could provide lunch, some snacks and even a simple bed. For Junbesi, head north and down to the valley floor. Follow the valley to cross the suspension bridge. This leads to the trail on the northern bank of the Junbesi Khola.

Route from Ringmo to Phaplu
The junction for the path to Phaplu is obvious at Ringmo but don't believe local assurances that Phaplu is only a couple of hours away. It'll take more than three hours and probably almost five.

The trail is well constructed and passes though some very pleasant forest. An hour or so out of Ringmo another path branches off the main trail. This descends to the river and the bridges below to join the track from Junbesi to Phaplu. However, it's better to continue along the main trail, the branch that contours leading to Phaplu without any serious climbs. After many more bends the airstrip at Phaplu comes into view.

THE CHUGIMA LA/CHO LA   [MAP 16]

Safety

Although the crossing of the Chugima La (5420m/17,782ft) has become popular, it does cross a glacier which could be dangerous. Note the general information on glaciers (see p231). If it has snowed recently either avoid the pass or take great care descending/ascending the smooth slabs on the Gokyo side of the pass. If it has snowed heavily or the weather is unstable avoid the pass altogether. A recent tragedy occurred in this area after freak storms had dumped more than two metres of snow on the Khumbu. On the night of 8th November 1995 more than 40 people, including 13 members of a Japanese trekking group, were killed in an avalanche on the Chugima La route.

The rock approaches are steep but present no real problems. However a light fall of snow on the glacier creates a treacherously slippery surface as it begins to melt in the sun. Porters are never provided with crampons, instead they tie thick string around their shoes at the ball of the foot. This concentrates the load at that point and provides more grip, a handy trick that everybody without crampons should adopt. String can usually be found at Lobuche and Gokyo, as well as on either side of the pass, where it has been discarded.

Crossing between Gokyo and Lobuche in one day is very tough, possibly the hardest and longest day on any trekking itinerary. It's much more pleasant to break it up. From Lobuche, Dzonglha, with its solitary lodge, is a few hours' walk and means a few hours' less the next day. Dragnag and Na now also have lodges. Well-equipped campers may want to stay on the glacier.

Route From Lobuche

Follow the track towards Tuglha but do not continue across the creek: stay on the right (west) side. After a flat area there's an obvious track that contours around the huge spur to another flat area about an hour away. Up this broad gully is the route to Lobuche Peak Base Camp. Continue straight ahead for the route to the Cho La, climbing to the top of the ridge and then dropping down to an area with many streams. After crossing the biggest of them on a stone bridge the path heads gently up a tiny valley.

Dzonglha (4850m/15,912ft) This is a summer yak herding station on the left, or south, side of the miniature valley. There are two new lodges here, convenient for trekkers crossing the Chugima La. In the quiet seasons ask at Tughla (where the sister of one of the owners also runs a lodge), Lobuche or Gorak Shep to check that at least one of the lodges is open. If camping, there are suitable watered spots from here up to the beginning of the steep climb.

The approach There are two routes up the pass but one is disused now. As the path gets steeper you cross the main stream which can be tricky. Head up to the crest of the moraine that points into the huge rock face. The route (for from here there is no trail as such) climbs up big boulders and slabs staying close to the wall on your left (west). There are a few cairns to look out for and eventually a flattish area is reached. The route continues to climb still staying close to the rock wall which is now to your south since the trail has taken a 90° turn.

If you have crampons head for the glacier as soon as you can see a way onto it, otherwise continue up to where the rock meets an almost flat snowy area. From here the tip of Everest is just visible and down-valley Baruntse begins to look formidable. Little of this wild mountain is normally visible.

Great care is necessary as you pass the bergschrund, the gap between the glacier and the rock. It's partly filled with rocks and sometimes crossed by unsafe snow bridges. There's no path here and the route passes within a metre or two of it.

The glacier Stay to the very southern edge of the glacier. Never cross to the middle. Sometimes the footprints stay high on the south bank and at other times they drop down a little. It's very important to keep a good look out for crevasses, although they do not often occur on this side of the glacier. The highest point of the pass is at the far end of the ice. Leaving the slippery glacier for the security of hard rock is always a relief.

CHUGIMA LA/CHO LA TO GOKYO   [MAP 15: p183]

Down to Dragnag Before continuing down, have a look at the route possibilities in the valley below. The main valley descends gently to the south to Na while the route to Gokyo crosses a couple of ridges via a shallow saddle before entering a steep valley that is partly out of view. The rock descent is via rounded ledges, wide but often slippery. Staying on a track, or sometimes even finding one, is hard. If heading to Dragnag and Gokyo the climb up the last ridge seems to be never-ending – demoralising for the very tired but the views to this point are rewarding. Once over the shallow saddle it's down, down, down, main-ly on the north side of the khola, although the path always looks better on the side that you are not on.

Dragnag (4700m/15,420ft) This collection of yak sheds has grown in the last couple of years to include two real lodges which are nor-mally open while the Chugima La is passable. Gokyo is still an hour or two from here over rough ground.

Crossing the Ngozumpa Glacier Just north, around the corner, is a prominent cairn on the crest of the moraine which you should head for. Scan the glacier and look for signs of the most direct route. If the large tarn is still there the trail is north of that. The path across is well used but not always obvious and there are older paths further down (glaciers move!). Don't attempt to cross in thick cloud. The walking is tough for tired feet but eventually climbing the moraine on the oppo-site side you drop between the First Pond and the Second Lake.

Route from Gokyo to Lobuche
If you're beginning from Gokyo, start early. From just below the Second Lake look for the trail over the moraine in a small notch. It is essential to find exactly where it begins.

Once across the pass itself, the walking in the valley is very pleas-ant. If you have reached Dzonglha and are contemplating continuing, Tuglha is about an hour away but involves a descent that would be tricky in half-light. Alternatively, two hours or so of hard walking will bring you to Lobuche.

THE KONGMA LA   [MAP 17]

The Kongma La (5535m/18,159ft) is a pass that provides an interesting high route between Chukhung and Lobuche. It takes a tough day to walk, and is longer than the lower route via Dingboche. If free of snow, it's a non-technical pass. It requires only a little confidence and steady feet for the last short section to the crest. A walking-stick may be handy. It's more pleasant to do in the Chukhung-Lobuche direction because the walk up is on grass, leaving the rock-hopping and loose scree for the descent. It's really worth camping by the high lakes or even slightly above the pass itself (views in both directions) for the stunning sunset and sunrise.

Route from Chukhung to Lobuche Contour and cross the large stream issuing from the ablation valley just west of the Nuptse Glacier. Then there's a long climb up the huge grassy ridge. There is no trail, instead aim for the point where the high, sharp rocky spur peters out into the grass. Pick up the track on the western side of this ridge at a high yersa which has some rock shelters and a water source. There are several ways up and the main track from here is easy to lose. It stays above the marshy/icy grass flats, then heads left (north-west), parallel to some bluffs where you may see Himalayan thar nimbly cavorting over the sheer rock faces. The track then curves and ascends right to round a big knob of rock (on the right side of it).

The lakes After a couple of climbs and short descents, the lakes are the next stage with the highest being the most beautiful. The sun arrives around here wonderfully early in the morning which makes up for the night temperatures (usually well below 0°C). Even when the lakes are frozen there's a tiny spring by one of the smaller ones.

The Kongma La The track to the pass goes to the right (north) of the highest lake to start the diagonal traverse of the steep face. The pass itself is littered with cairns up each ridge, and 50m to the north up the ridge is a small ledge perfect for a single tent. Bring a block of ice up from the lake as there's no water.

The route down drops only a little while heading right (almost due north) for a long way before beginning a slide down scree. From the ablation valley, crossing the Khumbu Glacier takes another tiring hour before Lobuche appears.

Route from Lobuche to Chukhung

To locate the trail across the glacier from the Lobuche side, head downstream about 200m to a large rock right beside the stream. Perpendicular to the stream at this point there are a couple of tracks on the moraine that head for a small notch. Once across the glacier, take care not to lose the path heading up to the pass.

PEAK 5886m (19,311ft)   [MAP 17: p114]

This peak is marked as 5880m on the Schneider map; the lakes below are unmarked. Accessed via the short north summit ridge from east or west sides, it could also be used as a possible glacier pass-hop. There is the odd hole and step in the ice, and a sling plus 10m cord would aid retreat off the scenic lunch spot. Since there are lakes on either side, camping here is easy. A good nose to follow and adventurous, steady feet required.

(Opposite) Top: Lobuche (see p174). **Bottom:** Gorak Shep (see p175). **Overleaf:** Seen from the Kongma La, Pumori is the peak on the far right with the popular Everest viewpoint, Kala Pattar (the 'Black Rock'), rising from the grassy cone immediately below. The tiny dots on the dry grass in the extreme left are the lodges and tents of Lobuche.

CHUKHUNG PEAK (5857m/19,216ft)   [MAP 11: p171]

This is the peak north of the peak commonly called Chukhung Ri (5559m/18,238ft), the Kala Pattar of Chukhung. The ridge between these two is too dangerous to traverse in its entirety; instead it's a gully scramble on the east side directly to the summit. Either way the ablation valley to the east provides access and exit. It is possible but strenuous to ascend both Chukhung peaks in a day, good preparation for Imjatse/Island Peak or the Amphu Labtsa. An axe, stick or ski pole would be handy. Views are staggering and include Chomo Lonzo (north of Makalu) and Gauri Sankar.

AMPHU LABTSA (5787m/18,986ft)   [MAP 11: p171]

The Amphu Labtsa is a tough and dangerous pass, nothing akin to the Cho La or Thorong La (Annapurna area). It's a mountaineering proposition that leads into some particularly isolated country. You need a climbing-experienced guide who has crossed the passes many times, good equipment and a rope. Each year several porters get frost-bite and ill-prepared trekkers have died here.

The pass is well concealed, visible only as you near it or from Imjatse/Island Peak Base Camp. It's best attempted early in the morning to lessen the danger of avalanche and rockfall. This means camping below at Amphu, a short half-day's walk from Chukhung. This grass/stone area gets very little sun making it one of the coldest parts of the entire valley and it also lacks water. The nearest easily accessible water is a clear spring just west of where the trail joins the Imjatse/Island Peak Base Camp path. Other possible sources are two small lakes above the faint trail and there's also glacier runoff or ice.

Routes to the Pass

There are two routes each with a sub-route or two. From both sides both routes look sheer but on the way up the route unravels. For the snow/ice route beginning in Amphu, head up the glacier and across the big crevasses to the avalanche-smoothed diagonal gully – the route up. It is possible to stay mainly on rock for the first part even if at first this does not appear to be the case. Then there is a short exposed traverse before the final petit basin to the crest. If you're coming over from the Hongu it's difficult to reach the top of the pass in the correct spot and

(**Opposite**) : Views from the Mera La. Anyone planning to camp at altitude needs to be extremely well equipped.

many lengths of rope testify to the number of parties that decided it was easier to simply abseil down a vertical wall than attempt to find the easiest crossing point. From a distance look for the two low spots. In the centre is a small notch that is slightly higher – the pass.

If snow-free, the higher **rock route** (5900m/19,357ft) is an alternative. Pick up the trail on the way up. One steep section often requires a short rope pitch. From the summit there is a tricky rock trail down. Sometimes it is possible to descend partly on the glacier beside, staying near the rock.

To Mera
Along the shore of the larger lake of Panch Pokhari is a small trail that descends to the other lakes. The trail crosses briefly to east bank of the Hunku/Hongu Khola to skirt the lake marked 5004m on the *Shorong Hinku* map. Otherwise the trail remains on the west bank. See p233 for the Mera La.

PASS 5443m (17,857ft)   [MAP 15: p183]

This lies above Gokyo between Gyazumpa and Ngozumpa. The glacier to the north has an even set of crescent crevasses so stay on the edge or on the rock. It is a bit of a scramble to the top but descent down the other side is pleasant.

MINGBO VALLEY   [MAP 10: p167]

Just above and opposite Pangboche, the Mingbo Valley is an infrequently explored but spectacular valley. Reaching a satisfying distance into it requires an overnight camp and perhaps some acclimatisation.

'Here I am in the clouds at 15,000ft. White wisps rush past clearing momentarily to reveal jagged black mountains before me. The fragrant smell of alpine grasses is overwhelming; the oneness with the landscape almost brings tears of joy. There's such immense peace and silence. No airplanes, no cars, no human sounds except the scribble of my pen and the crinkle of my jacket. Melting snow sculpts the rugged slopes and rocks fall from the big castle mountains. Rumbling power'.

Malia's Diary (Mingbo)

Leaving Pangboche descend to the bridge, then follow the trail accurately marked on the National Geographic and *Khumbu Himal* maps to the stream just before Mingbo. Here a trail branches off to roughly follow the stream to Ama Dablam Base Camp. The path straight ahead leads to Mingbo with its *goths* which are usually locked. Over the ridge from the Base Camp or 10 minutes north of Mingbo is the outline of the old Mingbo airstrip which was used to ferry supplies to the Tibetan refugees leaving Tibet after China invaded. A glance at the approach will reveal why it is disused now. It was another 'Hillary job'. Several small paths continue up the valley and the keen can scramble to around 5700m on the larger of Ama Dablam's southern ridges.

Mingbo La (5800m/19,029ft)

Groups occasionally use this pass rather than the more standard Amphu Labtsa after climbing Mera (p233). The approach from the Hinku Valley up the Hunku/Hongu Nup Glacier is straightforward although crevassed. Conditions on the Mingbo side vary; sometimes the fluted face drops off at perhaps 60 degrees and requires at least two pitches to reach the glacier proper, sometimes it is tamer, and occasionally it is virtually impassible.

From the pass look for the small trail on the ridge descending from Ama Dablam. Once off the glacier you will have to cross some rough terrain and climb up to this.

THE BHOTE VALLEY

The Bhote Valley (see p24) is closed to trekkers above Thame since it is close to the Chinese border. Foreigners wandering into China this way are simply deposited in jail until Beijing can be contacted. The valley, because it is closed, has generated some special allure but in fact it is very similar to the other main valleys. There are no lodges and no year-round occupied villages above Thame Teng.

With the new trekking regulations (in theory) opening up all of Nepal to specially organised trekking groups, there may soon be tours to the Nangpa La, the trading pass on the Tibetan border. Other areas that would undoubtedly be interesting to explore are Panbug-Na (as marked on the Schneider map) and perhaps the Sumna Glacier.

From the Renjo/Henjo La

From Gokyo to the top of the Renjo/Henjo La (5417m/17,772ft) is described as a day trip from Gokyo. On the Bhote Valley side the descent isn't easy. With snow or ice it could be quite dangerous. The pass itself is long. You can descend in two places to head left (south) along smoothed, slightly exposed slabs close to the bluffs above. Beware of yetis throwing stones down. Then, when you can, head for the lake aiming to go around it on the northern shore. The overflow stream leads to another lake area where there's a *phu* (herding station) with a good small rock shelter. From this point your route depends on your destination. For Thame continue to another *phu* where there's a real track down.

To Nangpa La

Despite the fact that yaks are used for the crossing of this pass into Tibet, it is no ordinary trek. It's tough, even for yaks, judging from the number of carcasses along the track. The trek from Gorak Shep to Everest Base Camp is a trifle compared to the slog over the Nangpa Glacier.

There's shelter and a spring at **Lunag/Lonak** (5070m/16,634ft), the only roofed buildings in either direction for a long way. From here the ground begins to get rougher and water can be hard to find. The scenery also becomes wild. At **Dzasampa** the ablation valley ends and it's time to cross into the middle of the glacier. Conditions are quite variable and it's not difficult to turn an ankle on the rocks which look firmly fixed to the slopes of verglas (glass-ice) but aren't. As you work your way up, concentrating on finding a safe route, the surrounding mountains begin taking on mythical shapes. The rubble gives way to a smooth white glacier with contouring hair-line cracks every 10m or so. The pass is marked in true Tibetan fashion and the view is enough to inspire any explorer. The nights up here are even colder than at the Six Lakes/Cho Oyu BC area.

Rolwaling

INTRODUCTION

Rolwaling means 'the furrow left by the plough', a very suitable name for this steep-walled valley. It's a rugged yet beautiful area inhabited by friendly Sherpas. Unlike their Khumbu cousins, they form a single isolated community with just one main village. Above the inhabited area the valley divides into several largely unexplored glaciated valleys dominated by formidable 6000m/19,685ft peaks. The highest mountain in the area is the holy Gauri Sankar, an ice-castle that can be admired even from Kathmandu.

Permits

Despite the dotted line marking the route on many trekking maps, the Trashi Labtsa (5755m/18,881ft) is a mountaineering challenge not a teahouse trekking route. It's far more dangerous than the Kongma La or Cho La. Officially only groups who have a permit to climb the trekking peaks Ramdung-Go (5930m/19,455ft) or Parcharmo (6273m/20,580ft) can trek in the Rolwaling valley and, for safety reasons, it's very unlikely that this valley will be opened to individuals.

Safety

It would be insane to try to cross the Trashi Labtsa by yourself. Several climbers have disappeared while alone in this area. Crevasses are a real danger and there are some areas in the icefall that may need an abseil. From Thame or Beding you will need at least three days' food and should carry reserves for two more days, plus enough fuel to melt snow or ice for water. For small parties ice-axes and crampons are needed by all, plus a rope with a few ice-screws and slings and gear for a short abseil.

Route planning and acclimatisation

The Rolwaling valley is a destination in its own right but most trekkers combine it with a visit to the Khumbu. Commercial trekking groups usually approach the valley from Dolakha or Barabise, attempt the trekking peak Ramdung-Go for acclimatisation, then cross the Trashi Labtsa. For proper acclimatisation 12 nights should be spent between Simigoan (2000m/6562ft) and the first night above 5000m/16,404ft. Since the highest village (Beding) is at 3700m/12,139ft this means many days camping. Independent trekkers will find crossing from the Khumbu to the Rolwaling makes more sense logistically than the other way around. From Thame (suitably acclimatised) it is possible to reach Dolakha/Barabise in just under a week and taking 8-9 days would be quite leisurely. Extra time will allow exploration of the valleys that head the Rolwaling and the wall of mountains to the south.

There are two route possibilities for starting (or finishing) the trek (see Map B: p204; Map C: p208). Dolakha (near Charikot) is a few km off the Jiri road and the walk to Simigoan takes 2-4 days following the Tamba Kosi. Barabise is on the Arniko Highway and from here to Simigoan takes 4-6 days. Between Simigoan and Beding there is also a choice of routes.

Note that the route is described crossing the pass from Thame to the Rolwaling and on to the road-heads at Dolakha/Charikot and Barabise. Information relevant to travelling in the reverse direction is also given, marked by '▲'.

Facilities

Since it's usually groups with tents that pass through here, there's no organised system of lodges but finding food and a place to stay at villages en route isn't difficult. However, there are a number of nights where camping is unavoidable and camping supplies are far more difficult to find than in the Khumbu.. Don't expect them to stock things like noodles, muesli and milk powder. It's best to carry in all you need and it's worth considering employing a porter unless you're approaching from the Khumbu.

THE ROLWALING VALLEY   [MAP A: p199]

Leaving Thame The trail leaves from the little lodge beside Thame Gompa (visible from Thame village). Take the upper tracks at each of the main junctions and you pass several small yersa deserted, except during summer.

Tengpo (4350m/14,271ft) is a couple of hours from the gompa. This large yersa has a number of minuscule two-storey houses. It's overlooked by the spectacular south faces of Teng Kangboche. There's ample spring water year round and plenty of places to camp. If, however, your party is well acclimatised then it's a better idea to camp closer to the pass.

The track continues but is smaller now. Looking back there's an unusual view of Ama Dablam with the fluted cirque and glacier of the Mingbo La clearly visible and with Makalu almost hidden behind Ama Dablam. There are good camping areas around the point from where the views of Ama Dablam start to disappear. Further up the track stays above the valley base and heads to the black rock spur (north-western side of the valley), where there are more camping places but these lack water after a spell of dry weather. Over and slightly down the other side of the moraine (the route does not follow the valley by the black rock ridge) there are several more rocky sites.

To the north is an icefall and to the left of this are several rough moraine ridges. Partially ascend one and head up, keeping to the left of the icefall. There should be a rough track to follow. Above are another two groups of campsites called **Ngole/Mgole** (5100m/16,732ft) with interesting overhanging rock shelters that porters may prefer to use rather than camping in the open.

▲ **Crossing in the reverse direction** Note that when coming down from the pass to these camps you must keep to the left and avoid descending to the obvious and large valley floor.

The Trashi Labtsa/Tesi Lapcha (5755m/18,881ft)
Access to the pass involves passing areas of frequent rockfall so an early morning start is best. In the early morning the rocks may still be frozen in place but as the sun hits them they expand, loosen and come thundering down. On a winter's day things might be stable but on a warm October afternoon it's like Russian roulette. It's said by the Sherpas that Lama Sange Dorje crossed this pass and the name Trashi Labtsa bestows a certain protection on travellers.

Onto the glacier There are two obvious routes. You can head left, down and under an icefall close to a large avalanche cone from

Rolwaling Valley

Parcharmo. However, the quicker and more popular route is simply to stay on moraine-covered ice and head up the ice valley. This could also be totally snow covered. Once up here the lay of the land becomes clearer. To the left, almost on Parcharmo's flanks, is a small diagonal icefall that fails to meet the smooth, white, almost flat glacier below. The upper part meets a rock wall that stretches from the right of the glacier to above you. Make for the point where the icefall and the wall meet, which involves an ascent of the steep unstable scree slope below the wall. Beware of heavy rockfalls here. Known as Tashi Phuk, there's some shelter for a camp under the wall. Sometimes stepping onto the icefall is easier. Groups often use a rope here although with crampons and good glacier conditions it may not be necessary.

From here the going is easier and it's a simple plod to the top of the pass. Crevasses are not normally a problem but if there has been a lot of snow recently then use a rope. Parcharmo's snow bulges rise to the left and you should watch out for falling rocks from Tengi Ragi Tau (6940m/22,769ft) to the right.

The pass (5755m/18,881ft) New vistas unfold at the pass which is a small flat rock rib running out from Tengi Ragi Tau/Kangi Tau marked by small cairns and a few prayer flags.

The descent is steeper than the ascent and requires care – there are several crevasses and a bergschrund. Head directly down, to where the glacier flattens out and meets the white Drolambao Glacier, divided by a line of moraine rubble. Once down stay close to, or on, the nearest medial moraine. Most groups camp somewhere around here but if you're making good time then you may be able to reach the next camp. Don't cross to the far side of the glacier – the route marked on the *Rowaling Himal* Schneider map is the 1950s route, now out of use, considered too dangerous and impractical.

From this point several routes have been used. Some trekkers have crossed the Drolambao Glacier before it starts to break up (and off!), then descended against the wall of Dragkar-Go but this requires some abseils and appears to descend a very dicey ramp. On my explorations, after descending some distance, I could not find a practical way down that did not need several ropes. Much better is to continue following the moraine, then cross over the broken ice to the left to another line of moraine debris formed by a glacier entering from Bigphera-Go Shar. This leads, sometimes easily, sometimes hazardously, off the glacier/ icefall onto solid rock. Conditions vary tremendously just here and at times it may require an abseil of up to 25m. Below, perhaps slightly to the right, is a massive lump of rock with obvious camping spots perched on top of it.

Ja Bua/Noisy Knob Camp (5000m/16,404ft) To reach this camp, follow the small diagonal gully below (not the bigger gully, filled with debris, under the seracs). Depending on conditions and your skill, a rope may be necessary here. This camp's a classic, perched almost under the falling seracs and above the Trakarding Glacier. A warm night will surround you with the roar of avalanches, the crash-tinkle of seracs and continual groans of the glacier ghosts.

▲ **Crossing in the reverse direction** This camp is situated on the large blunt knob of rock clearly visible projecting at the far end of the Drolambao Icefall, dividing it and the next icefall. It's shown on the *Rolwaling Himal* Schneider map. The route up the knob is from the Bigphera-Go Shar side.

The Trakarding Glacier

Continuing on, the most frequently used route is on the north side where there's a definite track but moving down on the south side is equally feasible. You could perhaps even head for the ablation valley early. If on the north side then once you're well down, the glacier cairns lead to the south side, while a vague path continues. Don't follow this path. You must cross to the south to traverse around the lake. The old northern route is extremely dangerous. Some of the steep moraines extend to sheer rock faces and are shelled with a virtually continuous hail of stones and rocks.

Once on the south side of the glacier, climb up on a rough track, eventually reaching the steep crumbling moraine (groups use a rope down here). There's grass and a big flat dust bowl with a track across it here. Then it's up again to avoid the huge bowling alley that drops into the head of the lake.

At the top, walk south-west a little before crossing among the boulders. The descent is steep but with great views of the Tsho Rolpa (4550m/14,927ft) and the mountains towering above it.

Down the ablation valley is **Kabug** with its small cave, water and pleasant camping area. **Sangma** and the areas below the lake are also pleasant camping areas, especially for a day or overnight trip up to Bombok (or higher) beside the Ripimo Shar Glacier. The bridge below Sangma is sometimes dismantled for winter.

Na (4183m/13,724ft)

After a few hours of pleasant walking down the valley, cross the bridge to Na. This is a large yersa, a summer village set under an incredible wall of mountains on the sunny northern side of the valley. It's deserted soon after the potatoes have been harvested, the fields left for the yaks and naks to pick over and add their dose of fertiliser.

It's a short half day's walk on the north bank to Beding, still with the spectacular Chobutse/Tsoboje (6689m/21,945ft) rising behind. The forests en route are striking for the size of the trees, even in areas that get very little sun. This is how the area around Namche, and even as high as Dingboche, must once have looked. As Beding becomes visible it is framed against one of the twin peaks of Gauri Sankar (7146m/23,445ft), or Jomo Tseringma as the Sherpas call it.

Beding (3700m/12,139ft)

Beding is a picturesque cluster of buildings centred around the gompa, with a well-kept stupa in the river bed. Although it's the only real village in the upper Rolwaling Valley, it's not permanently occupied. During the coldest winter months the entire population huddles down in the gunsas (Gyabrug to Nyimare). In the summer, some villagers move up to cultivate potatoes at Na and others roam higher with their grazing yaks.

The people seem to manage their village well without outside interference or government offices but there's no health post. There is a school, opened in 1972 by Hillary and bridges erected with Japanese aid. The way of life here has changed less than for the Khumbu Sherpas in recent years. Trade with Tibet has to some extent been replaced with trekking-related jobs here too but since only groups pass through, there are no trekking lodges. (Nevertheless almost every resident will more than willingly put a few people up in style.) Local people find employment as sirdars, cooks and especially as high-altitude sherpas on expeditions. Lowland porters sometimes quit en masse on the Trashi Labtsa so there's often lots of portering work for local people. The Rolwaling Sherpas are not as poor as Sherpas in non-tourist areas and the relative wealth has manifested itself in modernisation of many houses, expanding them to Khumbu proportions.

Trading with Tibet is still carried out on a small scale for salt, tsampa, yaks and naks, dried meat and Chinese manufactured goods. The trade route is over the Manlung La (5616m/18,425ft) which is reached

---

Gauri Sankar/Jomo Tseringma (7146m/23,445ft)

This twin-peaked mountain is revered by both Hindus and Sherpas. For the Hindus, Sankar (the north summit) represents the god Shiva who is married to the goddess Gauri, the south summit. For the Tibetan Buddhists, it is the palace of the white goddess Tseringma, and is second in importance only to Mt Kailash in Tibet.

From the Rolwaling Valley it's a reclusive mountain, barely visible. But from the distance its omnipotence and beauty are impressive and it can even be seen from Kathmandu on a clear day. In the climbing world it was also revered as one of the last virgin 7000er's. It was not until spring 1979 that the higher summit was conquered, and the south summit followed in the autumn. For an eloquent description of this second climb read *Sacred Summits* by Peter Boardman.

up the impossible-looking slabs a little to the north of Beding. The glaciated pass is most frequently used in summer and affords amazing views of the mountain known to the Sherpas as Jomo Garu (7181m/ 23,559ft). This beautiful peak is more commonly known as Menlungtse, the name Shipton gave it in 1951.

Routes to Simigoan There are two routes: the direct lower winter route via Gyalche (a short day's walk down but tough coming up), or the high scenic Daldung La route (for which it's best to allow two days). Snow in winter virtually precludes using the high route because the track is mostly in shaded areas where the snow is slow to melt. In addition, except in the early part of the season, this route is uninhabited until Simigoan.

To the Dzigri Khola, the boundary of the high Rolwaling Valley, both routes follow the same trail. The path is sunny and pleasant, always on the north bank, sometimes through forest, and, lower, sometimes in stunted bamboo. Prayer flags mark the wooden bridge (3200m/10,499ft).

The low route The trail, narrower now, continues on the north bank to cross the Tongmarnang, a stream originating directly from Gauri Sankar. There are numerous cairns along this part of the route. A little further down, the trail crosses to the south bank and starts its long roller-coaster ride to Simigoan. There are infrequent small campsites and a few Simigoan yersas: simple wood and bamboo shelters.

▲ **Trekking in the reverse direction** The high route is especially rewarding on the way in, with stunning views of Gauri Sankar and perhaps even a glimpse of Menlungtse. It's also an introduction to altitude, and a rather harsh one for many people but relief should come when crossing the Rolwaling Chhu. For this reason it is preferable to stay at Shakpa (2650m/8694ft), rather than Simigoan, and it reduces the climb the next day over the Daldung La (3976m/13,044ft).

SIMIGOAN TO DOLAKHA/CHARIKOT   [MAP B: p204]
Simigoan (2000m/6562ft)
This is a large agricultural village, spread way down the hillside: Sherpa in the higher parts and Tamang in the lower section. There is a campsite but signs giving directions to it are only along the route coming up to Simigoan. Alternatively, camping by the gompa offers superb views (but rubbish left by groups is a problem here). Although there's no real lodge, the local people offer accommodation.

To leave Simigoan descend through the village, pass the small police check post with its tiny sign in English (easy to miss early in the

morning) and continue down. At the edge of a flattish cultivated area is a junction almost overlooking cliffs. It's worth asking someone around here to check that you're on the correct trail. Go right (north) here on what may look like the slightly less used trail. This descends steeply, writhing down a steep wide gully to the suspension bridge across the Bhote Kosi at 1520m/4987ft. As you cross the bridge you can see the site of the old bridge upstream.

On the west bank, the trail to the north leads to Lamabagar/ Chhogsham and the police post controlling traffic to Tibet. The trail to the south leads (in just a minute) to Chetchet and a teashack. The route down follows the impressive Bhote Kosi (Tibetan River) with the path, in places, held together by concrete. Further along the valley, the Bhote Kosi becomes the Tamba Kosi (Copper River). The tide marks on the river rocks show the height of the torrent that rages through during the monsoon. For this reason there's a second higher route to Gongar, used when the river is at its most dangerous, which branches up half an hour below Chetchet. Around here the waterfalls and the gorge are particularly impressive.

Gongar (1400m/4593ft)
This is just a small village but tea is available. Around the corner, a few hundred metres upstream, is the new bridge across the Gongar Khola. On the main part of the far bank the trail divides: the lower path passing a huge house just below is for Charikot, and the upper path goes to Barabise (see trail description on p206).

The trail roughly follows the river, sometimes traversing and sometimes with short climbs to avoid bluffs. Jagat is approximately the halfway point to the old suspension bridge at Manthale. Here, particularly on the east bank, are some shops and frequently fruit, usually *suntala* (mandarin oranges) can be found. The valley starts to widen out although en route to Suri Dhoban there are still some narrow traverses that preclude the use of animals instead of porters.

Suri Dhoban/Dhovan (1020m/3346ft) has teashacks and bhattis
and is a normal overnight stopping place for Rolwaling Sherpas heading to or from Kathmandu. Across the fine suspension bridge up-valley is one of the trails for the route over the Yalung La, up the Khare Khola. The route down passes a post office little bigger than a postage stamp. The trail continues more or less along the river bank and after a cluster of houses crosses to the west bank on a suspension bridge. At the Sangawa Khola is a small but often busy village with a bhatti or two. The trail that zig-zags up the hill goes to Laduk and is heavily used. Take the suspension bridge across the Sangawa Khola instead and continue south.

Piguti/Biguti On the west bank of the river, this trading town even has a bank (no foreign exchange department) and a few Nepalese-style lodges. The trail continues south, staying on the west bank of the river (not marked on the Schneider map). The path widens (it's more like a road here) and runs through fine forests for a short time.

Malepu (880m/2887ft) The village is by the bridge across a small khola and has lodges and shops. It's a regular overnight stop since, with tired legs, the climb to Dolakha and Charikot can be soul-destroying in the afternoon sun.

The ridge is tough and unrelenting for the climb of almost 800m. There are several paths leading off to villages but the trail heading up is usually the correct one and the volume of traffic heading to the town means you're unlikely to get lost.

Dolakha (1650m/5413ft)

This is a large, beautiful and historic town with a few stupas and some flagstone-paved streets. Once it was a main town on the trading route from Tibet to the Indian plains and it still has a Saturday market. Becoming a roadhead has increased prosperity here but not ravaged the town as has happened elsewhere.

Dolakha, sometimes also called Charikot, and the new Charikot further up the ridge share the title of headquarters for the Dolakha District, which stretches from here to the Tibetan border. Consequently there are a number of government departments and there's a hospital being built, funded by Korea, which will be staffed by a Korean doctor and two nurses. At present it's open only two days a week.

▲ **Starting at Dolakha** If the bus you were on was heading to Jiri you'll be dropped off at Charikot. Depending on the time, you can either start trekking along the 3.5km dirt road to Dolakha, or stay in Charikot. Both have simple lodges and great views of the dominant Gauri Sankar and Menlungtse slightly to the east.

At the group pace, Simigoan is about four days' walk away, or a quicker 2-3 days. Returning in a hurry, two days is plenty of time. For the first expeditions, walking from Kathmandu to the Khumbu or Rolwaling, Dolakha was six days into the trek.

GONGAR TO BARABISE [MAP B: p204; MAP C: p208]

This is one of the classic routes which has been superseded by the Jiri road. As a route into the Rolwaling, it still has advantages because it offers a degree of helpful acclimatisation. It's also little changed since the early days of trekking and is very much a route suited to the expedition approach or to individual trekkers happy to eat dal bhat and learn some Nepali. Simigoan to Barabise is a pleasant four day walk including perhaps a half day rest at Bigu Gompa. It could be shortened to two-and-a-bit days by strong legs in a hurry.

Routes There are several possible routes from the Bhote/Tamba Kosi to Bigu Gompa and on to Barabise. See the *Lapchi Kang* Schneider map. The route described here leaves the Bhote/Tamba Kosi after crossing the Gongar Khola on a good trail that is not marked on the Schneider map.

Leaving Gongar Take the upper of the equal-sized paths, heading up and around on the south bank of the Gongar Khola. Shortly after a stupa is a small but interesting Hindu shrine. Although virtually nothing is marked on the Schneider map, this is a well-populated, mainly Tamang area. The trail passes through several villages during the several hours to Dulang (1900m/6234ft). Around here, since there are so many small trails, it pays to repeatedly ask the way. Ask for Bigu or Bigu Gompa, otherwise villagers tend to direct you to Laduk and the slightly shorter route out to Charikot.

Bulung (2150m/7054ft)
This sprawling village is a few hours further on. You may meet the pleasant high school teacher or some of the friendly children, many of whom are more interested in practising their English than in the usual begging. Bulung has some shops but since few visitors pass through they are not obvious. You'll need to ask a villager where they are and, if you need accommodation, asking around will soon turn something up. On leaving the village there are superb views of Gauri Sankar.

All the main trails lead to **Laduk** (1700m/5577ft) which, once out of Bulung and around the major ridge, is visible below. Stay high on the terraces and look for the large high school that sits above Laduk. The main trail continues directly from the school and is the one that contours and descends slightly. Laduk is a large centre with many shops. The porters prefer to walk here from Charikot rather than Barabise since the Tamba Kosi route is considered shorter.

Continue contouring and descend, then drop to the Thuran Khola. After climbing steeply, head around the ridge on an easy-to-follow trail.

Chilangka (1900m/6234ft)
This little village spreads above and below the main trail with little to offer except a shop beside the path. Contour, staying fairly high, and cross the Jorong Khola on a log bridge. Then head up and out onto the hillside and a pretty forest. Contour to **Loding/Lading** (1800m/5904ft) and after it reach a prominent view-point. Look for Bigu Gompa: a mass of prayer flags. The best

route from here is to wander upstream along the east bank of the Kothale Khola and cross on a major suspension bridge although there are some temporary bridges.

Numerous trails lead through the villages stacked up the hillside so ask for the gompa, sometimes also called Tashi Gompa. It is also possible to by-pass the gompa, although it's one of the main reasons taking this route, by dropping to Amatal and continuing up the valley on the south bank of the Amatal Khola.

Bigu Gompa (2510m/8235ft)

This nunnery is impressively-located amid prayer flags and huge juniper trees at the top of the village. The gompa is an island of Buddhism in the surrounding Hindu area. Many of the nuns are Tibetan refugees, and some are very recent arrivals. There are some beautiful paintings in this gompa and the setting is very pleasant. It's possible to stay at the tidy, smoke-free guest house. Below, in Bigu village there's a paper factory that sells its products in Kathmandu.

Leaving the gompa, it's a fairly gentle descent passing through an area ravaged by forest fires, to the distinctive roofed bridge across a tributary. There are many water-driven flour mills above and this heralds **Ruphtang** (2300m/7546ft). It boasts a teahouse just up from the bridge and more teashacks a little further on. These are the last facilities en route to the pass, still a 1000m/3281ft haul away.

The Tinsang La (3319m/10,889ft)

The sometimes eroded and elusive trail stays on the north bank of the Amatal Khola. In the kharkas and forests of tall firs maintaining your sense of direction may not be easy. Just before the crest of the Tinsang La is beautiful flat pasture used for grazing in summer, and dotted with roofless huts in the fall and winter. It's a good place to camp with a reasonably good water supply.

The panorama here stretches from Gauri Sankar (7146m/23,445ft) and the closer rock cone of Jobo/Chobo Bamare (5927m/19,445ft) on the Tibetan border to Numbur (6959m/ 22,831ft) in the east, the Yul Lha (holy mountain) of Shorong. Unlike the gentle ascent, the route down to Dolangsa seems unrelentingly steep though it takes only an hour or less.

Dolangsa (2500m/8202ft)

This is an extensive village resting on a large flat area. There are a few bhattis and teashacks above and below the gompa. Winter here is a time of crafts: knitting and weaving bamboo mats and dokos.

There are numerous ways down to Barabise but more widely used is the route on the northern side of the Sun Kosi via Budipa. Once across a few streams, down a ridge and across another stream you come to the village of Kabre. Stay on the large well-defined trail on the north bank and cross a large tributary to Budipa.

Budipa (1200m/3937ft) There are some teahouses and shops in this village. You can stay either here or in Simle, the next village, so as to avoid having to spend the night in Barabise. The trail from Budipa contours above the river and around a sharp ridge before descending into Barabise, and the mess of modern civilisation.

Barabise (820m/2690ft)

Big, dirty and crowded, Barabise is a trading post for many Chinese goods that have found their way over from Tibet via the Arniko Highway or been smuggled in along the older trading routes.

▲ **Starting from Barabise** Route-finding for the first few hours is difficult so it's a very good idea to hire a local porter. As well as acting as a guide, he (or she) will enable you to start with a light load in a hot area with a 2400m/7874ft climb to the Tinsang La. Note that if you camp just below this pass (a few days later) you're likely to feel the altitude as a result of the rapid ascent. By the time you reach Bigu Gompa, however, all symptoms should have cleared.

Dudh Kosi to Sanam

KHARE

PHAKDING

Kusum Kangguru
6369m

TANGNAG

LAKE

Mera
6476m

SEE ALSO
MAPS 6 & 7
142 & 151

LUKLA

SURKE

PUIYAN

Dudh Kosi

Zatrwala/
Cheterala
4580 m

BUPSA
2350m

Panch Pokhari
(WATER)

SMALL PASS

KHARIKHOLA

SHUBUCHE

PANGKONGMA

NO WATER

SatuLa/Pangumla
3173m

GAI KHARKA

NAJI DINGMA

Surkie La
3085 m

KIRAUNLE

BOKSOM
GOMPA

Inuku/Hinku Khola

BUNG

GUDEL

Hongu Khola

216 MAP E

GOMPA

LIMSOLAR/DIURE

N

MAP D

SANAM

0   5Km

Khumbu to the Arun

INTRODUCTION

Nowhere in Nepal are the differences between ethnic groups so striking as on the walk out of the Khumbu to the Arun Kosi and Hille. Although the Sherpa and Rai peoples are both of Mongolian stock and speak Tibeto-Burmese languages, the fact that they live at different altitudes influences many areas of their lives. The Sherpas inhabit the higher regions, growing potatoes and barley or wheat, and have herds of cattle. Throughout the year they wear heavy dark woollen clothing. In contrast the ancient Rai people occupy land at a lower level growing rice, millet and maize. It's warm enough for cotton clothes and they often harvest two crops a year in the frost-free climate.

The route

Most trekkers will choose to walk from the Khumbu to Tumlingtar/ Hille/Basantpur, so the route is described in this direction. The reason for this is that the trekking is slightly tougher than the Jiri to Namche section – the hills are steeper and the lodges are spaced further apart. Being fitter and more used to the trekking lifestyle makes it easier.

It's quite possible to do this trek in the other direction beginning at Tumlingtar or Hille/Basantpur, although some previous trekking experience is useful. The hills to be climbed are initially more challenging than when coming in from Jiri. The first pass you come to is, in fact, the highest pass on the route.

The route to the Arun leaves the main Dudh Kosi trekking highway between Puiyan and Kharikhola to go east to Pangkongma. Then it crosses a series of passes: the Satu La (3173m/10,410ft), the Surkie La (3085m/10,121ft) and the Salpa Bhanjyang (3349m/10,987ft) and they all, of course, have deep valleys in between them. The most frequently trekked route then heads to Tumlingtar (for flights out) or to the road. In late 1991 the Hille road was extended to Basantpur giving a choice of two routes from Tumlingtar, of roughly equal length. To Hille the track follows the large Arun Kosi then climbs, while for Basantpur you climb out of Tumlingtar for the ridge walk. The other possibility is to head to Dingla and Bhojpur airport.

Timing

The amount of time required for this walk varies considerably. Namche to Hille/Basantpur can take 10 to 12 days. Walking in, with the usual initial lack of fitness, may even add another day. Flying from Tum-lingtar reduces this by two days.

There are no places en route that warrant a full day's stop, although this is no reason not to spend a day or two relaxing on the way, or have some short walking days. On the way out the super-fit and hill-hard-ened could reduce Namche to Hille to five and a half very tough days.

Facilities

Between the Dudh Kosi and the Arun there's a scattering of lodges, and family homes masquerading as lodges, that offer food and a bed. These have sprung up only recently and their varied standards add to the plea-sure of trekking along this route. Do not expect apple pie or pizza here. In fact, don't expect even a menu in some places, just a share of what the family is eating. Some lodges have no special accommodation; you sleep in the same room as the family (a sleeping-mat can be useful). Others are modelled on the lodges on the Jiri-Namche route. There are also a number of stone shelters, mainly used by porters who cannot afford to pay for accommodation, so camping is an alternative.

The Arun Valley itself has few facilities specifically for trekkers. Instead there are many bhattis and tea shops catering for the multitude of porters that transport goods up and down the valley. Often, families curious about foreigners will invite trekkers to stay. Sleeping out on the banks of the river under the stars is another possibility. Early starts are easier to accomplish, leaving the hot midday for a siesta and swim-ming. The nights are warm at this altitude so a sleeping bag and a piece of plastic sheeting are all that's necessary.

The route description below follows the trail in the Lukla to Hille direction. At the end of each section there are notes for trekkers walk-ing in the opposite direction (Hille to Lukla), marked '▲'.

DUDH KOSI TO SANAM   [MAP D: p210]

From the main trail to Pangkongma The main Namche to Khari-khola trail can be left at Puiyan, Bupsa (possibly the best option) or Kharikhola. It is about half a day's walk to Pangkongma (sometimes called Pangum) from these places. If you're very fit you may be able to reach Naji Dingma from Bupsa in a day, or make Bung from Pangkongma or Shubuche. For most people, from Pangkongma or Shubuche to Naji Dingma is a long day and lunch should be brought from Shubuche.

Route from Puiyan Ten minutes north of Puiyan is a big boulder that makes an attractive view-point. From here the several trails south of Puiyan are visible. You can also see the rocky gully that the trail traverses. Just visible above is a trail which can be reached by a short scramble up the rocks and a slip to the path. This is part of the old route between Puiyan and Kharikhola, via Kharte. The present direct trail to Bupsa was constructed in the early 1980s. Head over the ridge and the Khari La (3081m/10,108ft) and down to the distinctive two-storey white house (a couple hours in total). Five minutes below is the main trail leading to Pangkongma, heading up the valley.

Route from Bupsa Go straight up the ridge behind the Solu Khumbu Trekkers' Lodge on a mainly mud trail. At the mani wall further up, just before the two-storey white house, turn right and contour or drop to the main trails ahead and below. The Bupsa-Pangkongma trail is narrow but well-used and contours with some ups and downs. A couple of days before the Namche Saturday market the trail is crowded with heavily laden porters heading for the bazaar.

Route from Kharikhola The locals recommend going via Bupsa, although there is a direct trail from Kharikola after the maze of fields.

Pangkongma
Two approximately parallel mani walls mark the entrance to this village. Walk to the left and head up to a group of four houses, two of which are lodges – the **Himalayan Trekkers' Lodge** and the **Trekkers' Kitchen**. The village has a wonderfully-located 1970 Hillary school and a gompa.

▲ Pangkongma to Bupsa Pick up the trail at the parallel mani walls just below the lodges and head north-west. Bupsa can be seen on the ridge slightly north and Kharikhola below on the southern wall of the valley. On the far side of the valley you may perhaps be able to make out the trail heading up to the Trakshindo La.

Over the Satu/Pangum La (3173m/10,410ft)
Follow more mani walls up to the trail. The pass is about half an hour further up. The views are spectacular (if you can find an unobstructed view-point) and across the valley it's possible to see Naji Dingma, about two-thirds of the way up the next ridge.

From the pass keep to the left and after half an hour of gentle descent you reach the settlement of Shubuche which has two simple lodges and a shop.

▲ In the opposite direction Take the left track one minute past the teahouses of Shubuche, when going up.

The trail continues straight to the end of the ridge, crossing a fence or two then drops off, turning slightly south. It's a very steep, knee-jerking descent to the suspension bridge. Once across the Inukhu Khola at 1850m/6069ft, there is a pleasant picnic or camping spot with water available.

The long ascent begins. The first habitation is Gai Kharka. Although this means 'cow pasture' the area is now under cultivation. Apart from a new water tap there are no facilities for trekkers. Half way through the settlement head to the north or left side of the cultivation. The climb continues relentlessly to **Naji Dingma** a flat grassy knoll at 2650m/8694ft. Here, among the few houses are two tea houses and a small shop.

Over the Surkie/Sipki La (3085m/10,121ft)
The ascent continues on a damp and sometimes icy trail, through bamboo groves for an hour or so. At the pass the trail veers left and drops through a tangle of forest where it can be difficult to follow. If you lose the trail, descend for a few minutes looking for a path heading southeast. This drops gently, contouring slightly, for several hours.

After several mani walls and a couple of prominent chortens **Boksom Gompa** can be seen, ringed by tall trees. The gompa is almost in ruins. The main trail by-passes it and most of the spread-out village of Khiraunle, which has no shops or lodges. The trail continues southeast and slowly loses altitude. Don't cross the obvious valley below the gompa.

There are several shelters along here that could be used for camping. The village of Gudel can be seen on the distant main valley wall while Bung, still a few hours away, is directly opposite, although you can't see it.

Bung
This is a large and rich Rai village which spreads over the hillside. The main trail is possible to follow, through a small ravine then to a school, although it's easy to get lost. There are now three lodges: at the top, middle and bottom of the village.

This region is known for its *tungba*, an alcoholic brew served in a tall wooden vessel and drunk using a bamboo straw. Boiling water is poured over fermented millet to make this warming drink. If there's a really big celebration it's served in a barrel, everybody using their own straw. The more mature the millet, the smoother the taste with a special vintage (rarely served to tourists) being about a year old.

From Bung it's a short day's walk to Sanam or one very long and tough day to the next village which is over the pass. It's possible to camp after Sanam but not on top of the pass since there is no water there.

From Bung to Gudel Leaving the lodges at Bung means following a maze of small paths but luckily some junctions have signposts. After some clumps of bamboo there are many tracks and slips but most lead to the suspension bridge that crosses the Hongu Khola at about 1280m/4199ft. Take the left fork after crossing the bridge for the steep ascent to **Gudel**. The narrow path leads to fields, then past a few houses. Follow the stream when you reach it. As usual there are numerous ways through the village but aim for the ridge up to your right or southeast. Higher in the village head for the mani wall on this ridge. Gudel has no real facilities but a few people readily offer tea and food.

▲ **From Gudel to Bung** From Gudel one can see the trail from the bridge zig-zagging upwards. The smart three-storey house in the lowest small cluster of buildings is the **Sagarmatha Guest House**. The lodges have signs that are visible only to people coming from Namche, so you have to look back at each house to spot the lodge signs. Also note the large stream north of Bung: for several hours the trail above Bung stays approximately parallel to this but about half to one km away. Leaving Bung it's easy to get lost as there are numerous trails, but all lead close to Boksom Gompa (several hours away) and its distinctive ring of trees. The main trail is about half a km above this and soon passes some mani walls and chortens.

From Gudel to Sanam
The wide trail climbs gently but steadily, hugging the steep valley wall. Once the mani walls are out of sight, you come to a major junction and for a change you must follow the trail that contours, not climbs. At the next two major junctions however, take the upper trails.

Several hours from Gudel are two hamlets variously called **Gompa** and **Limsolar** or **Diure**. The people are friendly, offering tea and food, and on the way out is the **Alpine Club Lodge**. Further up there are several trail junctions that could be confusing, but they are simply old and new paths that rejoin a little later.

Sanam is half an hour further up the trail. The people are hospitable here, too, although poor and there are several 'lodges' (really just houses) where you can stay. Delicious dairy products are often available here. Note that from Sanam to Phedi is a long day.

SANAM TO TUMLINGTAR   [MAP E: p216; MAP F: p218]
Over the Salpa Bhanjyang (3349m/10,987ft)
This pass is a half day's walk from Sanam and is not at the obvious head of the valley but up a small valley to the right or south. Note that in dry conditions the Lidung Khola is often the last source of water until well over the pass.

Up the side valley, the track steadily gains altitude and passes two mani walls. A large weathered chorten graces the crest of the pass and marks the end of Sherpa areas. There are good views here but even better ones can be had by climbing to the south for a short distance.

The top part of the pass receives snow during the winter and the locals may wait several days after a fall before crossing. If the track is covered by snow, the route can be slippery and difficult to follow.

Going down the other side is easy. Follow the stone track that curves left, and continue roughly in the same direction, eventually to the new settlement of Kariti. It is possible to stay here. Water can be found to the north. Then the thin track climbs to the crest of the obvious razorback ridge. The descent down the other side is steep, equally sharp and often waterless although there are several stone shelters. A few hours down, still on the main ridge, is **Thulofokte/Jo Bare** with a few pleasant teahouses. Phedi is another hour or so down at the base of the ridge.

▲ **Crossing the Salpa Pass in reverse** It's a very tough day from Phedi to Sanam so an early start is required. It's not a bad idea to see if you can find a porter to help for this stretch, especially if you are not so fit.

Route-finding can be difficult after cresting the sharp ridge hours above Phedi but after the small flat areas the trail is obvious. Descending from the pass is easier. Follow the stream down and at the main valley, well down, the track to Sanam is on the north bank of the Lidung Khola. There's a camping place here. Later the trail starts traversing as Sanam is well above this river.

Phedi (1700m/5577ft)
Virtually at the confluence of two rivers, Phedi boasts two simple lodges. Take particular care of your possessions in the Sherpa-run lodge. From here on, with the exception of Tumlingtar, there are no lodges especially for trekkers, although you will receive plenty of offers for simple accommodation.

Phedi to the Arun Valley
Walking quickly it takes seven hours to reach Belawa Besi; ten hours at a more normal pace. The trail crosses the stream on your left, then climbs a little before crossing the main river and meandering between paddies and fields. It's possible to stay on the southern bank but there are trails on both sides of the river.

Later, at a major confluence joining from the south, is a growing trading post. Beyond this the trail down also stays mainly on the southern bank of the winding Irkhuwa Khola. Much later you climb a steep hill to two pipal trees; the *suntala* sellers often do good business here. From here the main track goes to **Dingla**, climbing, dropping and climbing again.

From Dingla there is a main trail to Tumlingtar but this town is easily bypassed for a more direct route to the Arun River. To do this leave the main track about 100m past the pipal trees and head across the paddies and fields to a cluster of houses. From here on it pays to ask directions frequently because there is a multitude of trails that look as if they could be correct. The basic idea is to gain a little height then contour around the blunt ridge, dropping and continuing around. The locals will usually point you in the right direction. You are heading for the bridge that crosses the Chirkhuwa Khola at **Balawa Besi**. You can stay here.

▲ **Coming up from Balawa Besi** Route-finding is not easy, walking from this direction. Since there is a considerable altitude gain with two long hard days, hiring a porter (at least for this section) is a wise idea.

After crossing the bridge turn right, parallel to the Arun, then the long climb starts. Head along and up, and repeatedly ask the locals for the track to Phedi and Salpa Bhanjyang. Once you find the main trail, and the two pipal trees, following the trail is easier.

Several hours up-river there's a major tributary to cross. On the other side look for an iron-roofed building in a cluster of others and cross to this, then follow the river bank. The track divides one minute later: take the immediate right turn, the slightly smaller path. The potential for getting temporarily lost around this area is high. This trail, still staying on the southern bank of the Irkhuwa Khola, leads to Phedi.

Dingla to Bhojpur The airport at Bhojpur is an alternative to Tumlingtar, although better as an entry point. The trail between Bhojpur and Dingla involves several ascents and descents and takes 6-10 hours.

THE ARUN VALLEY

Down to Tumlingtar

From here until the approach to Hille, the trail has few hills, at least no major climbs. The track now moves closer to the Arun and half an hour down crosses the river at Kartiki Ghat. Among the simple local lodges the suspension bridge is surprisingly easy to miss. Here a woman collects the bridge toll – and more if you are willing to pay. Between the bridge and Tumlingtar there are few tea shops and the track is narrow, considering the amount of traffic that passes by. The route uses the river banks and shore at every opportunity before rising to the plain where Tumlingtar is situated. It's still at least an hour's walk across the plain to Tumlingtar.

Tumlingtar (300m/985ft)
The string of hotels here cater to the locals arriving and leaving by plane, although a couple can do pancakes for foreigners that want them. If you're not flying out there's no compelling reason to stay the night here. However, if you are flying, find out what time the RNAC office opens and book or reconfirm your flight.

If you have a day or two to spare, Chainpur (see Map G p220) is only three or four hours' walk away. Chainpur brass pots, pans and dishes are made here. These are well-known for their quality and can be found in Kathmandu and even further afield. The brass comes from Singapore (and has done for the last 70 or so years) and is worked by skilled crafts' people. Since brass is valuable and not the lightest material to transport every effort is made to recycle old and dented objects. Some are salvaged from villages up to five days' walk away.

▲ **Starting from Tumlingtar** Arriving here from Kathmandu is like stepping back in time. The runway is grass-covered with a simple fence to keep the cows and goats away. The hotels are virtually the only buildings around so getting lost is difficult. The majority of the hotels are grouped along the main track. A couple more are slightly northeast by the pits dug for the manufacture of mud bricks. If your flight gets in early you could walk south for a swim (see Map G, p220) or even begin your trek. The main path heads north from the hotels and passes to the left, or west, side of the brick pits. The track is straight, passing the occasional house and shop. Once off the plateau the next significant point is the suspension bridge crossing the Arun, a short half-day's walk away. It may be possible to stay here at Kartiki Ghat although Balawa Besi is only a few minutes away.

TUMLINGTAR TO HILLE   [MAP G: p220]

Along the Arun Kosi
The Tumlingtar plain finishes with a descent to the Sabbhaya Khola, and a delightful spot for a siesta and swim. The water is refreshing and usually crystal clear. After the bridge there is a short climb over a ridge then you mainly follow the river bank again.

As with this tributary of the Arun, and several others further down, you have the option of crossing on the suspension bridge, or if the stream is low, wading across. Since the path to the bridge is difficult to follow you may well miss it and end up wading across anyway.

Mangmaya (250m/746ft)

At the Mangmaya Khola the trail heads away from the Arun to the small village beside the bridge. It's a long day's walk from Tumlingtar but there are a few simple bhattis here where trekkers occasionally stay when intending to climb the hill above during the cool of the morning.

Across the bridge take the trail to the left, although it's not very obvious, which leads up the hill; the trail to the right does not go to Hille. Now the route climbs out of the hot valley, through many villages where you can get hot and cold drinks. The path divides and rejoins many times on the way up. If the weather is clear, the views of Makalu and the surrounding peaks are inspiring. After gaining a ridge the trail levels off as it nears **Pakribas** and the British agricultural research and development project. The town of Pakribas is ugly; it's obvious that the roadhead is not far away.

Hille (1850m/6069ft)

It's back to the world of roads and shops loaded with wares trucked in. First impressions of this town may not be pleasing although after the peace of a few weeks' trekking, any town is liable to induce some form of culture-shock.

The last bus down leaves about 2 pm and usually goes as far as Dharan. If you've missed the 4 pm Dharan to Kathmandu bus, head for Itahari where many buses stop on the way to Kathmandu. An alternative is to go to the pleasant hill-town of Dhankuta, which the main road by-passes, and spend the night there.

▲ **Starting from Hille** If you've travelled non-stop from Kathmandu, you'll probably have arrived in mid-afternoon and feel a little the worse for wear. There are some lodges scattered along the road, nothing special but pleasant enough.

The start of the main trail to the Arun is not obvious. It begins at the top end of town, descending through what is almost a rubbish pit lined with dirty tea shops before opening out towards Pakribas. Ask directions frequently or follow a heavily laden porter. This is a major staging point for the goods heading up valley so there are numerous shops competing for the same market and the flow of porters is almost continuous. The goods are destined for villages scattered over a wide area and some are even traded across the border with Tibet. It's worthwhile hiring a porter (ask around at the lodges) for the hot stretch to Tumlingtar.

Trekking to Makalu Base Camp

INTRODUCTION

The route into Makalu Base Camp is frequently used by expeditions and a busy year sees up to five mountaineering groups attempting to climb the world's fifth highest peak. Now that the Barun-Makalu National Park has been set up trekking traffic is increasing. Lodges are developing to cater for individual trekkers but with large gaps in the facilities it's a long way off being a teahouse trek. Also, in contrast with many of the longer popular treks in Nepal visiting Makalu usually means retracing your steps – apart from a serious mountaineering alternative.

Safety and planning

This is not an easy or safe trek to do alone. Go with a few friends, experienced porters and, if there are more than a few members in your group, a sirdar or guide. From the last village to the shop at the Base Camp area is a five-day walk with absolutely no food or facilities available in between. The scenery around the Base Camp area is unbelievably stunning and once acclimatised there is much ground to explore. Five days up here would not be too long for an ambitious group. All this will require lots of food and porters to carry it.

The route after Tashigoan is not dangerous in good conditions but you should bear in mind that you're a long way from help if you need it. The trail crosses a series of small 4000m 'passes' with different names: the Shipton La, the Keke La, the Tutu La or La Cherma (Big Hill). It then drops into the Barun Khola valley at about 3000m/9843ft before gently ascending. If there has been snow (usually in March or early April) it's a tough walk in both directions and since several places in the Barun Valley are exposed to avalanches it's sometimes impassible. It takes a strong, well equipped party and some luck to battle spring snow. Avoid this season if you're not properly prepared and ready to take the chance of not getting through.

The best time to go is during the finest weather, October to the end of December. From mid-December there is a risk of a snow dump but this is rarely deep or too troublesome. During the winter months, January and February, the savage cold combined with mounting snow renders the route impractical. If there have been successive heavy falls this snow might only clear around mid-April. Trekking any time before that there is a very real risk of porters getting frostbitten, a risk simply not worth taking. During April and May the weather is inconsistent, sometimes gloriously fine or afternoon cloud rolling up the valley, and sometimes there is continual cover. Bear in mind also that the walk in, until the crossing of the Arun after Num, is at a low altitude in a famously hot area of Nepal and even in December the sweat will drip.

Sensible acclimatisation planning is difficult on this trek; use the planner below.

Day No	Altitude guide	Actual altitude	Itinerary and night stop
01	-	1000m	Fly to Tumlingtar, trek to Khandbari
02	-	1800-2000m	camp
03	-	1500m	Num
04	-	1500m	Seduwa
05	2-3000m	2000m	Tashigoan
06	2-3000m	3500m	Kauma - pass camp
07	3000m	3500m	Mumbak
08	3300m	3000m	Nhe Kharka - grassy camp
09	3600m	4700m	Shershon
10	3900m	5000m	Makalu Base Camp

The altitude strikes first at Kauma and Mumbak but at least there is relief descending to Nhe Kharka. The big and dangerous jump is to Shershon. Unfortunately, there are no suitable group camping places en route, although a small party could camp between them. A suggestion is to spend two nights at Shershon and on the free day descend a substantial altitude for a picnic. Note that AMS often hits on the second night after a large increase in altitude.

Maps
The most widely-available map for this area is the Mandala blue dycline *Dhankuta to Kanchenjunga, Mt Everest, Makalu and Arun Valley*. However it is very unreliable in places in particular for the entire route up the Barun Khola: the trail and the named points are partly on the other side of the khola. For the areas above the Base Camp, the National Geographic *Mount Everest* map or the Schneider *Khumbu Himal* are useful.

Supplies and facilities
• **Hille** This town is a typical roadhead with throngs of porters loading up with a huge variety of goods. Biscuits, noodles, milk powder, rice, sugar and other foodstuffs are widely available as at any Nepali market town. There are a few simple lodges suitable for trekkers.
• **Tumlingtar** There are some hotels catering to trekkers here but in the shops the variety of produce is not as good as at Hille. All staples are, however, available.

• **Khandbari** For provisions, this town is similar to Tumlingtar. It is the district headquarters with many salaried government civil servants so there are numerous shops. Two local lodges cater for trekkers.

• **Seduwa** Lodges are beginning to develop here and there are reliable shops that stock basic foodstuffs.

• **Tashigoan** There's no real shop but sleeping bags and jackets suitable for porters are available, charged out at what the market will bear.

• **Makalu Base Camp** During October and November, perhaps into early December, there is a five-bed lodge and shop open. Most supplies are available, even beer, all at premium prices. If you plan to use this place double-check at Seduwa and Tashigoan that it will be open.

Elsewhere there's the occasional very basic lodge and bhattis for dal bhat and tea. Biscuits and noodles are available in many small shops.

Porters

It is probably easiest to organise porters in Kathmandu to carry and look after the supplies en route to Hille. Finding more porters in Hille is also no problem. Note that porters dislike travelling solo in isolated areas; you can't expect a porter to return alone from the Base Camp.

TRAIL BRIEF

Hille to Tashigoan

From Hille it's approximately an eight days' walk to the last permanent village, Tashigoan. Flying in to Tumlingtar reduces this walk to five and a half days and is a sensible way to begin the trek. The usual route stays on the east bank of the mighty Arun Kosi, going via **Tumlingtar** and **Khandbari**. Approaching Khandbari, you leave the river bank as the shores steepen and the Arun thunders down wild gorges. The trail climbs a big lump of a ridge, sidling to the east of the main crest then crosses it on the descent to the village of **Num**. The track along this section is wide and well constructed, being part of the major trade route to Tibet which has unfortunately lost importance since the Chinese takeover of Tibet. Num is where you leave the trade route and the track descends to cross the Arun at an altitude of less than 1000m/3281ft. On the other side the ascent is steep, hot and tough to **Seduwa** and **Tashigoan**. There are also trails along the west bank of the Arun but as this is not a route normally used by long-distance travellers route-finding is difficult and there are no facilities, just a few villages. Groups are increasingly using this route on the way out.

(Opposite): Climbing Imjatse/Island Peak (6173m/20,252ft). This last stretch normally requires a rope, as does the glacier below it (see p231).

Above permanent settlements

The walk to the Base Camp usually takes porters some five days from Tashigoan, though a few of the days are quite short. Some expeditions change to local porters here, sending their original group back down. The locals are used to bargaining with expeditions and have a 'set' price for the trip which must be negotiated. It's slightly more expensive than the usual daily rates for porters. The porters have fixed stopping points and are reluctant to deviate from these. The pace is actually quite sensible because you gain altitude steadily but for most people the rate of ascent is still fast enough to induce some altitude sickness.

The first preferred camping spot is in an area that often lacks water. The last water source before it is a stream a few hours out of Tashigoan. Here there are some overhanging walls that provide primitive shelter and thrilling views. The next morning, a few hours up, is a picturesque tarn (lake), a good spot for a porter-style late breakfast. Then it's over a couple of passes where, even in light snow, route-finding may be tricky. Take care to look back and perhaps even write a few notes on the route, especially if you will be returning without porters – under snow it will look totally different. The descent leads into the rhododendron forest and a pleasant camp west of the main stream.

The track drops further offering relief if you're still suffering from the altitude. It turns upstream after descending to the Barun Khola. In this area the track stays close to the riverbank sometimes descending onto the rocks. There are a few dangerous sections of eroded and loose riverbank to be crossed and you should beware of falling stones. In snow, watch out for avalances.

From here the walk is pleasant and the track leads gently up, occasionally passing signs of summer habitation. The spectacular mountains on either side appear to get higher and higher, seeming to mock your ascent although looking back reveals how steady the climb is. The climax comes with the awesome view of Makalu, towering above you.

Makalu Base Camp

This is on the west bank of the Barun Khola with several sites being used, most of them with a good view of the lake. Expedition debris can be found and, apart from the lodge, there are a few roofless stone shelters. This is as far as ordinary porters with heavy loads normally go. Most expeditions, however, set up an advance base camp (ABC) further up the Barun Glacier just off the tributary descending from Kangchungtse/Makalu II (7640m/25,065ft). This is a little to the west of

(**Opposite**): Walking up to Amphu, with Imjatse/Island Peak in the background, dwarfed by the massive Lhotse-Nuptse wall (see p193).

point 5457m on the National Geographic 1988 *Mount Everest* map. In this bleak spot are more roofless stone shelters and a few flat tent spots laboriously cleared among the rubble.

Exploring the area

The peak in between the two 6400m/20,997ft peaks east of Makalu on the Tibetan border is not a difficult climb and offers fantastic views of strange mountains in Tibet. There's also good camping some distance from the base of the peak, at the end of Makalu's south-east ridge. Everest is hard to recognise from here. I even met an Everest summiteer who couldn't make it out. I didn't recognise it until I looked carefully at photos: the view is part of the rarely-seen Kang-shung Face.

The wild way out

This trip requires serious planning (see the 1988 National Geographic *Mount Everest* map) and mountaineering experience. The route is via Sherpani Col (6146m/20,164ft) or East Col (6183m/20,285ft) over the large, almost flat, snow field to West Col (6143m/20,154ft) which drops down a glacier to the 5200m/17,060ft head of the Hongu Basin. There are several ways out of this. You can go over the Mingbo La (5866m/19,245ft), or over the Amphu Labtsa (5780m/18,963ft) with its steep (or vertical, if your route-finding isn't spot-on) descent and couple of big open crevasses at the base. The third option is down the Hongu valley to Mera La and one more pass to Lukla. These routes should only be attempted by well-equipped, seasoned mountaineers. The survival rate among the inexperienced does not make nice reading.

The search for the yeti

Stories of a mysterious ape-like creature first started filtering back to Europe in the 15th century but it was the early Everest expeditions that brought the yeti to the attention of a world of newspaper readers. While Mallory, Wheeler and Bullock were exploring on the northern side of the mountain, at almost 6700m they saw giant footprints which the porters immediately recognised, saying they were from Metohkangmi or Yeti. Shipton renewed public interest in the controversy in 1951 by photographing footprints at about 5800m. The Sherpa he was with claimed to have seen a yeti 'from a distance of 25 yards at Thyangboche'. Subsequently several yeti expeditions were mounted. They never sighted one but tracks were found and faeces were analysed showing that the creature lived on small animals and plants. The famous 'yeti scalp' from Pangboche monastery was sent to a laboratory where it was found to have been made from the skin of a Himalayan goat.

In 1974, a Sherpa girl was attacked in Machermo and five yaks were killed, their necks broken. The girl claimed her attacker was covered in brown hair and nearby, police found tracks that were similar to those photographed by Shipton.

The yeti legend lives on but one thing is certain. With continuing human encroachment on the world's few remaining wilderness areas, if it does exist it's unlikely to be around for much longer.

APPENDIX A: ITINERARIES

The preceding trail guide was deliberately not written on a 'Day 1, Day 2' basis to encourage trekkers to travel at their own pace and not stop all in the same places. Some guidelines are, however, necessary for overall planning. Overnight stops are given in the tables below.

ACCLIMATISATION PLANNER

Awareness of the time taken for your body to acclimatise is the key to planning itineraries in this region. Although the process of acclimatisation begins even at altitudes as low as Kathmandu (1400m), planning only becomes important if heading above 3000m. The usually ignored medical recommendation is that a minimum of 2-3 days (and better 4-5 days) should be taken to reach 3000m or 10,000ft, followed by a daily altitude gain of 300m or 1000ft with a rest day every 900m or 3000ft, as shown on the table below.

Some people acclimatise slower than others but you should find that your body will tolerate deviations of plus or minus approximately 300m from these figures. Larger deviations may bring on symptoms. For example, if after Night 8 at 4200m/13,779ft you spend Night 9 at 5000m, this may cause some symptoms, although often a night later. Spending Night 8 at 4800m/15,748ft, however, is much less likely to bring on mild AMS especially if you stay a further night there to synchronise with the table again.

Night			Night		
	00	below 2000m/6562ft		07	3900m/12,795ft
	01	2-3000m/6562-9842ft		08	4200m/13,779ft
	02	2-3000m/6562-9842ft		09	4500m/14,764ft
	03	3000m/9842ft		10	4800m/15,748ft
	04	3300m/10,827ft		11	4800m/15,748ft
	05	3600m/11,811ft		12	5100m/16,732ft
	06	3900m/12,795ft		13	5400m/17,716ft

GETTING TO NAMCHE

	Jiri (sedate*)	Jiri (rapid)	Phaplu (medium)	Tumlingtar (sedate/medium)
01	Ktm→Jiri (bus)	Ktm→Jiri (bus)	Ktm→Phaplu§ (plane)	Ktm→Tum (plane)
02	Shivalaya	Bhandar	Jubing	Balawa
03	Bhandar	Sete (short day)	Surke	Phedi
04	Sete	Junbesi/Sallung	Monjo	Sanam (long day)
05	Junbesi	Kharikhola	Namche	Bung
06	Junbesi(rest)	Chourikharka		Naji Dingma
07	Nuntala	Namche		Pangkongma
08	Kharikhola			Surke
09	Puiyan			Monjo
10	Phakding			Namche
11	Namche			

* or group pace   § overnight at Ringmo

Note that it's possible to get from Jiri to Namche in 4 days but only if you are extremely fit. To walk from Kathmandu to Tumlingtar takes 3 to 4 days. For Tumlingtar to Namche, whether you are fast or slow, allow 10 days.

LUKLA TO NAMCHE

The table below shows the safe rate of ascent if you have flown from Kathmandu (1400m) to Lukla (2850m). The recommended maximum altitude for each day (as laid down by AMS specialists) is indicated. Ascending above Namche in four days, which is the schedule followed by most trekking companies, has been shown to cause troublesome mild AMS in about 50% of trekkers.

Altitude guideline*	Itinerary 1	Itinerary 2	Unwise option
01 2-3000m	Phakding/Monjo 2650m	Lukla 2850m	Phakding/Monjo
02 2-3000m	Namche 3450m	Phakding/Monjo	Namche
03 3000m	Namche	Namche	Namche
04 3300m	Namche	Namche	(higher)
05 3600m	(higher)	(higher)	

NAMCHE TO LOBUCHE/GOKYO

For acclimatisation, you should spend two nights at Namche (or three if you flew to Lukla), two nights at Tengboche or similar altitude and two nights at Dingboche or Pheriche, before reaching Lobuche and attempting Kala Pattar. Note that an alternative to spending three nights at Namche is to spend just two nights there and an extra night at Lukla.

Studies have shown that spending two nights at Namche, one at Tengboche, and two nights at Dingboche before reaching Lobuche causes mild AMS in about 50% of trekkers.

Altitude guideline*	Itinerary 1	Itinerary 2	Itinerary 3
00	(additional night at Namche for people who flew to Lukla)		
01 3000m	Namche 3450m	Namche	Namche
02 3300m	Namche	Namche	Namche
03 3600m	Tengboche 3860m/Khumjung 3790m		Namche**/Khumjung
04 3900m	Tengboche/Pangboche	Pheriche 4280m	Phortse/Phortse T
05 3900m	Dingboche/Pheriche	Pheriche	Dole 4040m
06 4200m	Dingboche/Pheriche	Duglha 4600m	Machermo§ 4410m
07 4500m	Lobuche 4940m	Lobuche	Gokyo 4750m
08 (day)	up Kala Pattar	←	up Gokyo Ri
08 4800m	Lobuche		Gokyo
09 (down)	Tengboche/Namche		Phortse T/Namche
10 (down)	Lukla		Lukla

This acclimatization plan seems to work quite well for most people but obviously the more time spent acclimatizing, the better you will feel. Conversely if you cut out just one of the nights listed above the risk of minor altitude sickness greatly increases.

* The altitude guideline shows the fastest recommended rate of ascent.

** or Thame
§ or Pangka

GRAND TOUR - NAMCHE TO CHUKHUNG, LOBUCHE & GOKYO

	Itinerary 1 (long)	Itinerary 2 (short)	Itinerary 3 (reverse)
00	(additional night at Namche for people who flew to Lukla)		
01	Namche	Namche	Namche
02	Namche	Namche	Namche
03	Tengboche/Khumjung	Tengboche/Khumjung	Namche/Khumjung/Thame
04	Pangboche/Tengboche	Pangboche/Tengboche	Phortse/PhortseT
05	Dingboche	Dingboche	Dole
06	Dingboche	Dingboche	Machermo/Pangka
	Chukhung Ri ↓	↓	↓
07	Chukhung	Lobuche	Gokyo
	↓	Kala Pattar	Gokyo Ri
08	Dingboche/Duglha	Lobuche	Gokyo
09	Lobuche	Pangboche/Phortse	Gokyo
	Kala Pattar	↓	Gokyo area
10	Lobuche	Machermo/Gokyo	Gokyo
11	Pangboche/Cho La	Gokyo	Phortse/Cho La
12	Machermo/Gokyo	Gokyo	Pheriche/Dingboche
13	Gokyo	Phortse/Dole	Lobuche
	Around Gokyo	↓	Kala Pattar
14	Gokyo	Namche/Monjo/Phakding	Lobuche
15	Phortse/Dole	Namche/Lukla	Tengboche
16	Namche		Namche/Monjo/Phakding
17	Namche		Namche/Lukla
18	Lukla		

RETURN - NAMCHE TO JIRI OR TO THE ARUN

	Itinerary 1 (medium)	Itinerary 2 (rapid)	Itinerary 3 (sedate)	Itinerary 4 (rapid)
00	Namche	Namche	Namche	Namche
01	Surke	Puiyan	Surke	Puiyan
02	Nuntala	Trakshindo	Pangum	Shubuche
03	Junbesi	Tragdobuk	Naji Dingma	Bung
04	Kenja	Bhandar	Bung	Salpa/Thulofokte
05	Shivalaya	Jiri	Sanam	Balawa Besi
06	Jiri		Phedi	Past Tumlingtar
07			Balawa Besi	Hille
08			Tumlingtar	
09			Arun Riverbank	
10			Hille	

APPENDIX B: TREKKING PEAKS

INTRODUCTION

The Nepal Mountaineering Association (NMA) has classified 18 peaks in Nepal as 'trekking peaks', a misleading name because all involve climbing. Ranging from 5650-6500m (18,537-21,325ft) some are, however, appropriate heights to combine within a trekking programme

Permits and costs

The procedure for obtaining a permit is streamlined in comparison to the months of planning required for expedition peaks. It's therefore possible to arrive in Kathmandu, organise a trekking peak trip from scratch and be on the trail in just under a week. At present the rules are biased towards larger groups because the fee is a flat rate – the same for one person as for ten. The noticeboards at the HRA, KEEP Trekkers' Information Centre and the Kathmandu Guest House are the best places to advertise for partners in Kathmandu.

The 18 peaks are divided into two categories: 12 'A' group peaks above 6000m/19,685ft and 6 'B' group peaks below 6000m/19,685ft. 'A' group permits cost US$300/£200 and 'B' group, US$200/£135. An NMA-registered sirdar must accompany the group for the entire trek and if you wish he can act as guide, rather than overseer. This is to ensure that every climbing trip is organised as a fully guided group trek, involving porters (who must all be insured) and tents, and costing at least US$20/£13.50 per person per day. Some trekking companies are willing to waive this rule.

Equipment and safety

If climbing in a trekking company group headed by a climbing guide, then harnesses and ropes will be used on every one of the peaks below, whether for crevasse danger or steep slopes. If climbing without a guide, recognising your personal limits is important. Some of these peaks are 'easy' but what this really means is that to be safe you don't need a sackful of karabiners, ice-screws, snow-stakes and rock racks – just a partner, rope, a few bits of protection, experience using this gear and an overriding urge to die of senility.

Routes described below cover the least difficult way up some of the main trekking peaks in the region. For proficient technical alpinists none of the routes is particularly challenging **under good conditions**. For safety-conscious amateurs, they have potential to provide satisfaction and experience without excessive danger.

Itinerary planning

Heading straight up to high altitude for the first time, even if following the recommended guidelines, is usually a shock to everyone's system. The effort required for walking, let alone climbing, uphill at 5000m is much greater than you might think. By far the best approach to climbing trekking peaks or the very high passes is to warm up first by heading high, say to Kala Pattar or Gokyo then down, sleeping a night or two much lower, eg Namche. Although this advice is not yet scientifically proven, HRA doctors and many climbers will attest to how much easier the next slog to high altitude is.

Glacier preparation

Everyone on the rope should always carry prussik loops/jumars and be familiar with their use. If you fall in a crevasse and do the job properly, knocking yourself out, then rescue, particularly by only one partner is an arduous, sometimes impossible, business requiring a pulley system and some gear. Crevasses can be completely invisible, especially in spring. Practise rescue moves and reacting quickly before entering dangerous territory.

Avalanche danger
Just as the Himalayan mountains are the largest in the world, so too are some of the avalanches. They should be treated with similar respect. Debris cones are a telltale sign that avalanches are frequent. Try to avoid going within 300m (or less) of these. One of the most dangerous times for avalanches is late winter if there is a massive dump of snow. Parts of Island Peak Base Camp can be hit in these conditions.

Glaciers for the uninitiated
When falling snow doesn't melt quickly enough, it accumulates, consolidates and is compressed to ice. Its weight forces it slowly downhill, literally bulldozing its way down to a warmer area where it melts.

The **neve** is the glacier's accumulation area, (the Western Cwm below Everest, for example) where snow falls in avalanches from the steep walls to the basin below and is squashed to ice. Next, as it moves down, it bends and catches on the valley walls, the uneven pressures forming cracks or **crevasses**. In the Himalaya these may be hundreds of metres deep, and in Greenland and Antarctica more than a kilometre. When snow falls, rather than fill the bottom of the crevasse, it often sticks to the top of the sides forming **cornices**. Instead it can cover the crack, sometimes with a snow bridge little stronger than a playing card.

Sometimes the ice drops down a steep slope and completely breaks up into a mess of building-sized blocks of ice, known as **seracs**. The infamous icefall above Everest Base Camp is a good example. Here the danger is not so much the huge cracks but of being squashed flat by them as they fall. The Drolambao Icefall on the Trashi Labtsa route is particularly risky.

The big glaciers shovel rocks up on themselves, especially where they meet another glacier. These rocks appear to be held in gravity-defying poses – that is until you put your weight on one whereupon it shoots away. Rocks tend to protect and extend the life of a glacier.

Technical climbing
Although some of the peaks are regularly climbed by groups many of the peaks are delightful technical mountaineering propositions. For an introduction see APA's *Insight Guide to Nepal*, and for more detailed information there's Bill O'Connor's *The Trekking Peaks of Nepal*.

IMJATSE/ISLAND PEAK (6173m/20,252ft)

The name was coined by Shipton, who thought this peak looked like 'an island in a sea of ice'. Finding a route to the top could be a challenge in itself were it not for the fact that as many as 25 people a day reach the summit during the busy season, October to November. This does not, however, detract from the fact that it's a hard climb that many people fail to complete, either because of a badly-planned acclimatisation itinerary, or because they set off too late in the morning or the winds become too strong. Often in spring, deep snow makes even reaching the Base Camp difficult.

Suggested itinerary
Before attempting this peak it's essential to include an acclimatisation trip (eg to Lobuche and Kala Pattar or any of the other Chukhung valley peaks). The table on the next page shows the absolute minimum number of days required to allow for relatively safe acclimatisation for most climbers. Night stops are shown.

Day No	Altitude guideline	Overnight stop
Fly to Lukla		
01	2-3000m	Phakding 2650m/Monjo/Lukla 2850m
02	2-3000m	Namche 3450m/Monjo
03	3000m	Namche
04	3000m	Namche
05	3300m	Tengboche 3860m/Khumjung 3790m
06	3900m	Tengboche/Pangboche 4000m
07	3900m	Dingboche 4350m/Pheriche 4280m
08	4200m	Dingboche/Pheriche
09	4500m	Lobuche 4940m
10	4800m	Lobuche
11	4800m	Chukhung 4750m
12	5100m	Base Camp 5150m
13	(day)	Climb Imjatse, return to Base Camp
14		(extra day for safety)
15		Pangboche
16		Namche
17		Lukla

Chukhung to Base Camp (5150m/16,896ft)

This walk takes a short afternoon on the well-defined track, accurately marked on the 1988 National Geographic map. The long thin base camp area is a real cesspit despite being cleaned up occasionally. Other problems here include the frequent howling winds and a lack of water in December and January, with only a trickle available a 10-minute walk above the camp near a couple of cairns on the rock fan south and above the Base Camp. As well as this it's not safe to leave a tent unattended, not so much because things will be stolen (although this is starting to happen) but because of the birds. They seem to enjoy ripping through even the toughest of tents so leave them packed up and, with all your other gear, well covered with rocks or leave someone to mind the camp. The high camp suffers from this problem as well, and so does the 8000m South Col on Everest.

The route up

As early a start as possible is best: before dawn or at dawn at the latest. It can be a long day and the wind sometimes arrives just before lunch. With an early start, quick parties may then return to Chukhung the same day. From the high camp, leaving just as the sun hits may be sufficient.

A trail heads clearly up the hill and then branches into direct and zigzag yak routes up to the high camp which is a series of tent platforms in several groups. From the high camp beside the steep stream, ascend the dry gully immediately to the left of the stream. After about a 50m ascent (measured vertically), cross the gully with the (frozen) stream in it and traverse, continuing around to the right. It's important here to find the correct route. Do not continue ascending the more obvious route or you'll come to a tricky white rock wall that is difficult to solo. Beware, also, of many misplaced cairns, some in the oddest of places. You should traverse around and continue ascending on black and brown rock to reach a further gully that steepens, bringing you onto the spur which shortly leads to the glacier.

There is a convenient spot to put on crampons but take care where you sit – it's amazing where some people have the audacity to shit. Well-acclimatised groups sometimes set up a camp just on the snow. From here there should be a nice cramponned track threading through the maze of gaping holes and crossing snow bridges to the flat, but still lightly crevassed, glacier above. If there's no clear track, route-finding can be difficult and possibly fatal without a rope. Head up the smooth, sometimes crevassed glacier and look for a line of weakness where the snow extends to the summit ridge. Beware of the bergschrund. The two general routes are either straight up or a diagonal traverse away from the summit. Groups always fix a rope although careful crampon and axe work alone may be enough in good conditions. The summit ridge presents the last surprise often with strong winds and in bad conditions a rope is necessary. Even with good snow many people will feel far happier with a rope.

The north ridge

Lots talk about it but few ever do it. Firm snow would make it a nice proposition with a rope and a few screws, stakes and a piton. Getting on/off the ablation valley by the Lhotse Shar Glacier can be tricky.

MERA (6476m/21,246ft)

Mera is one of the most popular of the trekking peaks and, despite being considered little more than a walk to the summit, it is also one of the most dangerous. It's often attempted by people who have flown in to Lukla and not given themselves adequate time to acclimatise. Several people each year pay for their lack of awareness (or their foolhardiness) with their lives. The following is a dangerous acclimatisation planner as followed by many groups. Don't book on such a trek!

Dangerous itinerary

Day No	Altitude guideline	Overnight stop
Fly to Lukla		
01	2-3000m	Lukla
02	2-3000m	Chutanga 3050m
03	3000m	High camp 4200m
04	3300m	Tuli Kharka 4300m
05	3600m	Tashing Ongma 3600m
06	3900m	Tangnag 4350m
07	3900m	Tangnag 4350m
08	4200m	Khare 5000m
09	4500m	Mera La 5400m
10	4800m	High Camp 5800m
11	4800m	High Camp 5800m
12	5100m	head out 3-5 days

The ignorance of the trekking companies that sell expeditions based on the above is hard to believe but many groups approximately follow this itinerary. Typically, out of a group of 10 members two to four might make the summit, perhaps eight or nine will feel sick and two or three mightn't even make the Mera La. In most groups at least one person will get ataxia and without immediate descent death is only a day or so away.

There are many itinerary alternatives that provide better acclimatisation preparation. If time is at a premium then consider visiting Namche first or flying in to Phaplu and taking the alternative Pangkongma route. While superior to the shortest itineraries these still bring you to altitude at a rate that is slightly too quick for some people. With more time why not walk in from Jiri (the bulk of the crew need only join you at Lukla) or for more adventure, try the Arun route via the Surkie La and Panch Pokhari. For better preparation first trek to Kala Pattar then over the Amphu Labtsa. There are many more variations, the only limits are time and your imagination.

Recommended itinerary

Day No	Altitude guideline	Overnight stop	
		Fly to Lukla	Fly to Phaplu
01	2-3000m	Phakding 2650m	Phaplu
02	2-3000m	Namche 3450m	Ringmo 2700m
03	3000m	Namche 3450m	Nuntala 2350m
04	3300m	Lukla 2850m	Kharikhola 2050m
05	3600m	Chutanga 3050m	Pangkongma 2850m easy day
06	3900m	Tuli Kharka 4300m	Tuli Kharka 4300m
07	3900m	Tashing Ongma 3600m	
08	4200m	Tangnag 4350m	
09	4500m	Tangnag 4350m	
10	4800m	Khare 5000m	
11	4800m	Mera La 5400m/Khare 5000m	
12	5100m	High Camp 5800m/Mera La 5400m	
13	5400m	High Camp 5800m/Mera La 5400m	

The Hinku and Hongu/Hunku areas are particularly isolated so groups planning to go faster than the recommended acclimatisation rate **must** carry a Gamow bag and should have trained Western medical personnel with them who have altitude experience.

To Mera over the Chetera La/Zatrwala La (4580m/15,026ft)

Note that the Chilli La/Zatr Teng (4943m/16,217ft) is infrequently used, being steeper and higher and impractical for loaded porters. Some place names on the *Shorong/Hinku* Schneider map are incorrectly placed according to locals: Gondishung is often referred to as Orshela, Dupishung is Gondishung, Lungsamba is Dupishung and Lungsamba is the name for the whole region, not a single place name.

The first camping place is often Chutanga. Although only three hours out of Lukla it's a sensible choice for the purposes of acclimatisation. The second camp (or the first if the group is acclimatised) is at 4200m/13,780ft where there's the last reliable water source until well down the double pass. This area can be entirely snow-covered in March-April. The trail traverses steep terrain but is straightforward if snow-free. In snow, however, a handline for porters in a couple of spots may be advisable.

Chetero/Tuli Kharka camp (4300m/14,107ft) is marked by a huge boulder that offers fine weather shelter for porters. Beyond the views open up spectacularly. Half an hour on is another camping place, part of the same kharka. The exposed trail is usually cairned although it descends several streams. The next possible camp, but more often a lunch stop, is the Tashing Dingma clearing. Tashing Ongma is the more usual camp. The trail (in October, the expressway) alongside the Hinku Khola is small but clear. At first, views here on either side are not very inspiring – rough, barren country, but ahead is the awesome Peak 43 (6769m/22,208ft) a real eye-catching pyramid and also a sacred mountain. Then the west face of Mera comes into view, sheer and horrible, but climbed once via a buttress by a Japanese expedition.

Tangnag (4350m/14,271ft) is a summer grazing area with the simplest lodges and shops beginning to develop. An acclimatisation day is essential here and a visit to the Sabal Tsho or the cairn (5271m) on the flanks of Kusum Kangguru can be rewarding, if the views are not already enough.

It's a slog to Khare 5025m/16,486ft, a regular camping spot, where another acclimatisation day or short trekking day is necessary. For the energetic there are plenty of exploring possibilities. Alternative camping spots are Dig Kharka or near the snout of the Hinku Nup Glacier. There are two trails on the western side of this glacier, a higher one (for the lake) and a lower trail that both lead around to near the Kangtaiga Glacier.

Conditions on the climb to the Mera La 5415m/17,766ft are variable. When the glacier is dry and the crevasses open, it presents few problems but in new snow a rope (at the very least for the leaders) is essential. A camp may be made either on top of the savagely-windy pass, or slightly the other side, but even with a slow ascent it's likely that you'll suffer the effects of the altitude.

Mera Peak
The standard route up is through a potentially dangerous crevassed area – note that the *Shorong/Hinku* Schneider map does not mark crevassed areas – to the top of the rock band, marked by a large cairn. Here it's possible to establish a high camp either in the snow or on the rock at 5800m. From here the views are outstanding, with Everest, Makalu, Cho Oyu and more piercing the skyline.

Mera has two peaks. The easier one attempted by most groups, is accessed by taking a higher line to the eastern 6461m/21,197ft peak, with its steep last 20ms or so. The true 6476m/21,246ft summit can either be reached by a drop and traverse, beyond many people by this stage, or by initially taking a more westerly lower line out of the high camp for a steep haul to the true summit. Note that both of these routes are crevassed.

Approaching Mera from the Surkie La
There are two routes to the Surkie La: from Hille/Tumlingtar via the Arun Kosi, or via Bupsa from Jiri or Phaplu. The trail junction, a little east of the Surkie La, is by a crumbling mani wall and soon leads on to the high and pleasant ridge, passing through pastures. A couple are suitable for camping if water is still available. The holy lakes of Panch Pokhri, where there is a Hindu shrine, also offer good camping but they would be a rapid ascent from the Surkie La to do in one day. Route-finding out of the lakes area is a little tricky. The trail now contours in and out of numerous gullies where, if the monsoon runoff has dried up, there is no water until the Mojang Khola/Drangka and quite a descent to the Hinku Khola. You can cross the bridge to Tashing Ongma or go up the valley to Mosom Kharka, where there's another bridge and a camping area. The trail then crosses the Hinku on temporary bridges, joining the regular route from Lukla.

Approaching Mera from the Pangkongma La
This is an alternative to the standard route over the Zatrwala if coming from Jiri or Phaplu or even from Lukla. Although the route from Lukla is longer, it would give useful acclimatisation time. The route to the Pangkongma La is covered on p213, then, just east of the pass is a trail that follows the ridge. This route is used occasionally but it is not always obvious. It joins the Lukla-Chetero La/Zatrwala approach around Chetero/Tuli Kharka.

After Mera
Some groups backtrack or head to Lukla for a quick exit. The more daring head east down the Mera La then north to reach the Khumbu via the Mingbo La (5866m/19,245ft), see p195, or into the Chukhung Valley via the Amphu Labsta 5787m/18986ft. The trail is unmarked on the *Shorong/Hinku* map but descends from just before point 4919 near the lake and joins the valley floor roughly where the 270 45' line intersects the Hunku Khola. Note that the logistics of getting fully-laden porters over the Amphu Labtsa early on in the expedition are difficult. It's

easier later in the trip when the majority of the supplies have been consumed and packs are lighter.

LOBUCHE (6105m/20,029ft)

This is the hardest of the trekking peaks that ordinary commercial groups attempt and while many clients attain the worthwhile false summit, very few make the real summit.

Base Camp

There are two routes to Base Camp. If you're coming down from Lobuche, where the track to Tuglha crosses the creek stay instead on the west bank. From the first flat area, that valley ascends to the Base Camp area via a short rope pitch. To reach Base Camp without using a rope continue around the huge spur between Tshola Tsho and Tuglha and at the large, roughly flat, area a cairned track heads up the valley. The Base Camp is pleasant with lots of snow for water.

The climb

Good conditions and a dawn or pre-dawn start is essential. The average angle for the entire climb is not steep but there are some highly crevassed areas and some bulges en route that require two axes, front pointing and belaying. The ridge route is sometimes easier.

PARCHARMO (6273m/20,580ft)

There is some confusion over the height of Parcharmo. The height given on the Schneider maps is 6273m, the Nepal Mountaineering Association state the height to be 6187m/20,298ft and surveyors on the first expeditions calculated it to be 6318m/20,700ft. However it's over the magic numbers 6000m and 20,000ft.

There's a reasonable view of the least difficult route up as you approach Parcharmo and from the Trashi Labtsa but a cursory glance here may lead you to underestimate the difficulties. Although of modest angle, the access to the ridge is crevassed and, further up, seracs tower. Basic equipment should include a rope with a few stakes and screws, and two axes (at least for the leader).

POKALDE/DOLMA RI (5794m/19,009ft)

When snow-free and with clear weather, the top of Pokalde is a great place to have lunch. Although below 6000m or 20,000ft, the view is reward enough for a few hours' scrambling.

There's a splendid base camp by the lakes below the Kongma La. From here, there are two easy routes up, with a traverse quite possible. Novices, however, may well feel more secure with a real rope and harness backed by slings and perhaps a simple rock rack.

The east ridge, high up, has a step a few metres high that the simplest of gear would make safe: a friend to push or catch you, and a 3m sling or 5m cord. An ice-axe or something to jam in a crack might also be useful.

The north ridge runs directly up from the Kongma La and is a little more hazardous. There are some exposed moves, requiring steady feet and nerves, that prudent climbers would not solo. Infinitely safer would be to take 10m of cord, a sling harness, a couple of slings and a tool or two.

If there's no snow lying around then both routes are solid rock, but beside a section of the north ridge is an ice/snow slope that is convenient to climb with crampons and axe. If there is snow, the conditions are infinitely more variable, requiring a real rope.

OTHER TREKKING PEAKS IN THE REGION

Kongma Tse (5817m/19,084ft)

Once called Mehra, this can be climbed from either the east side or from the south. The south route from the superb camping spot below the Kongma La goes up beside the glacier, at times on slippery rocks, then continues on steep rock to the summit ridge. A rope (plus limited gear) is widely considered necessary.

Ramdung-Go (5930m/19,455ft)

This is usually climbed from the north and combined with a crossing of the Trashi Labtsa. The southern approach is difficult to follow and crevassed but otherwise isn't technical.

Kongde (6187m/20,298ft)

This peak is seldom attempted. It's more of a climbing than a scrambling peak and requires a stocked rock rack and bivvy gear.

Kusum Kangguru (6369m/20,895ft)

Rarely climbed, its razor ridges provide challenge for the serious and well-prepared.

Kangchung (6103m/20,023ft)

The twin peaks of Kangchung are eye-catching from all the high points around the Gokyo region, sticking up like islands from the surroundings. The Schneider map marks a pass between the peaks and approaching from the south is fairly straightforward. The north side, however, is steep, not a pass at all. The climb can be solooed on good snow. With other than perfect conditions and a pension to look forward to, some snow and ice protection are necessary and perhaps two axes for the leader. The lower twin peak has a more gently-angled ridge but close inspection can reveal horrible double-sided cornices. A rope is required. These peaks would make excellent trekking peaks, so in the forlorn hope that the trekking peak list will be expanded they are included in this description.

APPENDIX C: HEALTH

STAYING HEALTHY WHILE TREKKING

In the developed countries, we take for granted clean drinking water, hygienically packaged food and comprehensive sewage systems, none of which exist in the villages of Nepal. New-arrivals to Asia will be lucky to escape a visit to Nepal without some form of upset stomach, although in many cases this is quite mild and soon clears up of its own accord. It seems to make little difference whether you trek with an expensive group package or independently, staying in lodges. Most group cooks working for the bigger agencies have completed a basic hygiene course. Their assistants, however, usually have not and the conditions under which food is prepared are far from perfect. Some lodge owners have attended basic hygiene courses, their working conditions are better and they attempt less adventurous dishes. Lodge hygiene, however, has improved significantly in the last few years.

DIET

The food you will eat in the mountains is nutritious and healthy. The diet is carbohydrate-weighted, exactly what is needed, with protein coming mainly from eggs, nuts, beans and dal. Walking every day, breathing harder and the cold at higher altitudes all mean that you'll burn far more calories than normal. Don't be afraid to eat as much as you like!

A vitamin tablet every few days will do no harm (women may want to take an iron supplement) but a daily vitamin tablet probably does little more than make the drug companies even richer.

WATER PURIFICATION

All water from taps, streams and rivers in Nepal (even at high altitudes) is contaminated to some degree and should not be considered safe to drink without purification. Only spring water and water made from clean snow is safe without being treated. There are several methods of purifying water but, first, it helps to know who your enemies are. The most difficult to kill of the various pathogens are the cysts that cause giardia and amoebic dysentery; even one or two can cause the disease. These can survive in very cold water for several months and can even survive when the water freezes. High concentrations of chemicals are required to penetrate their protective shell. They are, however, killed immediately by bringing water to the boil. Bacteria and viruses are less resilient. Larger numbers are needed before infection occurs and they are destroyed by very low concentrations of chemicals.

Boiling
Water that has been brought to the boil, even at 5000m/16,404ft, is safe to drink. It need only be pasteurised (heating to 75°C/162°F), not sterilised (boiling for 10 minutes). At 5800m/19,000ft water boils at around 81°C/177°F so hot drinks, like tea, coffee and hot lemon etc, are all safe.

Iodine-based methods
● **Iodine tablets** The active ingredient is tetraglycine hydroperiodide. If the water is very cold allow 30 minutes rather than the usual 10; if it is cloudy double the dose (ie 2 tablets per litre). These tablets are convenient and easy to use but are not generally available in Kathmandu. The two brand names are: Potable Aqua and Coghlan's Drinking Water Tablets.

• **Polar Pure** This method relies on dissolving a small amount of iodine directly in water. It is very effective and cheap. The iodine crystals come in a glass bottle with a filter to prevent the crystals from falling out of the bottle. There's a temperature sensitive strip on the side to determine the dose needed.

• **Betadine/Povidone** This method uses a non-iodine based molecule to bind free iodine. For a 10% solution use 8 drops per litre of water. If the water is 20°C wait 15 minutes before drinking; if very cold, one hour.

• **Lugol's Iodine Solution** Unless purchased in the West, the solutions come in different concentrations that are often not indicated on the bottle. The solution could be 2%, 4% or 8%. In addition, the free iodine (the active ingredient) is dissolved in potassium iodide so the total amount of iodine consumed is much higher than necessary. However, if you have no choice, it's definitely better than nothing. For 2% solution use 5 drops per litre of water and leave for 15 minutes before drinking. If the water is very cold, or cloudy, then it should be left 30 minutes or 10 drops should be used.

Note that iodine solutions are messy, so put the bottle in several plastic bags, and the iodine (except Betadine) should be kept only in a glass bottle.

Chlorine based methods
• **Sierra Water Purifier** This uses super-chlorination, a high dose of chlorine that is later neutralised by adding hydrogen peroxide. It's very effective.

• **Chlorine based tablets** (Steritabs, Puritabs) If used alone, they aren't effective against giardia. However if used with a fine filter (to remove the giardia), half a tablet is adequate. Note that standard Micropur tablets are not effective for trekking conditions.

Water filters
There is quite a variety on the market and some now include an iodine resin. Follow the manufacturer's instructions carefully, especially with regard to cleaning and maintenance. The drawbacks with filters are their size, weight and cost.

Using bottled water
This can be obtained along the trail at some points, but only very rarely above Namche. Because it must be carried in, its price rises dramatically. The leftover bottles are also unsightly and difficult to dispose of. Using purifying methods is a far better solution. Boiled water is sometimes available in the lodges but it requires valuable firewood to prepare.

AMS - ACUTE MOUNTAIN SICKNESS

Commonly called altitude sickness, AMS can affect all trekkers in Lukla and above. It's caused by going up too high too fast and can be fatal if the warning signals are ignored. Your body needs time to adjust to the smaller quantity of oxygen that is present in the air at altitude. At 5500m/18,044ft, the air pressure is approximately half that at sea level, so there is half the amount of oxygen (and nitrogen) in it (see table below). For treks below an altitude of about 2400m/7874ft, AMS is not normally a problem.

Barometric pressure table

Altitude		mmHG	Pressure	Altitude		mmHG	Pressure
Sea level		760	100%	5000m	16,404ft	404	53%
1000m	3281ft	670	88%	5500m	18,044ft	380	50% *
2500m	8202ft	554	73%	6000m	19,685ft	356	47%
3000m	9843ft	520	68%	7000m	22,966ft	314	41%
3500m	11,483ft	489	64%	8000m	26,247ft	277	36%
4000m	13,123ft	460	60%	8848m	29,028ft	249	33% **
4500m	14,764ft	431	57%	* (Kala Pattar) ** (Everest)			

Altitude sickness is preventable. Go up slowly, giving your body enough time to adjust. The 'safe' rates of ascent for the majority of trekkers involve spending 2-3 nights between 2000m/6562ft and 3000m/c10,000ft before going higher. From 3000m you should sleep at an average of 300m/c1000ft higher each night with a rest day every 900m/c3000ft. These rates are marked on the sample itineraries on p219. Be aware of the symptoms and only ascend if you are symptom-free.

MILD AMS SYMPTOMS - NEVER GO HIGHER!

You need have only one of the following symptoms to be getting altitude sickness, not necessarily all of them.

● **Headaches** are very common among trekkers. A headache often comes on during the evening and nearly always worsens during the night. Raising your head and shoulders while trying to sleep sometimes offers partial relief. A bad headache may be relieved by taking a painkiller: aspirin (Dispirin), paracetamol, Ibuprofen (Aduil) or acetamenophen (Tylenol). Never take sleeping tablets. Headaches arise from many causes (dehydration, for example) but if you develop one assume it is from the altitude.
● **Nausea** can occur without other symptoms but usually develops with a bad headache. If you are better in the morning, take a rest day; if you still feel bad descend.
● **Dizziness (mild)** If this occurs while walking, stop out of the sun and have a rest and a drink. Stay at the closest teahouse.
● **Appetite-loss**, or generally feeling bad, is common at altitude after too rapid an ascent.
● **Dry raspy cough** This may sometimes be painful.

In other words, anything other than diarrhoea or a sore throat could be altitude sickness and you should assume that it is. If, for example, your headache is due to dehydration ascending further is not dangerous but if it's due to AMS the consequences could be serious. You cannot tell the difference so caution is the safest course. Don't try to deceive yourself and accept that you body needs more time to adapt. There basic AMS rule is: **Never go higher with mild symptoms.**

What to do about mild AMS symptoms If you find mild symptoms developing while walking, stop and relax (with your head out of the sun) and drink some fluids. If the symptoms do not go away completely then stay at same altitude. **If symptoms get worse, go down**. Even a small loss of elevation (100-300m/328-984ft) can make a big difference to how you feel and how you sleep. You should descend to the last place where you felt fine.

If symptoms develop at night then, unless they rapidly get worse, wait them out and see how you feel in the morning. If the symptoms have not gone after breakfast then have a rest day or descend. If they have gone, you should still consider having a rest day or at least only an easy day's walking. Continued ascent is likely to bring back the symptoms.

Note that there is a time lag between arriving at altitude and the onset of symptoms. In fact, statistically it is more common to suffer mild symptoms on the second night at a set altitude than on the first night.

Altitude sickness must be reacted to when symptoms are mild: going higher will definitely make it worse. You trek to enjoy, not to feel sick.

What to do if mild AMS symptoms continue If you have troublesome mild symptoms, descent for a few hours may be more beneficial than staying at the same altitude. The following case is a good example. A climber bound for Island Peak experienced mild AMS in Pheriche (4280m/14,042ft) and wisely decided not to go higher. Three days later he had improved and continued to

Chukhung (4750m/15,584ft), even though he was not 100%. Here, his mild AMS returned and he was advised to go down to Dingboche (4350m/14,271ft) for the rest of the day. On arrival, he immediately felt better, had lunch and for good measure spent the rest of the day by the bridge below Dingboche. He returned to Chukhung late that day, had the best sleep since Lukla and suffered no problems the next night at the Base Camp (5150m/16,896ft).

SERIOUS AMS SYMPTOMS - IMMEDIATE DESCENT!

- **Persistent, severe headache**
- **Persistent vomiting**
- **Ataxia** - loss of coordination, an inability to walk in a straight line, making the sufferer look drunk.
- **Losing consciousness** - inability to stay awake or understand instructions.
- **Liquid sounds in the lungs**
- **Very persistent, sometimes watery, cough**
- **Difficulty breathing**
- **Rapid breathing** or feeling breathless at rest.
- **Coughing blood**, pink phlegm or lots of clear fluid.
- **Severe lethargy**
- **Marked blueness of face and lips**
- **High resting heartbeat** - over 120 beats per minute.
- **Mild symptoms rapidly getting worse**

Ataxia is the single most important sign for recognising the progression of AMS from mild to serious. This is easily tested by trying to walk in a straight line, heel to toe and should be compared with somebody who has no symptoms. Twenty-four hours after the onset of ataxia a coma is possible, followed by death, unless you descend. Take note of the second basic AMS rule: **Immediate and fast descent with serious symptoms.**

The patient must be taken as far down as possible, even if it is the middle of the night. If you are above Pheriche, go down to the HRA post there. The patient must be supported by several people or carried by a porter since his or her condition may get worse before getting better. Later the patient must rest and see a doctor. People with serious symptoms may not be able to think for themselves and may say they feel OK. They are not.

Medical conditions at altitude
High Altitude Cerebral Edema (HACE) This is a buildup of fluid around the brain. It causes the first four symptoms on the two lists above. HACE can occur in 12 hours but normally takes 1-3 days. At the first sign of ataxia begin descent. If the condition has developed doctors usually give 4mg of dexamethadrone 6 hourly, Diamox* (250mg) 12 hourly and 2-4l/min oxygen**. A Gamow Bag*** will be used if available. See overleaf.

High Altitude Pulmonary Edema (HAPE) This is an accumulation of fluid in the lungs and can be serious. It is responsible for all the other mild and serious symptoms. Immediate descent is vital and Diamox (250mg) may be given 12 hourly, Nifed orally (10mg, 8 hourly) and 2-4l/min oxygen. A Gamow Bag should be used if available. Before much was known about AMS, HAPE was often mis-diagnosed as pneumonia and since the treatment was antibiotics, rather than descent, most people died.

Periodic breathing Less oxygen in the blood affects the body's breathing mechanism. While at rest or sleeping your body seems to feel the need to breathe less and less, to the point where suddenly you require some deep breaths to recover. This cycle can be a few breaths long, in which after a couple breaths you miss a breath completely. Alternatively it may be a gradual cycle over a few minutes, appearing as if your breathing rate simply goes up and down regularly. It is experienced by most trekkers at Namche, although many people are unaware of it while asleep. At 5000m/16,404ft virtually all trekkers experience periodic breathing, although it is troublesome for only a few. Studies have so far found no direct link to AMS.

Swelling of the hands, feet, face and lower abdomen An HRA study showed that about 18% of trekkers experience some swelling, usually minor and women are more susceptible. It is not a cause for concern unless the swelling is severe, so continued ascent is OK. Rings should be removed.

Altitude immune suppression At base camp altitudes, cuts and infections heal very slowly but the reasons for this are not known. For serious infections, especially brochitis, descent to Namche level is recommended.

High Altitude Flatulence Emission (HAFE) This is commonly known as HAF (High Altitude Farts). The cure - let it rip! You're not a balloon that needs blowing up.

*Diamox (Acetazolamide) This is a mild diuretic (leads to increased urination) that acidifies the blood to stimulate breathing. Generally it is not recommended to take it as a prophylactic (ie to prevent AMS, before you have symptoms) unless you ascend rapidly, unavoidably (eg flying to a high altitude, Lhasa, for example, or on a rescue mission), or unless you have experienced undue altitude problems previously. It is a sulfa drug derivative, and people allergic to this class of drugs should not take Diamox. The side effects are increased urination and tingling sensations in the lips, fingers or toes but these symptoms are not an indication to stop the drug. It can ruin the taste of beer and soft drinks.

The recommendations are to carry Diamox and consider using it if you experience mild but annoying symptoms, especially periodic breathing if it continually wakes you up. The dosage is 125 mg (half a tablet) every 12 hours for one to two days. Diamox actually goes to the root of the problem: so if you feel better, you are better. It does not simply hide the problem. However this does not mean that you can ascend at a faster rate than normal, or ignore altitude sickness symptoms since it is quite possible to still develop AMS while taking Diamox.

Note that it used to be recommended that you needed to start taking the drug before ascending for it to be most effective. This has, however, now been found not to be necessary.

** Oxygen Supplementary O_2 does not immediately reverse all the symptoms but it does help significantly. Descent in conjunction with O_2 is more effective.

***Gamow Bag This is the latest device to assist with severe AMS. Basically, it's a plastic tube into which the patient is zipped. A foot pump is used to raise the pressure inside the bag simulating a lower altitude.

The acclimatisation process
When you move to a higher altitude your body quickly realises that there is less oxygen available and its first reaction is to get you to hyperventilate. More oxygen (O_2) is inhaled but more carbon dioxide (CO_2) is breathed out and with the O_2-CO_2 balance upset the pH of the blood is altered. Your body determines how deeply to breathe by the pH level (mainly the dissolved CO_2 in your blood). If you exercise hard at sea level, your muscles produce large amounts of CO_2 so you breathe hard and fast. While resting, your body is using little energy so little CO_2 is produced. When this balance is upset your body may believe that it needs to breathe less than it really does. Over several days it

tries to correct this imbalance by disposing of bicarbonate (carbon dioxide in water) in the urine. (Since it's not very soluble you need to drink plenty). Diamox assists by allowing the kidneys to do this more efficiently thereby enhancing some people's ability to acclimatise. In addition, after a day or two, the body moves some fluid out of the blood thus increasing the haemoglobin concentration. After 4-5 days more new red blood cells are released than normal.

Rates of acclimatisation
Individual rates of acclimatisation are dependent on how fast your body reacts to compensate for the altered pH level of the blood. For slow starters Diamox can provide a kick-start but for people already adapting well its effect is minimal.

Even Sherpas who live in Kathmandu occasionally get AMS upon returning to the Khumbu. Studies have shown that people who live at moderate altitudes (1000m-2000m/3281ft-6562ft) are acclimatised to those altitudes. They are much less susceptible to AMS when ascending to around 3000m/9842ft (ie going to Namche). However the benefits decrease once higher and they should follow the same acclimatisation programme as others.

Trekkers who fly from sea level to Kathmandu and then almost immediately fly to Lukla are more likely to suffer AMS than people who have spent a few days in Kathmandu (1400m/4593ft) on the way. Unfortunately it is usually these people who are in a hurry to go higher. This is why group trekkers are initially more susceptible to troublesome AMS than individual trekkers, who often walk from Jiri or spend time in Kathmandu first.

Effects of long-term exposure to altitude
If you stay at altitude for several weeks there are more changes: your muscles' mitochondria (the energy converters in the muscle) multiply, a denser network of capillaries develop and your maximum work rate increases slowly with these changes. Expeditions have run medical programmes with some interesting results. Climbers who experience periodic breathing (the majority) at base camp never shake it off and have great difficulty maintaining their normal body weight. Muscles will strengthen and stamina is increased but not the muscle bulk. Interestingly Sherpas who have always lived at altitude, never experience periodic breathing and can actually put on weight with enough food.

How long does acclimatisation last?
It varies, but if you were at altitude for a month or more your improved work rates could continue for weeks so you'd still feel fit upon returning to altitude. You could not, however, ascend faster than normal if you return to sea level for a few days since you'd be susceptible to HAPE.

If you have been up to 5000m/16,404ft and then go down to 3500m/11,483ft for a few days, returning rapidly to 5000m/16,404ft should cause no problems. Thus, having been to Lobuche and Kala Pattar, then rested for two days in Namche, you should be able to ascend to Gokyo or a trekking peak quickly.

Sleeping at altitude
Many people have trouble sleeping in a new environment, especially if it changes every day. Altitude adds to the problems. Apart from the condition known as periodic breathing (see above), the decrease of oxygen means that some trekkers experience very wild dreams. This often happens at Namche, on the way up.

Appetite
Altitude causes some people to lose an interest in food but you should try to eat as much as you can since your energy consumption, even at rest, is significantly higher than normal. Your body needs to generate heat to combat the constant cold, especially while sleeping. Very energetic trekkers, no matter how much they eat, will often be unable to replace the huge quantities of energy used.

DIARRHOEA

This is a very common problem in developing countries, especially Nepal, and few trekkers escape without some (usually mild) form of diarrhoea. Ideally, you should visit a doctor for a stool test if it doesn't clear up in a few days. While trekking, however, this is usually impossible so some self-diagnosis may be necessary.

Many people over-react and start taking medication at the first loose stool. Diarrhoea will not normally kill you so urgent treatment is neither necessary nor always recommended. It's better to wait a few days and see if it goes away on its own. Unless the diarrhoea is particularly severe (eg as with food poisoning) there is no need to stop trekking. Just drink lots of water and listen to your body: if you feel hungry, eat, and if you don't then take soup and light foods. If the diarrhoea is still troublesome after a few days and you are fairly sure what type it is you may want to treat it. Note that this isn't, however, absolutely necessary.

Travellers'/bacterial diarrhoea

Hitting many new arrivals to Asia, it's caused by eating food that contains strains of bacteria different to those that your body is used to. The onset is often accompanied by or even preceded by a fever and/or chills and nausea, followed by fairly sudden, frequent, watery diarrhoea and often cramps.

Treatment There are two methods of treatment. First, it's worth waiting to see if your body can fight it off on its own. Tough Nepalese bacteria, however, may need stronger measures. Most effective is to begin a short course of **Norfloxacin**, available under the name of Normaflox in Nepal. The dose is 400mg, every 12 hours, for 3 days. An often recommended drug is Bactrim/Bactrim DS or Septra but as there are now resistant strains these are not nearly as effective.

Mild food poisoning

This comes on suddenly and severely, with vomiting and diarrhoea, about 4 to 8 hours after eating contaminated food. Luckily, it usually lasts less than 24 hours and recovery is quick, although you may feel weakened. There are no drugs that can help - the body just has to eject all the contaminated food and rid itself of the poison. Rest and drink plenty of fluids. Oral rehydration solutions are helpful.

Giardia

Common in Nepal, giardia is caught from infected water, especially in Kathmandu and from high mountain streams near areas where yaks graze. It generally takes 7-10 days to develop and does not come on suddenly. The classic symptoms are sulphurous (rotten egg) smelling farts and burps. Additional symptoms that make it easier to distinguish from other types of diarrhoea include a rumbling upset stomach, bloating and cramps. There is usually no fever, chills or nausea. Giardia can also be virtually symptomless: just a slightly upset stomach with occasional soft stools or even constipation. Some forms may go away on their own after several weeks but treatment is usually required.

Treatment There's a choice of two drugs. **Tiniba** can be bought at all Nepalese pharmacies without a prescription. The name of the active chemical is Tinidazole. The dose is 2 grams, ie 4 x 500 mg, taken all at once. It's better taken in the evening because the usual side effects (nausea and a strong metallic taste in the mouth) may be slept off. Do not mix with alcohol. This dose is about 90% effective but, if you feel positive that you have giardia, the same dose may be repeated 24 hours later.

Alternatively **Flagyl/Metronidazole** may be used. The dose is 250mg, three times a day for 5 to 7 days. This should also not be mixed with alcohol.

Amoebic dysentery

The onset of amoebic dysentery may be sudden and severely weakening - sometimes to the point where the sufferer is barely able to leave the toilet. However, it usually starts slowly, a mild diarrhoea that comes and goes, something that can almost, but not quite, be ignored. This is when it is most dangerous because although the symptoms can eventually clear up, your system is still infected and being slowly damaged. If you suspect you might have amoebic dysentery, have a stool test when you return to Kathmandu. Only 1% or less of all diarrhoea cases are caused by amoebic dysentery.

OTHER HEALTH PROBLEMS

Dehydration

Trekkers lose large quantities of water, not just through sweating but by breathing harder at altitude. Water vapour is exhaled with each breath and the thinner air means more breaths are required. If the fluids lost are not replaced, dehydration will result making you feel lethargic and sometimes resulting in a headache. The symptoms are similar to AMS so the easiest way to avoid confusion is to always keep hydrated.

A happy mountaineer always pees clear! If your urine is a deep yellow or orange colour you are not drinking enough. Even if you are not feeling thirsty you should still try to drink more. This can include any liquids (soups and tea but not alcohol) and as much water as possible. Many people find that with supper they often drink more than a litre of water, catching up on what they should have drunk during the day.

The Khumbu Cough

Few trekkers manage to escape this one. The extra amounts of cold dry air that you need to breathe in at altitude irritate your bronchi (windpipes). Your body reacts to this as it would to an infection like flu, producing large quantities of phlegm, a mild cough and a runny nose. Since there is, in fact, no infection it's pointless taking antibiotics but throat lozenges help so take plenty along.

Bronchitis

This is also an inflammation of the bronchi but it's caused by an infection. Differentiating between this and the Khumbu Cough is difficult but it may be accompanied by a fever and an even more productive cough. Since it can be a viral or a bacterial infection, taking antibiotics will not always help and is not particularly recommended. It's best to get some rest or return to a lower altitude, eg Namche, and see a doctor.

Snow blindness

This is sunburn of the cornea, a painful affliction that feels like hot sand in your eyes. Porters often get snow blindness. It is entirely preventable by wearing sunglasses that block UV light. This precaution is most important not just in snowy areas but also at altitude since the concentration of UV light increases with altitude.

If you lose your sunglasses, make yourself two cardboard eye-shields shaped like glasses with two narrow slits for vision. These are surprisingly effective at cutting down UV.

Frostbite

When flesh freezes the results are very serious. Amputation may be necessary. Frostbite occurs usually in fingers or toes and takes time to develop unless bare flesh is exposed to winds at low temperatures.

Treatment In the early stages of frostbite, fingers or toes feel numb, clumsy and lose power. If it's still possible to move them a little they should be warmed up immediately as they are on the verge of freezing. Warm slowly and evenly. Blood temperature is the optimum warming temperature and once defrosted you must promote blood circulation. Rewarming is painful and blisters will probably form. When deep freezing has occurred the flesh turns white or even blue and fingers or toes become wooden, incapable of movement. At this stage don't begin rewarming until in a position where refreezing cannot occur since this is even more damaging. See a doctor as soon as possible.

Boils
More common during the monsoon, these are usually the result of a staphylococcal skin infection. Non-urgent but see a doctor.

Unwelcome bed companions
If you're using your own sleeping bag then it's very unlikely you'll have problems. Renting sleeping bags always carries a very small risk of scabies but not fleas or bedbugs, and this can be further reduced by airing the bag for a day or two in the sun. If you ever use local blankets the risks increase considerably.

● **Bedbugs** Bites are normally small, itchy and in neat lines. Bedbugs do not normally live in sleeping bags because when they are aired there is nowhere to hide.

● **Fleas** All local dogs are carriers and fleas also hide in quilts, blankets and old carpets. Occasionally trekkers pick them up. The small, red, itchy bites are usually congregated around areas such as the tops of your socks, waist, armpits or sleeves. You should try not to scratch and wash yourself and your clothes thoroughly. If you can find some flea powder, use this as well.

● **Scabies** Caused by a microscopic parasite this is luckily rare amongst trekkers. It can be caught from sheets or rented sleeping bags (but only if they have not been aired properly) or contact with an infected person, sometimes another trekker. To avoid scabies you should always use a sheet sleeping bag within your sleeping bag. The itchy red spots look like pimples without the pus and may, at first, be confused with flea bites. As the parasites multiply, the marks spread widely. Go to Kunde Hospital or the Pheriche Clinic, if possible, or visit a health post. Treatment is a head-to-toe dousing with Scabex. All clothing should be washed and thoroughly aired and your sleeping bag should be left in the sun for a several days. It takes a few days for the symptoms to disappear and a second treatment may be necessary.

Leeches
These monsoon terrorisers are able to put a sizable hole in you completely painlessly. Found in profusion in damp forest, leeches are adept at penetrating socks and even boot eyelets. Do not try to pull a leech off but apply salt, iodine or a lighted match and it'll quickly drop off.

Blisters
Since you spend most of the time on your feet, looking after them properly to avoid blisters is of paramount importance.

Prevention Start with boots that have been worn in. This means not just for a short walk on level ground but with a pack in hilly country.

If a blister starts to develop while you're trekking you can usually feel it. There'll be some rubbing, localised pain or a hot spot. Stop and investigate, even if it occurs during the first five minutes of walking or just in sight of the top of the hill. The trick is to detect the symptoms before the blister develops. Apply moleskin or Second Skin, or a strong adhesive tape (Leukoplast, available in Nepal). Check that the hot spot is not being caused by the seam of a sock or a seam in your boot. Once you've applied a dressing, recheck it periodically to ensure that the problem is not getting worse.

Treatment If you develop a blister there are several approaches. If it's not painful then surround it (don't cover it) with some light padding, eg moleskin, and see how it feels. If it is painful you may want to drain it. Clean the skin, sterilise a needle by holding it slightly above a flame for few seconds and pierce the blister. Do not cut away the blister skin until it has dried out and is no longer useful for protecting the delicate skin underneath. Put protective tape over it with some cotton wool as padding. Some people, however, put the tape straight over the blister, with no dressing.

Vaginal infections
If you have experienced these before it is worth bringing a course of the medication you were last prescribed to Nepal in case the infection recurs.

FIRST AID KIT

This is a basic list to cover the more common ailments that afflict trekkers. Climbing groups, expeditions and trekkers going to isolated areas will need a more comprehensive kit. Quantities stated are for one person.

Easily purchased in Kathmandu:
● **Diamox** This comes in two forms, 250mg tablets (in Nepal) and 500mg time-release capsules. One strip of 10 tablets is plenty.
● **Norfloxacin** See 'diarrhoea' for dosage. This is a powerful drug that can also be used to treat urinary tract infections.
● **Tinidazole/Tiniba** 8-10 tablets.
● **Jeevan Jal** (oral rehydration salts). 1-3 packets for the replacement of salts and fluids lost by vomiting and diarrhoea. Fanta, Coke or Pepsi (with the fizz taken out) and soup are also helpful but not in excessive quantities.

You may also consider taking **Erythromycin** for skin infections or bronchitis. The dose is 250mg, four times a day.

Better purchased in the West:
● **Moleskin/Second Skin/zinc oxide based tape (Leukoplast)** - for blisters. Cheap low quality tape is available in Nepal.
● **Painkillers** Aspirin (Dispirin), paracetamol or acetamenophen (Tylenol) or Ibuprofen (Aduil). These are useful as mild painkillers for headaches, for reducing fever and reducing tenderness or swelling in joints (aspirin is particularly effective at this). Some brands are also available in Nepal.
● **Plasters/Bandaids** Assorted plasters and perhaps a stretch bandage would be useful. If you have had knee or ankle trouble previously a good support bandage is well worth bringing.
● **Betadine/Savlon** Antiseptic for cuts.
● **Throat lozenges** Bring several packets for the Khumbu Cough. They are also available in Kathmandu.

RESCUE PROCEDURES

Assessing the situation
On a standard trek in the Solu Khumbu there are few situations where the only solution is a helicopter rescue. For severe AMS immediate descent is vital rather than even an hour or two's wait. In most cases, walking or being carried to Syangboche or Lukla is quite feasible and porters can carry phenomenal loads in short relays. During the high season, the HRA doctors can be summoned surpris-

ly quickly from most places in the Khumbu. In the lower reaches, the doctor at Kunde (year round) can be contacted. In addition, there are always a surprising number of doctors on treks themselves.

If somebody has had a serious accident, don't panic. If there is bleeding, apply pressure over the wound, keep them warm and take stock of the situation. Look at all your options logically and carefully.

Summoning a helicopter

The process of summoning a helicopter can take 24 hours or longer once the message reaches Kathmandu because there must be a guarantee of payment (by a trekking company or your embassy). How quickly the helicopter comes also depends on the weather.

There are radio posts at the National Park HQ, the HRA post and at several of the army posts. When sending a message include as much clear detail as possible: your names and nationalities, the exact location, the reason for the rescue request (this will assist the doctor sent) and an assessment of the seriousness. Helicopters require a flat area to land on, below approximately 4500m/14,764ft.

APPENDIX D: FLORA AND FAUNA

The best all-round guide to the flora and fauna in this region is *The Story of Mt Everest National Park* by Margaret Jefferies. It's available in Kathmandu and well worth taking along on your trek.

FLORA

From October to the spring the Khumbu is dry and brown, almost desert-like. In contrast, during the monsoon the greenery is surprisingly intense and flowers dapple hillsides. The wide range of flora includes the rhododendron, gentian, primrose, edelweiss and the beautiful mountain poppy. The forests of the deep Khumbu valleys comprise blue pine, fir, and juniper with birch and rhododendron forests at lower altitudes. Above the tree line is dwarf rhododendron and juniper scrub. The latter is prized by the Sherpas for its fragrant and instantly recognisable smell when burnt, a scent that soon becomes very familiar. The highest plant of all is the tiny snow rhododendron.

WILDLIFE

In the Khumbu few wild mammals live above the tree line and even fewer are regularly seen.
● **Himalayan thar** A large and handsome goat adept at rock climbing. The males are around a metre high and sport a luxuriant coppery brown coat, with a paler mane. They are often seen during the first day or so of the walk above Namche, eying trekkers with disdain.
● **Snow leopard** Hauntingly beautiful solo cats, virtually never seen by trekkers.
● **Wolf** Although rarely seen, wolves live at the top of the tree line. Their coat is thick and sandy or grey and they use their bushy tail to keep their nose warm while sleeping.
● **Weasel** Quick eyes may see a blur of tan fur around grass and rocks near villages above Namche, even to as high as 5500m/18,044ft.

● **Himalayan mouse hare** A small tail-less mammal that is surprisingly tame.
● **Musk deer** Well under a metre high, this delicate deer is occasionally seen near Dole or around Tengboche in the dark forest. It is illegally hunted for its musk, produced by a gland in the male and used for making perfume. The male has large distinctive fang-like teeth.
● **Common mouse** At night in the lodges there's the telltale pitter-patter across the roof and the occasional scream (not of mouse origin!).

DOMESTIC ANIMALS

In the warmer lower hills a variety of animals are kept. Chickens are kept mainly as egg-producers. There are dogs; and goats are numerous, being sacrificed and eaten during important Hindu festivals and ceremonies. They are very destructive, stripping the ground and shrubs bare of leaves and are responsible for much of the deforestation close to villages. Buffaloes provide milk and meat, and pull ploughs. At high altitudes they are replaced by yaks, naks and various crossbreeds.

BIRDS

Nepal is on some major migration routes and is famed for its varied birdlife. Since the local people don't hunt birds, and they are all protected in the park, with keen eyes you should seen the majority of the birds mentioned below. Serious birdwatchers should consult: *Birds of Nepal* by RL Fleming or *Birds of the Central Himalayas* by Dorothy Mierow, both usually available in the Kathmandu bookshops.
● **Lammergeier/bearded vulture** This large and beautiful soaring bird is a scavenger, often seen gliding along the mountain sides above Namche, searching for carcasses.
● **Griffon** - similar to the lammergeier, but slightly heavier, with a shorter and wider tail.
● **Golden eagle** This raptor hunts pheasants, snow cocks and smaller mammals rather than being a scavenger. It is smaller and more agile than the other soaring birds.
● **Danphe/Impeyan pheasant/Monal** The national bird of Nepal, often seen in pairs. The male sports nine iridescent colours and is plump, almost heavy. The female is a plainer brown and white. Good places to spot them are along the trail to Thame and Tengboche, and around Phortse.
● **Blood pheasant** The male has a red throat, red and white tail and bright red legs. They are seen around Tengboche and Dole.
● **Tibetan snow cock** Both male and female are striped: black, white, grey and brown with orange legs. Easy to approach, they congregate in noisy groups at altitudes above Namche right up to the snow line, especially on freshly dug fields.
● **Snow pigeon** They fly in compact flocks and as they wheel around in the sky their colour alternates between light and dark.
● **Yellow-billed and red-billed chough** Black with red legs, choughs are curious and playful but have the annoying habit of attacking tents, ripping the material with their beaks. Together with crows, they are known as 'gorak' by the Sherpas.
● **Jungle crow** Black and slightly scrawny, crows are great camp scavengers.
● **Tibetan raven** ('Caw caw'). Completely black, these ravens attain nightmarish proportions in the Khumbu.

APPENDIX E: NEPALI WORDS & PHRASES

Many Nepalis, especially those used to dealing with foreigners, can speak some English. It is, however, really worth making the effort to learn even a few Nepali phrases since this will positively affect the attitude of the local people towards you and you'll be made all the more welcome.

Derived from Sanskrit, Nepali shares many words with Hindi and is also written in the Devanagari script. For many of the people you speak to (Sherpa, Rai etc) Nepali will, in fact, be their second language. Whilst Nepali is not a particularly difficult language to learn up to a basic level, Sherpa is much harder.

Nepali includes several sounds not used in English. The transliterations given below are therefore only approximate. However since pronunciation varies across the country your less-than-perfect attempts will probably be understood as just another regional variation.

Namasté

Probably the first word learnt by the newly-arrived foreigner in Nepal is this greeting, which is spoken with the hands together as if praying. Its meaning encompasses 'hello' and 'goodbye' as well as 'good morning', 'good afternoon' or 'good evening'. *Namaskar* is the more polite form.

General words

How are you?	*Bhaat khanu-boyo?* (Have you eaten your dal bhat?)
Fine thanks	*Khai-é* (I have eaten)
Please give me	*..... di-nus*
Do you speak English?	*Angrayzi bolnoo-hoon-cha?*
yes/no	(see below)
thank you	*dhan-yabad* (not often used)
excuse me (sorry)	*maf-garnus*
good/bad	*ramro/naramro*
cheap/expensive	*susto/mahongo*
Just a minute!	*Ek-chin!*
Brother/sister	*Dai/didi* (used to address anyone of your own age)
Good night	*sooba-ratry*
Sweet dreams	*meeto supona*

Questions and answers

To ask a question, end the phrase with a rising tone. An affirmative answer is given by restating the question without the rising tone. 'No' is translated as *chaina* (there isn't/aren't any) or *hoi-na* (it isn't/they aren't).

What's your name?	*Topaiko* (to adult)/*timro* (child) *nam ke ho?*
My name is	*Mero nam ..... ho.*
Where are you from?	*Topaiko/timro dess kay ho?*
Britain/USA	*Belaiyot/Amerika*
Australia/New Zealand	*Australia/New Zealand*
Where are you going?	*Kaha janné?*
I'm going to	*..... janné*
Are you married?	*Bebah bo sokyo?*
Have you any children?	*chora chori chon?*
boy/girl	*chora/chori*
How old are you?	*Koti borsa ko boyo?*
What is this?	*Yo kay ho?*

Directions

Ask directions frequently and avoid questions that require only 'yes' or 'no' as a reply.

Which path goes to ....?	........*janay bahto kun ho?*
Where is ...?	.....*kaha cho*
lodge/hotel	*bhatti*
shop	*possol*
latrine	*charpi*
What is this village called?	*Yo gaon ko num kay ho?*
left/right	*baiya/daiya*
straight ahead	*seeda jannus*
steep uphill/downhill	*bhiralo matti/talla*
far away	*tadah*
near	*nadjik*

Numerals/time

1 *ek*; 2 *du-i*; 3 *tin*; 4 *charr*; 5 *panch*; 6 *chho*; 7 *saat*; 8 *aatt*; 9 *nau*; 10 *dos*; 11 *eghaara*; 12 *baahra*; 13 *tehra*; 14 *chaudha*; 15 *pondhra*; 16 *sora*; 17 *sotra*; 18 *ottahra*; 19 *unnice*; 20 *beece*; 25 *pochis* 30 *teece*; 40 *chaalis*; 50 *pachaas*; 60 *saati*; 70 *sottorri*; 80 *ossi*; 90 *nobbi*; 100 *say*; 200 *du-i say*; 300 *tin-say*; 400 *charr say*, 500 *panch say* ; 600 *chho say*; 700 *saat say*; 800 *aatt say*; 900 *nau say*; 1000 *hozhar*

How much/many?	*kati?*
What time is it?	*kati byjhay?*
It's three o'clock	*tin byjhay*
hours/minutes	*ghanta/minoot*
today	*ajaa*
yesterday	*hidjo*
tomorrow	*bholi*
day after tomorrow	*parsi*

Food and drink

Restaurant/inn	*bhatti*	cheese	*cheese*
Please give me...	......*di-nus*	boiled egg	*phul*
mineral water	*khanni-paani*	omelette	*unda*
tea	*chiya*	salt	*noon*
coffee	*coffee*	spicy hot	*piro*
milk	*dood*	no chillis	*korsani china*
boiled milk	*oomaleko-dood*	sugar	*chinni*
beer	*beer*	honey	*maha*
rice spirit	*ruxi*		
Cheers!	*khannus!*	It tastes good	*Ekdum meeto*

chicken	*kookhura-ko massu*
buffalo	*rango-ko massu*
pork	*sungur-ko massu*
rice	*bhaat*
lentils	*daal*
vegetables (cooked)	*takaari*
potatoes	*aloo*
bread	*roti*

APPENDIX F: GLOSSARY

ama	mother
bergschrund	gap where a glacier parts from a rock wall
bhanjyang	pass
bhatti	simple hotel
bivvy (bivouac)	small shelter for camping
Brahmin/Bahun	Hindu high priest caste
cairn	pile of stones marking a route ('stone men')
chang	home-brew made from barley or rice
chhu	river
chimneying	climbing a vertical crack just greater than body width
chomo/jomo	mountain goddess
chorten	Tibetan stupa (see below)
chotar	prayer flag pole beside house
crampons	spikes that strap on boots to aid walking on ice
crevasse	dangerous cracks in a glacier
cwm	shaped like an amphitheatre
dal bhat	staple meal of lentils and boiled rice
deorali	pass
dhai	curds
dingma	clearing
doko	woven, load-carrying basket
drangka	stream
ghat	river bank or bridge
goan	village
gompa	Buddhist temple (literally: 'meditation')
goth	shelter or temporary house
gunsa	'winter place', where early crops are grown
himal	snowy mountains
jumars	device used for climbing up a fixed rope
kang	mountain
kani	entrance arch
kharka	grazing ground
khola	stream
kosi	river
kund	lake
la	pass
lho	south
mani wall	wall of stones carved with Buddhist mantras
mantra	prayer formula
neve	smooth high snow-field, accumulation area of a glacier
nup	west
phu	high altitude herding station
piton	spike hammered into a rock crack for climbing security
pokhri	lake
prussiks	loops of cord used to climb a vertical rope
rakshi	local distilled spirit
ri	peak
satu	flour
serac	large block of ice typically found in an icefall
shar	east

Sherpa	of the Sherpa people
sherpa	trekking group assistant
solja/suchia	salt-butter tea
stupa	hemispherical Buddhist religious monument
suntala	mandarin orange
tal	lake
tarn	small lake without entry or exit stream
trisul	trident carried by worshippers of Shiva
tsampa	roasted barley flour
tse	peak
tsho/cho	lake
yersa	crop-growing area above main village

APPENDIX G: BIBLIOGRAPHY

TRAVEL GUIDES

Armington, Stan *Trekking in the Nepal Himalaya*, Lonely Planet Publications, Australia, 1991

Bezruchka, Stephen *Trekking in Nepal - A Traveler's Guide*, 6th edition, Cordee, UK/The Mountaineers, USA

Nakano, Toru *Trekking in Nepal*, Yama-Kei Publishers, Japan 1984/ Allied Publishers, India 1985

O'Connor, Bill *The Trekking Peaks of Nepal*, Crowood Press, UK 1989

Swift, Hugh *Trekking in Nepal, West Tibet, and Bhutan*, Hodder & Stoughton, UK 1989

Nepal, Insight Guides, APA 1989

MAPS

Khumbu Himal, Freytag-Berndt und Artaria, Vienna, 1978 and 1985

Lapchi Kang, Freytag-Berndt und Artaria, Vienna, 1974 and 1985

Mt Everest, National Geographic Magazine, 1988

Planimetric Map of Satellite Images, for National Remote Sensing Centre (Nepal) by Institute for Applied Geosciences, Germany 1986

Rolwaling Himal (Gaurisankar), Freytag-Berndt und Artaria, Vienna, 1981

Shorong/Hinku, Freytag-Berndt und Artaria, Vienna, 1974, 1979 and 1987

TRAVELOGUES/HISTORY

Bernstein, Jeremy *Wildest Dreams of Kew*, George Allen & Unwin UK 1970

Boardman, Peter *Sacred Summits*, Hodder & Stoughton, London 1982

Bonington, Chris and Clarke, Charles *Everest the Unclimbed Ridge*, Hodder & Stoughton, London 1983

Bonington, Chris *Everest South West Face*, Hodder & Stoughton, London 1973

Bonington, Chris *The Everest Years*, Hodder & Stoughton, London 1986

Eggler, Albert *The Everest Lhotse Adventure*, Geo Allen & Unwin, UK 1957

Franco, Jean *Makalu*, Jonathan Cape, London 1957

Gillman, Peter *Everest - the best writing and pictures from 70 years of human endeavour*, Little, Brown & Co, London 1993

Hillary, Edmund *Nothing Venture, Nothing Win*, Hodder & Stoughton, London 1975

Holzel, Tom and Salkeld, Audrey *The Mystery of Mallory and Irvine*, Jonathan Cape, London 1986

Hillary, Louise *High Time*, Hodder & Stoughton, London 1973

Hornbein, Thomas *Everest the West Ridge*, Vikas New Delhi 1982

Howard-Bury C.K. *Mount Everest: The Reconnaissance* 1921

Hunt, John *The Ascent of Everest*, Hodder & Stoughton 1953

Kolhi, Capt. M S. *The Himalayas - Playground of the Gods*, Viking India 1983

Kolhi, Commander M. S. *Nine Atop Everest*, Orient Longman New Delhi 1969

Norton E.F. *The Fight for Everest: 1924*, Edward Arnold, 1925

Salkeld, Audrey *People in High Places*, Jonathan Cape, London 1991

Shipton, Eric *That Untravelled World*, Charles Scribner's Sons, NY 1969

Shipton, Eric *The Six Mountain-Travel Books*, The Mountaineers, Seattle 1985

Tichy, Herbert *Cho Oyu By Favour of the Gods*, Methuen & Co, London 1957

Tichy, Herbert *Himalaya*, Anton Schroll, Vienna 1970

Tilman, HW *The Seven Mountain-Travel Books*, The Mountaineers, Seattle 1983

Unsworth, Walt *Everest*, Oxford Illustrated Press, UK 1989

Verghese *Himalayan Endevour*, Times of India 1962

Von Furer-Haimendorf, Christoph *Exploratory Travels in Highland Nepal*, Sterling Publishers, New Delhi 1989

Weir, Tom *East of Kathmandu*, The Travel Book Club

RESEARCH

Bista, Dor Bahadur *Fatalism and Development Nepal's struggle for Modernisation*, Orient Longman, Calcutta 1991

Jefferies, Margaret *The Story of Mt Everest National Park*, Cobb/Horwood, Auckland 1985

Bhatt, Dibya *Natural History and Economic Botany of Nepal*, Orient Longman, New Delhi 1977

Fisher, James F. *Sherpas - Reflections on Change in Himalayan Nepal*, University of California Press, Berkeley, 1990

Lachapelle, Paul A, *Report on human waste management in Sagarmatha National Park* for University of Vermont, Burlington VT and School for International Training, Kathmandu 1995 (kindly provided)

Mierow, Dorothy *Birds of the Central Himalayas*, 1988

Ortner, Sherry *Sherpas through their Rituals*, Cambridge UP 1978

Schaffner, Urs *Road Construction in the Nepal Himalaya: the Experience from the Lamosangu-Jiri Road Project*, ICIMOD 1987

Sharma, Pitamber *Assessment of Critical Issues and Options in Mountain Tourism in Nepal*, 1989

Stevens, Stanley *Sherpa Settlement and Subsistence - Cultural Ecology and History in Highland Nepal* for University of California

The Himalayan Journal 45 1987-88, Oxford University Press Bombay, 1988

MEDICINE

Medicine for Mountaineering ed. Wilkerson, 3rd edition, The Mountaineers, Seattle, 1985

Management of Wilderness and Environmental Emergencies ed. Auerbach and Geehr, second edition, C.V. Mosby, Toronto 1989

Mountain Sickness, Peter Hackett, American Alpine Club

INDEX